ENCYCLOPEDIA
of
ARTS
AND
CRAFTS

This wardrobe was given to William Morris and Jane Burden for their wedding in 1859. It was designed by Philip Webb and painted by Burne-Jones with a scene from *The Prioress' Tale*.

ENCYCLOPEDIA
of
ARTS
AND
CRAFTS

The International Arts Movement 1850-1920

Consultant - Wendy Kaplan

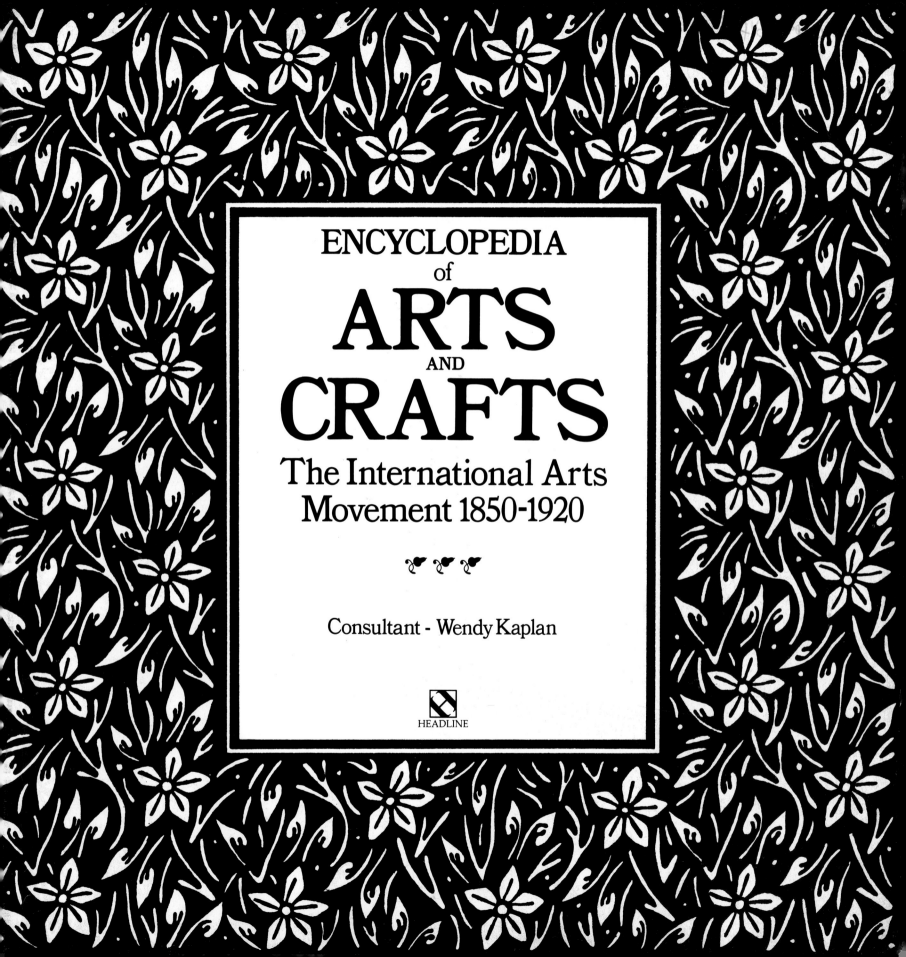

HEADLINE

A QUARTO BOOK

Copyright © 1989 Quarto Publishing plc

First published in Great Britain in 1989 by
HEADLINE BOOK PUBLISHING PLC
Headline House
79 Great Titchfield Street
London W1P 7FN

British Library Cataloguing in Publication Data
Encyclopedia of arts and crafts ; the
    international arts movement 1850-1920.
    1. Architectural design. Arts and Crafts movement
I. Bayer, Patricia
724.9'1

ISBN 0-7472-0180-3

This book was designed and produced by
Quarto Publishing plc
The Old Brewery, 6 Blundell Street
London N7 9BH

Senior Editor: David Game
Project Editor: Mary Trewby
Editor: Charlotte Plimmer

Designer: Neville Graham

Picture Researcher: Anne Marie Ehrlich

Art Director: Moira Clinch
Editorial Director: Carolyn King

Typeset by Ampersand Typesetting Limited, Bournemouth
Manufactured in Hong Kong by
Regent Publishing Services Ltd
Printed by Leefung-Asco Printers Ltd, Hong Kong

CONTENTS

THE AUTHORS

PATRICIA BAYER *(Pottery)* has worked at the Metropolitan Museum of Art, New York, and the Virginia Museum of Fine Arts, Richmond. She is an authority on the decorative arts of the 19th and 20th centuries and co-author of *Lalique*.

❧ ❧ ❧

BEVERLY BRANDT *(Introduction, Interiors, Architecture and Afterword)* is Assistant Professor of Design at the College of Architecture and Environmental Design, Arizona State University. The subject of her doctoral thesis was the Boston Society of Arts and Crafts; subsequently she has published widely on the Arts and Crafts Movement in specialist journals.

❧ ❧ ❧

HAZEL CLARK *(Textiles and Wallpaper)* gained her doctorate in textile design history and is a founder member of the Textile Society. She teaches at Ravensbourne College, London, and lectures widely on textile history.

❧ ❧ ❧

PETER DORMER *(Glass)* is the author of a number of books on 20th-century applied art and is a regular contributor to a wide range of design magazines.

❧ ❧ ❧

PETER HINKS *(Metalwork)* was formerly director of the Jewellery Department of Sotheby's London. He is author of *Nineteenth-Century Jewellery* and *Twentieth-Century British Jewellery*.

❧ ❧ ❧

GILLIAN NAYLOR *(Furniture)* is a Senior Tutor in the Department of Cultural History, Royal College of Art, London. She is the author of several books, including a survey of the Arts and Crafts Movement, and studies of the Bauhaus and the work of William Morris.

❧ ❧ ❧

JEAN-FRANÇOIS VILAIN *(Graphics)* writes for Arts and Crafts Quarterly and the Arts Pottery Journal.

❧ ❧ ❧

WENDY KAPLAN *(Consultant)* writes and lectures extensively on the decorative arts both in the UK and in the USA. Recently she was director of the Boston Fine Arts Museum exhibition "The Art that is Life".

INTRODUCTION

❧ ❧ ❧

THE ARTS AND CRAFTS MOVEMENT developed in England as a protest against the character of mid-Victorian manufactured products and slowly evolved during the period between 1850 and 1920 into an international campaign for design reform that affected all aspects of the environment, from architecture and gardens to interior furnishings, finishing materials and fittings. Throughout its lifespan, its supporters argued that design affects society – that the character of the living and working environment moulds the character of the individual.

These were devout reformers who feared that mid-nineteenth-century design had gone astray. They not only condemned the shoddy workmanship, indiscriminate use of materials, inefficient forms and elaborate ornamentation that characterized most mid-Victorian manufactured products, but believed that such products had a deleterious effect upon society.

By initiating a programme of reform, they hoped to improve the quality of design and thus to strengthen the character of the individual and of society as a whole. To achieve their goal, they strove to ensure that traditional methods of handcraftsmanship would survive, despite competition with machine production, to ameliorate the working conditions of artisans and craftsmen, and to encourage artistic collaboration among workers. Their intention was to improve the quality of life for everyone by restoring integrity to the objects common to daily living.

The clamour for design reform had begun largely in reaction to the falling standards of taste as exemplified by products shown at international exhibitions. These enormous world fairs, which took place regularly throughout the nineteenth century, were six-monthly celebrations of industrial technology and of the potential of the machine. Beginning with the Great Exhibition of 1851, which was held in London, they stood as testimonies to the changing aesthetic and technical standards of an era. They allowed representatives from industrialized nations throughout the world to display their best products, inviting comparison and stimulating competition. And, they provided a means for thousands of visitors to judge the impact of the Industrial Revolution upon every aspect of daily life.

Products ranged from mass-produced, everyday wares to

The Great Exhibition, held in London in 1851 featured displays which included raw materials, machinery and manufactured products, executed in more than 50 different styles, often used in eclectic combinations. The stylistic chaos that reigned within the Crystal Palace characterized design for the next half century.

Organized by Albert, Queen Victoria's husband, the Great Exhibition was the first, major world's fair. The event was open to all industrialized nations, and was housed in an innovative building designed by Joseph Paxton. The progressive nature of Paxton's pre-fabricated, iron-and-glass Crystal Palace contrasted with the retrospective character of most of the exhibits found within.

one-of-a-kind presentation pieces. Those in the former category often introduced newly developed materials or patented mechanisms; those in the latter were remarkable primarily for their size, complexity and cost or investment of labour. Stylistically, most demonstrated a reliance upon the past, their retrospective appearance contradicting the fact that they embodied the latest developments in technology.

Although such fairs were intended to glorify the accomplishments of the Machine Age, to design reformers they invited more criticism than approbation. Surveying the manufactured products on display, many disapproved not only of what was being made, but also of *how* it was made, and, with a degree of enthusiasm that belied their relatively small numbers, they set about changing both.

They questioned whether it was appropriate to utilize new materials and processes in order to create elaborate works that recalled, with varying degrees of accuracy, the historical styles of the past. They pondered the relative merits of machine production as it affected form, ornament and finish. They weighed the manner in which materials were selected and used. And they objected to the fact that most goods were manufactured in stages, using a so-called "division of labour".

The negative effects of this sort of division were eloquently described by a Boston design reformer, Frederick Allen Whiting, who explained its impact upon traditional crafts such as chair-making. At one time, he wrote, "Every chair was lovingly wrought out by hand by a man who was interested in his work for its own sake [who] believed that everything has an inherent beauty which it is the craftsman's duty and privilege to bring forth, and who defends, because of the power of expression it gave him, his craft with his skill of workmanship as earnestly as he would have defended his honor...A chair made under such circumstances and traditions, by such a craftsman", Whiting continued, "was fit for two centuries of use, and bore in its every line and part, evidence of human thought and feeling."

By contrast, in his day, Whiting stated, "we now have a very different picture – that of the manager in his office who receives an order for 100 of No. 674, which he passes on to the foreman who distributes the orders to John for the legs, to Silas for the backs, to William for the frames, and so on...each man turning out the [given part] on his special machine. Then the different pieces are sent to the assembling rooms to be put together by 'specialists' whence they move on again to still others who sandpaper, putty, scrape or fill, varnish or polish. The completed chairs – 100 or 1,000 of them – are as identical and as perfect as accurate machinery can make them, but with hardly a touch of human interest left by one of the many hands through which they have passed."

Whiting was decrying the erosion of individuality. The comprehensive vision of the independent pre-Machine Age craftsman, true or false, had been replaced by the limited perspective of the machine operator who laboured in relative isolation. Designers seldom had contact any longer with the craftsmen who implemented their ideas, and few workers ever saw the finished product. Manufacturers had little exposure to the consumers who used their wares, and could not therefore assess their reactions. What had once been an integrated, cyclical process had become segregated and linear, and the resulting lack of communication caused standards of design and construction to deteriorate.

Reformers hoped to improve design by restoring conditions they believed had been typical before the Industrial Revolution. They addressed such issues as the training, education and working conditions of the designer or craftsman; the aesthetic or technical attributes of the end product, and the manner in which products became available to the public. In addition, they considered the effect which products common to daily living had upon the user's environment and the appropriateness of the product for its intended purpose. Whether or not they were interested in changing every stage of the design process, all of the reformers hoped for essentially the same outcome: the restoration of dignity to the maker, integrity to the product, discrimination to the user and artistic cooperation throughout the design process.

Although the questionable standards of mid-Victorian manufactured products undoubtedly justified the need for reform, the ideals of English design reformers would never have gained international acceptance without the benefit of a strong and widely publicized philosophical argument. This was propounded chiefly by three ardent advocates, AWN Pugin, John Ruskin and William Morris who, by word and deed, spread the message not only within Britain, but throughout the industrialized world.

The design reformer's major premise, that the character of the living and working environment moulds the character of the individual, evolved from a related idea promulgated by Pugin in the 1830s. A designer, writer and the son of a French emigré architect, Pugin believed that the character of a nation was expressed by its architecture and applied arts. He recommended that English architects and designers should abandon their allegiance to Graeco-Roman models in favour of

Gothic examples from the late Middle Ages, the greater suitability of the latter, he argued, stemming from its association with a Christian rather than a pagan culture. He made this case passionately in such books as *Contrasts* and *The True Principles of Pointed or Christian Architecture*.

In addition to their symbolic appropriateness, Pugin maintained that Gothic and other styles from the Middle Ages were superior for their integrity. He admired the functional nature of the plan, the expressive quality of the façade and the integration of structure and ornament that characterised medieval architecture. He suggested that such features were absent from contemporary British architecture and he recommended that architects and designers could learn valuable lessons by studying the work of their medieval predecessors: "There should be no features about a building which are not necessary for convenience, construction or propriety".

With a similarly pragmatic attitude, he stated: "all ornaments should consist of enrichment of the essential construction of the building", advocating a degree of decorative restraint. His belief in the moral and aesthetic superiority of the Gothic style inspired a generation of architects and designers (many of whom trained supporters of the Arts and Crafts Movement) and stimulated enthusiasm for the Gothic Revival style in Britain and abroad.

Like Pugin, John Ruskin, architectural critic and first Slade Professor at Oxford (1868), equated the character of the nation with that of its architecture. He believed that the nature of contemporary British architecture would improve if it were designed to express qualities exemplified by the Romanesque and Gothic styles. In the *Seven Lamps of Architecture* (1849), he identified those qualities as Sacrifice, Truth, Power, Beauty, Life, Memory and Obedience, and explained how each might be conveyed by form, ornament or construction.

In the *Seven Lamps of Architecture*, Ruskin provided aesthetic recommendations, arguing in favour of simplified massing (Power), naturalistic ornamentation (Beauty), historicism of style (Obedience), and an honest use of materials (Truth). He also addressed the issue of construction, demonstrating that he was as concerned with the process of building as with the finished product. He suggested that architecture must reflect the thoughtfulness and feeling of each individual involved in its construction. "I believe the right question to ask, respecting all ornament," he wrote in *The Lamp of Life*, "is simply this: Was it done with enjoyment...was the carver happy while he was about it?"

Ruskin continued to explore this theme in *The Stones of Venice* (1851-53), an influential work in three volumes that provided an in-depth analysis of Venetian architecture from the Middle Ages. In one section, an essay entitled "On the Nature of Gothic", Ruskin summarized the qualities that gave medieval architecture its distinctive character. These included Rudeness (imperfection or lack of precision), Changefulness (variety, asymmetry, and random placement of elements), Naturalism (truthfulness or realism as opposed to conventionalization), Grotesqueness (delight in the fantastic), Rigidity (conveyed by sprightly or energetic forms and ornament), and lastly Redundance (achieved through the repetition of ornament). He viewed each quality as an extension of the craftsman's personality, and each was essential to achieving an architecture of character.

AWN Pugin's passion for the Gothic style developed in part after his conversion from Protestantism to Catholicism. His work in the Gothic Revival style ranged from fanciful adaptations to relatively accurate recreations which often rivalled in authenticity the original models upon which they were based. Shortly after completing the Medieval Court for the Great Exhibtion, Pugin lost his mind and died.

As long as the "division of labour" degraded the "operative [or worker] into a machine," architecture would fail to achieve the qualities of medieval architects. He advocated changing the design process to foster an environment of "healthy and ennobling labour." To achieve such an atmosphere, he proposed "three broad and simple rules" to be applied by architects, designers and manufacturers: "1. Never encourage the manufacture of an article not absolutely necessary, in the production of which Invention has no share. 2. Never demand an exact finish for its own sake, but only for some practical or noble end. 3. Never encourage imitation or copying of any kind, except for the sake of preserving records of great works. Without dictating a specific formula for design reform, Ruskin established an ideal; and for the next 70 years, that ideal, as set forth in "On the Nature of Gothic", continued to inspire reformers.

The leader among these was William Morris, who began to study at Oxford in 1853, two years after the Great Exhibition and in the year when "On the Nature of Gothic" first appeared. As a student, Morris developed a profound affection for the culture of the Middle Ages, stimulated by his familiarity with Ruskin's works, his appreciation for Oxford's medieval architecture, and his travels in France to the cathedral cities of Amiens, Beauvais and Chartres. His sensitivity to his surroundings was strengthened by a two-year apprenticeship in the Oxford office of the Gothic Revival architect, George Edmund Street. Although he abandoned architecture to take up painting, the time Morris spent in Street's office was invaluable, for it was there that he developed a lifelong friendship with the senior clerk, Philip Webb whom he had met at Oxford.

This friendship was one of several fortuitous connections made by Morris at Oxford. While there, he also met a fellow painter, Edward Burne-Jones, who became his room-mate and travelling companion, and still another painter and poet, Dante Gabriel Rossetti, both of whom, with him, were later to be members of the Pre-Raphaelite Brotherhood. Like Webb, they shared Morris's passion for the culture of the Middle Ages. They were inspired not only by its architecture, art and craft, but also by of artistic co-operation which had fostered their creation.

The commitment of these friends to the artisanry and atmosphere of the Middle Ages was tangibly expressed in Red House, the marital home designed by Webb for Morris and his bride, Jane Burden. The house is as significant for the manner in which it was built and furnished as for its warm and unassuming appearance. Proudly handcrafted by workers

William Morris was both a philosopher and a practitioner. His designs were less important than his ideas, yet both have continued to inspire generations of followers. Morris was engrossed in every detail of the design and production process, often devoting hours to the mastery of a single printing or weaving technique.

The first wallpapers designed by William Morris appeared in the 1860s. The papers emphasize the flatness of the wall and avoid a false illusion of depth. Most are naturalistic, featuring flowers, birds and beasts, and juxtapose large- and small-scale motifs.

involved throughout the building process, it was in essence a communal labour of love to which Morris's entire circle of artistic friends contributed. A unified whole, related from large-scale to small, from site to hardware, and from exterior to interior, it has become a monument of the Arts and Crafts Movement, not so much for what it is, but for what it symbolizes.

The collaborative effort manifest in Red House prompted the formation in 1861 of Morris, Marshall, Faulkner & Co. "Fine Art Workmen in Painting, Carving, Furniture and the Metals". The company specialized in ecclesiastical and residential commissions, and its reputation flourished as the result of exposure at various international exhibitions. It was organized somewhat in the manner of a medieval guild; its members, including Burne-Jones, Webb, Rossetti and Ford Madox Brown, developed their designs, carried them through to completion, collaborated with one another and dealt closely with clients, deriving satisfaction all the while from their work process and its outcome.

In 1875, Morris assumed full responsibility for the firm, abbreviating its name to Morris & Co. The enterprise produced a wide range of interior furnishings, finishing materials and fittings, and provided advice regarding interior decoration. Among Morris's many personal responsibilities during the 1870s, 1880s and 1890s were the design and production of over 600 chintzes, woven textiles and hand-blocked wallpapers, a task that involved his researching dyes, weaves and printing techniques. As designer, craftsman and entrepreneur, his goal was ambitious: to provide a tasteful and affordable alternative to the products of the Industrial Revolution, which he condemned as "masses of sordidness, filth and squalor, embroidered with patches of pompous and vulgar hideousness".

Morris's considerable talents extended to poetry, printing, preservation, writing and politics. In his later years, he devoted much of his time and energy to the cause of social reform, formally allying himself to socialism in 1883. At the Kelmscott Press, which he operated from 1891 to his death in 1896, he hand-printed utopian polemics, such as his novel *News from Nowhere.* "What business have we with art at all", he often asked, "if we all cannot share it?" This query prompted scores of his followers to embrace socialism with enthusiasm, convinced that design reform was impossible to achieve unless preceded by social, political and economic changes.

Throughout his career, Morris struggled to reconcile his artistic ideals with his political inclinations. His commitment to the creation of products that reflected the highest standards of design and construction seemed constantly at odds with his desire to produce them at a cost that middle-class consumers could afford. His dedication to utilizing the aesthetic and technical skills of craftsmen to their fullest potential, in a Ruskinian atmosphere of "healthy and ennobling labour", conflicted with the necessity of using machine production wherever possible to eliminate the drudgery of certain tasks and to reduce production costs. It was a dilemma that he never fully resolved while director of Morris & Co, and it continued to plague his followers in the years to come.

Although his firm may have been only a qualified success from an economic standpoint, it served, nevertheless, as a testimony to the merits of artistic co-operation. It inspired a host of imitators throughout England in both urban and rural locations, where small groups of architects, designers, craftsmen and critics banded together in organizations dedicated to design reform. Among these were the Century Guild, founded in 1882 by the architect Arthur Heygate Mackmurdo, the Art Workers' Guild, formed in 1884 by pupils of the architect Richard Norman Shaw and which still exists, and the Guild of Handicraft, organized in 1888 by the architect Charles Robert Ashbee.

Many of them were patterned on medieval guilds, and, as such, established certain aesthetic and technical standards to be maintained by their supporters, who were sometimes ranked according to their level of expertise in a particular craft. Some groups assumed educational roles, offering lectures, workshops and classes. Most held regular exhibitions to promote the work

According to the arts-and-crafts reformers, many nineteenth-century factories utilized a "division of labour" to increase the speed of production. Thus designers and craftsmen were often unable to carry an idea to completion, and consequently, lost interest in the quality of the end product. Design reformers hoped to improve the craftsman's outlook — and thus to upgrade the quality of objects produced — by restoring the process of "crafting" objects.

THE GUILD OF HANDICRAFT.

ITS DEED OF TRUST AND RULES FOR THE GUIDANCE OF ITS GUILDSMEN, TOGETHER WITH A BRIEF NOTE ON ITS WORK CARRIED UP TO THE CLOSE OF THE YEAR 1909 AND PREPARED FOR THE USE OF ITS MEMBERS AND FOR THE TRUSTEES, BY C. R. ASHBEE.

Left. CR Ashbee's Guild of Handicraft was located in Chipping Campden in Gloucestershire. Supporters of these utopian communities believed that craftsmen benefited from life in the country: there, they could work in a clean, quiet, healthy atmosphere in close proximity to Nature while learning traditional methods of handcraftsmanship from local craftsmen.

Below. CR Ashbee's metalwork features handles and legs which have an attenuated, almost waxen, quality. These are attached to simple, subtle, softened forms which appear to be derived from Nature. Ornamentation, when used, is also naturalistic, yet the results are always abstracted and highly personalized.

of members and to elevate public taste. The most venerable of these was the Arts and Crafts Exhibition Society, which used the name suggested by the bookbinder TJ Cobden-Sanderson. During the lifespan of the Arts and Crafts Movement, similar guilds and societies developed throughout Britain, Europe and North America, and were the primary means by which the ideals of the movement were disseminated.

One of the oldest and most influential of the American groups was the Society of Arts and Crafts in Boston (SACB), which was established in 1897 and is still in operation. Modelled after the Arts and Crafts Exhibition Society, it began as a small group of 71 architects, designers, craftsmen, philanthropists and connoisseurs, but within 20 years it had attracted an international membership of close to 1,000. The SACB provided an important philosophical connection between the British and American branches of the Arts and Crafts Movement, which was fostered by Charles Eliot Norton, the first president of the SACB and a professor of fine arts at Harvard.

While travelling in Europe between 1855 and 1857, Norton met John Ruskin, initiating a social and professional relationship that lasted for 45 years. Their friendship was fuelled by a variety of shared passions and mutual concerns, including respect for the culture of the Middle Ages, dedication to the preservation of ancient architecture, and belief in the restorative powers of the countryside. Their dismay at the encroachment of industrialization upon rural areas paralleled their concern for the working conditions of the contemporary craftsman. To both, early Italian cathedrals were symbolic of a more joyous and productive age, and, as a buffer against the assault of the present, each surrounded himself with the artefacts and arts of the past.

Later, while living abroad with his wife and young family, Norton also came to know Morris, Rossetti, Burne-Jones and the essayist, Thomas Carlyle. As a result of these contacts he became a life-long supporter of the goals and campaigns of the Arts and Crafts Movement. Norton endeavoured to revive the arts-and-crafts spirit in Boston and throughout the United States.

Few who acknowledged the need for design reform could escape the compelling arguments of writers such as Norton, Pugin, Ruskin or Morris, whose works continued to inspire supporters into the second decade of the twentieth century. The challenge for their supporters lay first in translating their ideals into reality, and then in convincing the public of the advantages offered by the products of the design reform movement. One means was through public exhibitions of

John Ruskin (1819-1900) was an historian, educator and writer, whose essay, "On the Nature of Gothic", set the moral and philosophical tone for the entire Arts and Crafts Movement. His position as an arbiter of mid-Victorian taste was established by his prolific writing and lecturing as Slade Professor at Oxford University.

Above right. Charles Eliot Norton (1827-1908) graduated from Harvard University, Boston, in 1848 and two years later embarked on a literary career, contributing to the *Atlantic Monthly* and editing the *North American Review*. In 1874, he was appointed Professor of Fine Arts at Harvard, and his dedication to design and social reform culminated in his leadership of The Society of Arts and Crafts in Boston.

Right. Charles Eliot Norton and John Ruskin were contemporaries and kindred spirits, whose friendship would last for 45 years. In his letters, Norton referred to Ruskin as "mi magister dulcissime, homo honestissime et rarissime ...", stressing Ruskin's life-long influence as a friend, teacher and mentor.

CHRONOLOGY OF THE ARTS AND CRAFTS MOVEMENT

1841

AWN Pugin publishes *The True Principles of Pointed or Christian Architecture*, London.

1849

John Ruskin publishes *Seven Lamps of Architecture*, London.

1851

Ruskin publishes *The Stones of Venice*.
The Great Exhibition is held in London.

1856

Owen Jones's *The Grammar of Ornament* is published in London.

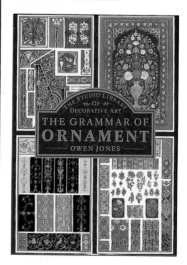

The Grammar of Ornament

1859

William Morris commissions Philip Webb to design Red House; the house's furniture made and decorated by Webb, Morris, Burne-Jones and Rossetti.

1861

Morris, Marshall, Faulkner & Co is formed (becomes Morris & Co in 1875).

1876

Centennial Exhibition held at Philadelphia.

1877

New York Society of Decorative Art founded.

1879

Associated Artists formed by Candace Wheeler and Louis Comfort Tiffany in New York.

1880

Charles Eliot Norton publishes *Historical Studies of Church Building in the Middle Ages*.

1882

Century Guild founded by AH Mackmurdo.
Oscar Wilde tours the United States of America giving lectures on Aesthetic ideals.

Left. Red House.
Right. Candace Wheeler.

1884

The Art Workers' Guild formed around architect Richard Norman Shaw.
The first issue of *The Hobby Horse* published by Century Guild.

1888

CR Ashbee's Guild of Handicraft formed in London.
Arts and Crafts Exhibition Society founded; first exhibition held in London in October.

1890

Morris establishes the Kelmscott Press.
Charles Rohlfs opens furniture workshops in Buffalo, New York.

CHRONOLOGY OF THE ARTS AND CRAFTS MOVEMENT

1891

George Stickley goes into business with his brother as a furniture maker in Grand Rapids.

1893

The first issue of *The Studio* published in London.
Frank Lloyd Wright sets up architectural practice in Chicago.

1895

Newcomb College Pottery established in New Orleans.

1896

William Morris dies.
CR Mackintosh wins competition for Glasgow School of Art building, Scotland.

Glasgow School of Art.

Left. Elbert Hubbard. Above. Stickley Workshop decal.

1897

First international Arts and Crafts exhibition held at Copley Hall, Boston.
The Society of Arts and Crafts (SACB) established in Boston.
International Exhibition in Brussels.

1898

Artists' colony set up at Darmstadt.
First Secession Exhibition held in Vienna.

1899

Adelaide Alsop Robineau publishes first issues of *Keramic Studio* in Syracuse, New York.

1901

Elbert Hubbard established Roycroft Guild in East Aurora, near Buffalo, New York.
The first issue of *The Craftsman* published by Gustav Stickley in Syracuse.

1902

Craftsman Workshops opened by Gustav Stickley in Syracuse.
Van der Velde opens the Weiner Werkstätte.

1907

Deutsche Werkbund exhibition held in Cologne.

1919

The Bauhaus founded in April in Weimar by Walter Gropius

Gustav Stickley was editor of *The Craftsman* which was central in the dissemination of the arts-and-crafts ideal in America. He designed simple, angular oaken furniture derived from Shaker models. Of all furniture designers he came closest to Morris's life-long goal of producing "useful" and "beautiful" home furnishings at modest prices.

THE CRAFTSMAN

VOL. VI   APRIL 1904   NO. 1

COPY 25 CENTS   PUBLISHED MONTHLY BY THE UNITED CRAFTS SYRACUSE · N·Y· U·S·A·   YEAR 3 DOLLARS

handicrafts, which were held regularly at local, regional and national levels, under the auspices of various design reform organizations, and dedicated to elevating standards of public taste. Since most were competitions as well as exhibitions, they also raised the technical and aesthetic standards of the participants by stimulating professional rivalry.

World fairs provided an opportunity for international exposure, although their emphasis upon current developments in machine technology seemed somewhat antithetical to the goals of the Arts and Crafts Movement. Initially, design reformers participated at these events in limited numbers. Morris, Marshall, Faulkner & Co, for example, were among the few to represent the cause at the International Exhibition held in London in 1862. But eventually, numerous adherents began to take advantage of the fairs to promote their work. They contributed hundreds of noteworthy displays, for example, to the palaces of manufactures, varied industries and art at the Universal Exposition held in St Louis, Missouri, in 1904.

This exposition was proof of the widespread and growing acceptance of the arts-and-crafts ideal, with exhibits from every part of Britain, most major cities in the United States and from many European countries, including Austria, Belgium, Denmark, France, Germany, the Netherlands, Italy and Sweden. Together with those from Canada, the Far East and South America, they demonstrated that the Anglo-American movement for design reform had become international in scope.

The acceptance of the movement outside Britain can be attributed to a variety of other influences. Its products and propaganda were featured in a growing number of periodicals with an international audience, including *The Studio*, *The Craftsman*, *Arte Italiana Decorativa ed Industriale*, *Art et*

Will Bradley (1868-1962) achieved international renown as a graphic designer. Known chiefly for his covers and illustrations for such publications as *The Inland Printer*, *The International Studio* and the *Ladies' Home Journal*, Bradley also flirted with interior decoration and furniture design, in the style of CR Mackintosh.

Initially, arts-and-crafts products were promoted selectively. However, merchandizers of all sorts eventually recognized the potential profitability of such "art produce", featuring the work of recognized design reformers, or commissioning them to design anonymously under a "house" name.

Décoration, Dekorative Kunst, and *Kunst und Handwerk,* as well as in influential books such as *Das Englische Haus,* written by the German architect Hermann Muthesius. The cause was the focus of international lecture tours during the last decades of the century by such leading names as Christopher Dresser, Oscar Wilde, Walter Crane, and C.R. Ashbee. Its attitude and approach were transmitted through travel or study abroad and through the interchange between nation and nation of skilled designers and craftsmen. Imported and domestic examples of "art produce" were sold at an increasing pace in retail stores, which ranged from sales-rooms associated with arts-and-crafts guilds or societies, to mail-order concerns, specialty shops, and department stores. The most influential was undoubtedly the Regent Street enterprise founded in London in 1875 by Arthur Lasenby Liberty.

While all of these played a part in furthering the arts-and-crafts ideal, the most effective means of dissemination remained the guild or society, patterned on British or American examples. Many organizations dedicated to design reform were established throughout Europe at the turn of the century, among them the Austrian *Werkstätten* and German *Werkbund* groups and societies such as the Dansk Kunstfudsforening (Danish Society for Industrial Arts) and the Svenska Slojdsforeningen (Swedish Society of Industrial Arts). Although they differed in structure and membership, all promoted high standards of design and craftsmanship and artistic cooperation. In doing so, they not only continued the campaign that had been launched by Pugin, Ruskin, and Morris, but anticipated the union of art and industry that was to become the focus of design reformers during the twentieth century.

Josef Hoffman who designed this elegant coffee pot was also a founder of the Wiener Werkstätte. The Werkstätte was an outgrowth of the design reform movement in Austria. It functioned like a collaborative guild whose members strove to produce tasteful and inexpensive metalwork, furniture, textiles and leather goods.

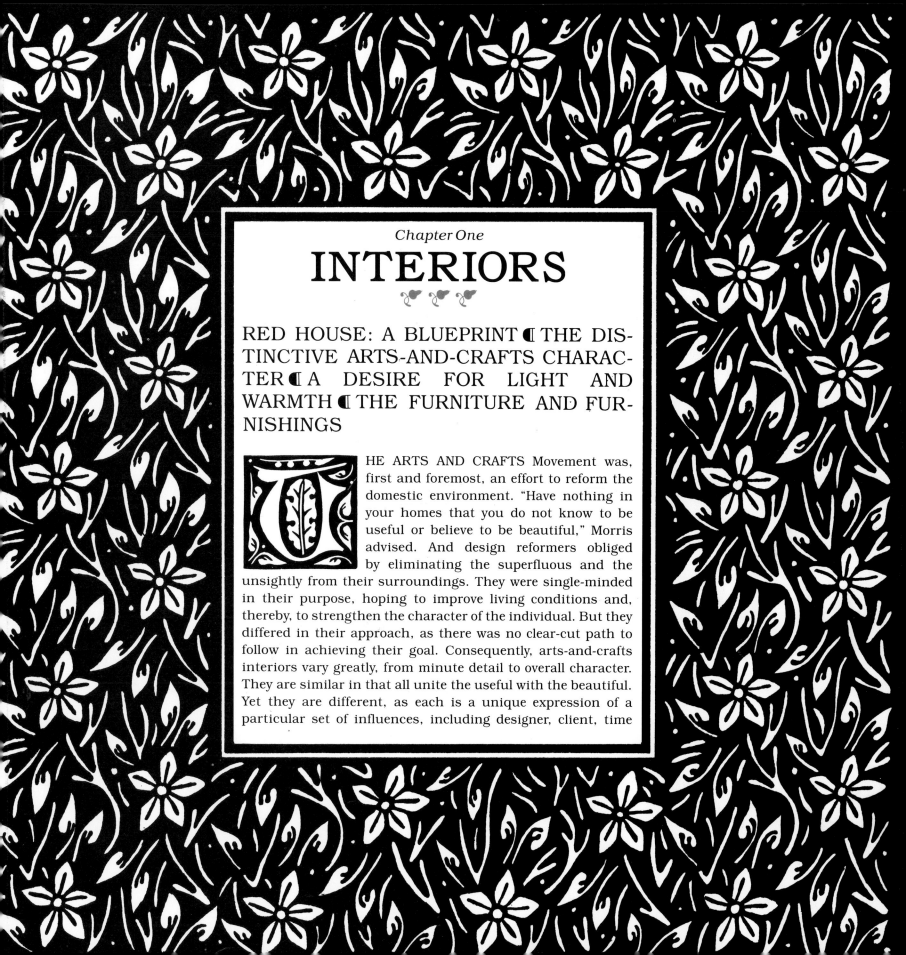

Chapter One

INTERIORS

RED HOUSE: A BLUEPRINT ❧ THE DISTINCTIVE ARTS-AND-CRAFTS CHARACTER ❧ A DESIRE FOR LIGHT AND WARMTH ❧ THE FURNITURE AND FURNISHINGS

THE ARTS AND CRAFTS Movement was, first and foremost, an effort to reform the domestic environment. "Have nothing in your homes that you do not know to be useful or believe to be beautiful," Morris advised. And design reformers obliged by eliminating the superfluous and the unsightly from their surroundings. They were single-minded in their purpose, hoping to improve living conditions and, thereby, to strengthen the character of the individual. But they differed in their approach, as there was no clear-cut path to follow in achieving their goal. Consequently, arts-and-crafts interiors vary greatly, from minute detail to overall character. They are similar in that all unite the useful with the beautiful. Yet they are different, as each is a unique expression of a particular set of influences, including designer, client, time

Above. Staircase, Standen, Sussex, England by Philip Webb, 1892-1894.

Right. Entry/stair hall, Red House, Bexley Heath, England, by Philip Webb, 1859-60. The miniature crenelations and spires of the railing are fine examples of Webb's simplified Gothic detailing and serve to unify interior with exterior. The light-filled staircase and massive, painted cupboard-and-bench are the focus of the relatively spartan entry hall.

period, location, and cultural milieu.

An arts-and-crafts interior can best be defined by establishing what it is not. It is never pretentious or intimidating in its scale, arrangements, or textures. It shuns overly realistic patterns, shoddy craftsmanship, and imitation materials. It is not slavishly imitative in its use of historical models, nor is it overburdened with archeological motifs or classical ornamentation. It is seldom stylistically pure and, above all, it rejects the worldly trappings of its Victorian contemporaries.

In these and other ways, the arts-and-crafts interior contrasts markedly with other Victorian examples. It is a product of the nineteenth century; yet it rejects many Victorian conventions governing aesthetics, construction, and materials. For these reasons, the arts-and-crafts interior is viewed as a precursor to those of the Modern Movement. It illustrates the first important stage in the evolution from the nineteenth-century aesthetic of "conspicuous consumption" to the twentieth-century argument that "less is more."

❦ ❦ ❦

Red House: a blueprint

THE PREREQUISITE CHARACTERISTICS of the arts-and-crafts interior were introduced by Philip Webb in Red House, a house at Bexley Heath in Kent designed in 1859 for William Morris and his bride, the Pre-Raphaelite beauty Jane Burden. In designing this innovative structure, Webb established several fundamental principles which influenced, to one degree or another, every subsequent arts-and-crafts interior designed over the next 70 years.

The first principle demonstrated by Red House is that, in form, ornament, and material, each interior must be a logical outgrowth of structure and plan. On the exterior, Red House is vaguely medieval and based upon rural vernacular examples. Its warm red-brick skin, asymmetrical L-shaped plan, and random window pattern give it an air of informality and welcome. These characteristics repeat on the interior: in the entry hall, lighting fixtures and newel post appear as modified miniature Gothic spires. Their forms echo the verticality of the steeply pitched hipped roof and the slender chimney stacks. The brick-and-plaster arches of the upper stair hall match the pointed arches of windows and doors on the façade. Such repetition unifies the structure throughout and indicates subtly the presence of an overall concept.

The second principle demonstrated is that each interior must have a distinctive character befitting its particular function; but it must, at the same time, provide a variation

upon a greater theme which links room to room. The dining room exudes warmth and gracious hospitality. The upper-floor salon provides a sunny, intimate refuge from the day's travails. The entry/stair hall is a practical transitional space, intended to guide the inhabitant efficiently from exterior to interior and from room to room. Each differs in scale and atmosphere, yet all are related through similar materials, details, and furnishings.

The third principle is that each interior must reveal its structural components honestly. In the upper-stair hall, brick, a traditional vaulting material, is used to define massive arches, while exposed timbers support the lofty, hipped ceiling above the stairs. The major planes of each room are emphasized by contrasting materials, patterns, or values, and interior window reveals, or recesses, call attention to the thickness of the exterior walls. The house presents its skeleton as proudly as its skin, allowing structural elements to appear ornamental.

The fourth principle is that each interior must use appropriate materials with integrity, from broadest surface to smallest detail. In the entry, tile provides a serviceable walkway; but softer wooden planks grace rooms intended for rest and repose. Fireplaces, designed of brick, ceramic tile, and metal, reflect light and heat into the room. And painted finishes on built-in storage pieces provide colorful, narrative decoration in the provincial manner.

Besides establishing these important principles, Red House presents a striking lesson in the application of historical models for contemporary use. The house reflects the shared passion of both architect and client for the Middle Ages, but it does so with modified, vernacular forms and simplified Gothic ornamentation. Both form and ornament acknowledge an historical source, but update its essential characteristics for use in a mid-nineteenth-century dwelling.

The fireplaces are but one indication of Webb's distinctive approach to historicism. They are Gothic in form, but mid-nineteenth-century in texture and scale. One features a breast of red brick which delineates with contrasting patterns a wide, pointed arch like those that shape the exterior doors and windows. Another incorporates the characteristic double-tapered, projecting hood of a fireplace found in a medieval fortified house. But unlike its massive, stone predecessor, it is executed in brick on an intimate, approachable scale. *Ars longa, vita brevis* ("Life is short and art is long"), a gilded inscription proclaims overhead where the brick hood joins the slanted, half-timbered ceiling – a reminder of Morris's quest to integrate life with art and art with life.

The entry hall, dining-room and salon are dominated by

massive cupboards, embellished with painted finishes and hand-forged hardware. These structural, multi-functional pieces are medieval in spirit, yet eminently suitable to the diverse activities of the mid-Victorian household. All include enclosed storage. Two incorporate seating. Two provide shelving for display, while one acts as a background for an illuminated scene.

Webb's use of vernacular Gothic models was prompted by more than an antiquarian enthusiasm for the Middle Ages. The house expresses his conviction, learned from such eminent neo-Goths as Charles Barry, AWN Pugin, GE Street and others, that English architects should reject foreign models in favour of those close at hand. In embracing the vernacular rather than the high-style, he suggests that professional architects could learn as much from the timeless simplicity of their anonymous, rural predecessors as they might from the great personalities of the Renaissance. He was weary, as were many other advocates of the English Domestic Revival Movement, of the ever-changing façades made fashionable during the nineteenth-century "battle of the styles".

In some ways, Red House interiors are more important for what they symbolize than for how they appear. The house was a communal labour of love, to which Morris's circle of artistic friends contributed. When they realized that Webb's unique structure demanded equally special furnishings, they set about making their own, working in the manner of a medieval guild. They refused to accept mass-produced,

Fireplace in upstairs drawing room, Red House, Bexley Heath, England, by Philip Webb, 1859-60. In shape, this fireplace resembles those found in medieval castles. The material, red brick, links interior with exterior, and the pattern, which varies from vertical to horizontal, exemplifies the sort of structural decoration advocated by design reformers.

readily available finishes and furnishings, and, in doing so, by-passed the accepted conventions for setting up house-keeping in the mid-Victorian age. Through all, their efforts were guided by Morris's desire for a house that expressed at every level truth, beauty, pragmatism and originality.

Morris, Webb and their Pre-Raphaelite associates were prompted by the attitude, "If you want something done right, you have to do it yourself." And their action had two long-lasting consequences. One was the formation in 1861 of Morris, Marshall, Faulkner and Co, which after 1875 was simply styled Morris & Co; it was always referred to as "the Firm" in correspondence. Promoted as "Fine Art Workmen in Painting, Carving, Furniture and the Metals", the enterprise was intended to benefit other design-conscious individuals who sought unconventional fittings and furnishings for their homes and workplaces. The other was the establishment of a precedent. Over the 70 years that followed, most arts-and-crafts architects showed a renewed interest in the interior appointments of the structures they designed, planning every feature from large-scale to small. They embraced enthusiastically the design of woodwork, stained glass and hardware, along with lighting fixtures, furniture, textiles and decorative arts. Their comprehensive approach gave arts-and-crafts structures an aesthetic cohesiveness absent from most other nineteenth-century buildings.

The principles exemplified by Red House became the credo of the arts-and-crafts designer both within Britain and abroad.

Above. Drawing room, Standen, Sussex, England, by Philip Webb, 1892-94. This elegant interior, with its delicately scaled furniture, and the window bay, painted wainscotting and repressed arch of the fireplace surround that recall Elizabethan examples, reflects the eclectic nature of the arts-and-crafts interior.

Left. Drawing room, Wightwick Manor, Staffordshire, England, Edward Ould, 1887. This is one of the more elegant interiors within Ould's half-timbered, mock-Tudor structure. The heaviness of the interior architectural features, adapted from traditional residential models, is counteracted by the products from Morris & Co., eighteenth-century antiques and oriental porcelains.

From Scandinavia to the Mediterranean, and from central Europe to the west coast of the United States, the quest for logic, unity, honesty and integrity informed the work of design reformers everywhere. Webb's principles, however, were more fluid than they were prescriptive. And, as a result, arts-and-crafts interiors internationally are characterized more by a general attitude than by a specific, recognizable style.

🌿 🌿 🌿

The distinctive arts-and-crafts character

EVERY INTERIOR of the design reform movement has a distinctive character, determined by such factors as cultural influences and local context. They can, therefore, appear collectively more different from one another than similar. But they share, nevertheless, several commonalities regarding the use of materials, the selection of patterns and finishes and the inclusion of certain planning features.

One similarity is the appearance of handcraftmanship, although this rustic pre-industrial look often did not incorporate much actual handwork, particularly in later years. But the ideal and symbolism were all important. From hand-sawn planks and hand-blocked wallpapers to metals pock-marked by the planishing hammer or corners enlivened by the draw-knife, the surfaces of the arts-and-crafts interior highlight the skilled touch of artisan or craftsman. These handcrafted finishes replace the lifeless, machine-produced veneers of the Victorian era. They are testimonies to the process of "manu-" facture, and, as such, are signatures of the individual worker. They are evidence of the maker's personality which, in turn, makes an interior more personable.

In most arts-and-crafts interiors, such handcrafted finishes appear in tandem with informal materials and textures. Rough-cut stone, rough-hewn beams, seeded glass, grainy woods and plain-woven wools, linens or cottons replace the polished, fragile textures associated with formal, high-style interiors. These humble, inviting materials are used in a fashion that accentuates their imperfections. They are durable and chosen to age gracefully. They welcome, and are enhanced by, daily interaction with the user.

While arts-and-crafts interiors glorify handcrafted finishes and informal textures, they also demonstrate a traditional approach to the construction of architectural elements and furnishings. Timbered ceilings evoke the framing techniques of the early housewright. Cut-stone floors, walls and fireplaces demonstrate the painstaking methods of the mason. Spindled backs recall the skills of the Windsor-chair maker, and

The Hall, Stanmore Hall, Harrow, Middlesex, England. A re-creation of the medieval Hall with the typically Morrisian wallpaper.

panelling, storage pieces and seat furniture made of solid woods with exposed joints reflect the techniques of the early joiner and turner. Even the approach to ornamentation tends to be traditional: run-mouldings, incised lines, chip-carving or painting add interest to surfaces when structural polychrome or integrated patterns are not already sufficient. In arts-and-crafts interiors, the forms of elements and furnishings might be progressive in their suave simplicity, but the manner in which they are wrought, assembled and embellished is often retrospective.

Their provincial sympathies are exemplified by the decorative motifs found on surfaces, textiles, furnishings and objects: many are of humble origin, associated for generations with the folk tradition. The decorative vocabulary consists of simple, geometric shapes and conventionalized natural motifs, used individually or as repetitive patterns or borders. Popular devices include the tulip, rose, leaf and bird. But chief among these is the heart, which appears on forms as diverse as leaded glass by Will Bradley, cupboards by CR Mackintosh, chair-backs by CFA Voysey, and firedogs by Ernest Gimson.

Justifications for the popularity of these folk motifs are at least threefold. First, they are compatible stylistically with the provincial nature of many arts-and-crafts designs. Second, they are as simple and direct in form as are the shapes and surfaces they embellish. And third, they evoke the positive,

Above. The Library, 9 Melbury Road, London, England. An excellent example of the tilework that was used in arts-and-crafts interiors.

Right. Dining room, Charles J. Page Residence, Westland Avenue, Boston, USA, by Herbert Langford Warren, 1887-88. The heavy furnishings and brick Romanesque arch betray Warren's years of employment in Henry Hobson Richardson's office. Later, Warren developed a reputation for such "artistic" interiors, which often featured the work of members of The Society of Arts and Crafts in Boston.

homely virtues that design reformers hoped to restore to daily life. But they are by no means used in a simplistic fashion; rather, they are manipulated in a sophisticated manner which belies their humble origins. In the hands of an accomplished designer, they assume an air of calculated *naïveté*.

Equally sophisticated are the patterns that are derived from natural sources and are often regional in their character. Morris's distinctive chintzes, wallpapers and carpets immortalize the wild flowers and vegetation growing along streams and in country gardens in south-east England. Mackintosh's sinuous wall stencils and embroideries provide variations upon the traditional "Glasgow rose" which flourished in Scotland's grey, damp climate. Frank Lloyd Wright's stained-glass windows, lighting fixtures and carpets capture with angular precision the essence of weeds, seed-pods and trees growing wild on the prairies of the American Midwest. And Candace Wheeler's appliqués and tapestries transform in subtle tone-on-tone the thistles, pine-cones, ivy and shells of the north-eastern United States. All of these have a freshness and originality that results from a close observation of Nature. But, by virtue of colour, composition, scale and modelling, they are transformed from commonplace to extraordinary.

A desire for light and warmth

IN DIMENSION, arts-and-crafts interiors range from grand to modest, yet all are inviting and approachable. Such qualities are the combined result of finishes and furnishings, but they are due as well to conventions regarding fenestration and planning. Like the interiors of the late Middle Ages or those of the Elizabethan age, arts-and-crafts interiors express a desire for light and warmth. In pursuit of such attributes, architects identified as priorities the size, shape and placement of windows and the location of the fireplace, the focal point within most spaces.

The fireplace was a hub of domestic activity, and its stature as such was frequently augmented by structural furnishings or fireside windows. Known as an inglenook, this enclosed fireplace bay became an intimate room-within-a-room. Its cosiness was often accentuated by a lowered ceiling or raised floor level. The importance of the inglenook as an arts-and-crafts planning feature was recognized by the German architect and critic Hermann Muthesius, who traced its origins to Anglo-Saxon homes in his influential book of 1904-5, *The English House*.

The treatment of the inglenook varies, but it can be found in "reformed" interiors throughout Europe and America. It appears in cottages and country estates designed by CFA Voysey; in the Prairie style homes and "Craftsman" bungalows of Frank Lloyd Wright or Gustav Stickley; in the Aesthetic or Colonial Revival interiors of the north-eastern United States, and in the Glasgow Style rooms by CR Mackintosh and his American emulator, Will Bradley. The inglenook is a ubiquitous feature in entries, stair-halls, drawing-rooms and dining-rooms. It serves both a practical and a decorative purpose, but, above all, it is significant for its symbolic connotation: it is the heart of the arts-and-crafts interior and is often located at the centre of the plan. Its symbolic importance may explain the prevalence of the heart-shaped motif on

"A Craftsman Dining Room" as featured in *The Craftsman*, USA, Gustav Stickley, c1904. "Craftsman" interiors resemble those of Frank Lloyd Wright, yet tend to be homier and more decorative, suited for middle-class tastes. Furnishings and interior elements are skeletal in character, with right angles and surfaces that are easy to mass-produce.

hoods, implements and furniture used in its proximity.

The intimate atmosphere of the arts-and-crafts interior is often determined by the ceiling, which is purposely lowered or detailed to accentuate the horizontality of the room. A lowered ceiling is often complemented by an ornamental frieze, a decorative horizontal strip defining the upper third of the wall. The frieze is frequently painted with a narrative mural or a large-scale repetitive border, but it might just as often be covered with stencilling or wallpaper to distinguish it from the wall surface below. In the nursery, it might include a motto or inscription, carefully selected to mould the character of the room's youthful occupant. The frieze in such cases becomes a permanent work of art, integrated into the very structure of the interior.

The furniture and furnishings

IT MAY, ON THE OTHER HAND, be plain, to contrast with built-in furniture, fabric, wallpaper or panelling below. A plain frieze is often trimmed by a picture moulding, plate rail or shallow ledge used to support small watercolours or prints, ceramics or carefully selected bric-à-brac. Defined by the frieze, these decorative elements appear as an extension of the interior architecture, rather than as distracting foreground clutter. The plain frieze can have a practical purpose as well: Voysey advocated the use of a light-coloured frieze to reflect natural daylight. Others, such as Frank Lloyd Wright, extended a frieze of uniform width from room to room to establish visual continuity throughout a structure.

Such continuity is perhaps the most striking, and indeed the most universal, aspect among interiors of the design reform movement. Finishes, textures, patterns and other elements might vary according to the demands of a client, but the architect always strove to unite the interior from large-scale to small. Each was viewed as an ensemble, to be co-ordinated from

Dining room, general interior, Gamble House, Pasadena, California, USA, Charles Sumner Greene and Henry Mather Greene, 1908. Interiors by the Greene brothers contain influences ranging from vernacular to oriental. Each element is crafted allowing the exposed joinery to assume a decorative role.

Library, Glasgow School of Art, Glasgow, Scotland, 1897-99, 1907-09, Charles Rennie Mackintosh. The exposed, wooden skeleton of the two-storey reading room makes the structure appear decorative. The interior expresses a quest for verticality and light in the manner of the Gothic, yet its detailing is progressive.

background to furnishings to accessories. A unified result depended upon the sensitive eye of the designer, who had to pay attention to every detail while orchestrating the whole.

Despite such commonalities, arts-and-crafts interiors differ greatly in overall appearance. They range from subtle to brilliant, from spartan to crowded and over-stuffed, and from eclectic to stylistically pure. They express a universal quest for logic, unity, honesty and integrity in design, yet each presents a personal interpretation of usefulness and beauty.

Colour, as one component of beauty, is treated variously by arts-and-crafts architects and designers. CFA Voysey, MH Baillie Scott, Carl Larsson or Will Bradley include large blocks of vivid colour to define interior planes boldly. Others, such as CR Mackintosh or Josef Hoffmann, utilize an achromatic palette of whites, greys and blacks enlivened by

Entry/stair hall, Gamble House, Pasadena, California, USA, Charles Sumner Greene and Henry Mather Greene, 1908. Sculptural in finish and presence, the staircase is exquisitely crafted. The continuous moulding that defines the treads and risers resembles the trim on a Japanese *hako-kaidan* or stairway chest.

strategic touches of brilliant colour. Another group offers a conservative approach: Philip Webb, Edward Ould, Stanford White or Henry Hobson Richardson incorporate chintzes, wallpapers or oriental rugs as subtle, multi-coloured accents. The majority, however, eliminate bright colour altogether, choosing instead to emphasize the dull tones of structural materials such as wood, stone, brick, plaster, metal or leather.

Such extreme variations in colour usage must be attributed to the preferences of client or designer, for the Arts and Crafts Movement *per se* did not dictate that one approach was more suitable than another. In some cases, designers were directed in their colour choice by external influences. The brilliant hues utilized by Voysey, Baillie Scott, Larsson or Bradley might have been inspired by the folk tradition. The black or coloured lacquers used by Mackintosh demonstrate his awareness of oriental finishes. The patterned textiles and wallpapers selected by Webb, Ould, Richardson or White complement the mellow tonalities of clients' collections of art and antiques. And those who stressed the coloration of natural materials consciously rejected the strident schemes popularized during the nineteenth century after the development of artificial aniline dyes.

Like colour, textiles are partially responsible for the usefulness and beauty of an arts-and-crafts interior. In some interiors every form is padded and every surface draped, while in later interiors and those designed by architects fabric and cushioning are kept to a minimum. The relative presence or absence of those elements affects profoundly the overall character of the room.

In some arts-and-crafts interiors, textiles are utilized as they had been throughout the nineteenth century. Comfortable seating pieces display buttons, tufts and trims, while draperies hang at the windows. Tapestries line walls above the dado, and patterned rugs cover the floor. Lambrequins adorn mantels, and cloths extend from table-top to floor. As a result, the features of the room and frames of seat furniture are obscured rather than exposed. Textiles used in so generous a manner are particularly evident in arts-and-crafts interiors in England, Scandinavia and the United States. They are especially prominent in interiors furnished by enterprises having a vested interest in their use, such as Morris & Co, Liberty & Co or Associated Artists.

What distinguishes these draped and upholstered interiors as products of the Arts and Crafts Movement are the woven or printed patterns that they contain. The patterns are modelled subtly and appear relatively flat to emphasize the flatness of the

The hall, Palais Stoclet, Brussels, Belgium, by Josef Hoffmann, 1905. Hoffmann's exquisitely detailed interiors have a strong unity of concept. He often clothed simple, geometric forms in costly materials, as here.

planes which they cover. They tend to be stylized and carefully composed in contrast to the undulating, naturalistic patterns of the Victorian age. Such stylization discourages the impression conveyed by large-scale, realistic patterns that the user is sitting or walking upon living specimens of flowers or foliage.

In contrast to such interiors, with their softened edges and curvilinear forms, are those that eliminate textiles wherever possible. In these relatively ascetic spaces, leather panels replace fixed upholstery, and trimmings of any sort are kept to a minimum. Stained-glass windows substitute for draperies to screen unwanted views or to filter natural daylight, and area rugs are placed selectively (if at all) on otherwise bare floors. These interiors reveal unabashedly every angle, plane and edge. In character, they contradict the more modest "feminine" aesthetic characteristic of the Victorian era.

These stark "reformed" interiors, designed by the Greene brothers, Wright, Stickley, Gimson, Hoffmann and others, present a strict interpretation of usefulness and beauty that thrives upon eliminating every superfluous detail. By restricting the excessive use of textiles, they established a precedent that has continued to be influential today. They are regarded by posterity as functional and proto-modern, in

Dining room, Haus Freudenberg, Nikolassee, Germany, by Hermann Muthesius, 1907-8. Muthesius incorporated many aspects of the English arts-and-crafts interior when he designed the dining room of his own house. The panelled wall bordered by mouldings and a patterned frieze, the coffered ceiling hung with elegant electroliers, the fireplace inglenook placed off-centre and flanked by a built-in cupboard all lend a touch of informality.

contrast to other arts-and-crafts interiors that utilized fabric in a more generous fashion.

During the life span of the Arts and Crafts Movement, this varied approach to the use of colour and textiles reflected the influence of other styles and movements currently in vogue. Some had little impact on arts-and-crafts interiors, while others affected everything from colour and texture to form and motif, to broader issues of planning and arrangement. Among these were the Gothic Revival and High Victorian Gothic, the Old English and Queen Anne, the Colonial and Georgian Revivals, National Romanticism and the English Domestic Revival Movement.

Such influences caused some design reformers to take an eclectic approach, assembling interiors that incorporated vestiges of several contemporaneous styles. But other designers regarded such stylistic eclecticism as antithetical to the goals of the Arts and Crafts Movement. They elected to pursue a purer approach which included only the slightest trace of any outside influence.

The presence of these influences demonstrates that arts-

and-crafts interiors were not created in isolation. All were products of the nineteenth century, and as such could not escape the dual stronghold of revivalism and eclecticism that had dictated the evolution of style during the late eighteenth and nineteenth centuries. Nor could they resist the beckoning of more progressive trends, such as the Art Nouveau style, the Jugendstil or the Secessionist Movement. These diverse influences infused the interiors of the design reform movements to different degrees, depending upon the stylistic proclivities of architect, designer and client.

Such stylistic eclecticism is illustrated by arts-and-crafts interiors that combine medieval architectural features with Jacobean wainscoting, oriel windows and elegant furniture reminiscent of Hepplewhite and Sheraton. In others, the forthright forms of joiner and turner co-exist with pseudo-oriental finishes and sinuous Art Nouveau ornamentation. Still others explore the "greenery-yallery" colour schemes, cluttered arrangements and oriental bric-à-brac promoted by the Aesthetic Movement. And in the north-eastern United States, some "reformed" interiors blithely mix Morris chintzes and Colonial antiques with Mission Style furnishings, Japanese fans and peacock feathers. Even the idiosyncratic interiors of Mackintosh or the Greene brothers include Chinese porcelains or oriental rugs. As in all interiors, these seemingly disparate elements provide a striking contrast of age and culture which serves to enrich the whole.

The Arts and Crafts Movement strove to improve life by simplifying the home and work environment, but it presented more options than restrictions to those wishing to achieve that goal. Design reformers, consequently, interpreted its principles broadly, and, as a result, the interiors of the design reform movements are often more challenging to analyse than are their more conservative academic contemporaries.

The complex character of the arts-and-crafts interior can perhaps be attributed to the fact that it expresses conflicting intentions: it reflects a nostalgia for attributes from the past, while it values a fresh perspective and an original approach. It seeks to provide an environment that is both warm and comfortable. But it argues convincingly that each interior must be efficient and easy to maintain. It incorporates whimsy and subtle humour, expressing a *joie de vivre* and an appreciation for the simple things in life. But it never forgets its mission nor its sobriety of purpose. It provides a congenial background for handiwork and other personal touches, but maintains that a spare, uncluttered atmosphere alone provides quiet and repose. Such dualities reflect its pivotal position in the history of design. It embraces the time-honoured achievements of the past, yet it anticipates the accomplishments of the Modern Movement.

Chapter Two

ARCHITECTURE

THE FUNDAMENTAL QUALITIES ❦ CON-
STRUCTION TECHNIQUES ❦ ORNAMEN-
TATION ❦ THE STRUCTURE AND ITS SITE
❦ A VARIETY OF PLANS

RTS-AND-CRAFTS architecture is not characterized by a recognizable style. Rather, it reflects an attitude shared by architects who supported the goals of the Arts and Crafts Movement. Although their background, training and philosophy varied, they were all champions of design reform, united by the belief that architecture must change in order to change society. Their formula for change was to design buildings that transcended fashion, expressing in its place values that were fundamental, universal, and timeless.

In supporting the design reform movement, they expressed the belief that their work profoundly affected the individual and society. Their altruistic goal was to develop an architecture of character that would, in turn, mould the character of the user. The connection between the two was noted by the English architect CFA Voysey, who stated, "Simplicity, sincerity, repose, directness and frankness are moral qualities as essential to good architecture as to good men." As this suggests, the challenge faced by arts-and-crafts architects was to expose architecture's moral fibre by removing the stylish cloak of historicism and revivalism that had obscured it since the Renaissance.

They were in constant search of ways to distinguish their work from that of their predecessors. In the process, they contemplated a variety of issues regarding function and appearance. They questioned what models, if any, should be used as a basis for aesthetic decisions. They pondered the role of materials, their coloration and their texture. They contemplated the nature of ornament, its appearance and its application. They considered not only functional aspects such as siting, planning and fenestration, but also technical issues regarding construction. They sought to address the physical needs of the user, as well as those which were psychological, emotional and spiritual. Above all, they strove to unify architecture, whether large scale or small, by eliminating the artificial divisions that separated structure from site, plan from facade, and interior from exterior.

Their quest to find new solutions to age-old problems

designates their work as the first important stage in the evolution of modernism. As they struggled to eliminate the superfluous and to release architecture from the stylistic strictures of the past, they initiated a process of design by subtraction. This attitude continued to affect modern architecture into the 1970s.

The development of arts-and-crafts architecture can be traced over a period of roughly 70 years. It began in England during the 1850s as an outgrowth of the Gothic Revival. Initially, it was concerned with reform of residential and ecclesiastical architecture, but by its demise in the 1920s, it had become international in its scope, affecting buildings of all types throughout Britain, Europe and North America.

The first generation of design reformers were inspired by the writings of AWN Pugin. They were neo-Goths who believed the morality of a nation to be inextricably linked with its predominant architectural style, and therefore they rejected imported Graeco-Roman models in favour of those that were domestic and Christian.

Pugin's argument in favour of the Gothic style was presented passionately in *Contrasts* and in *The True Principles of Pointed*

Garden façade, Red House, Bexley Heath, England, by Philip Webb, 1859-60. This modest, unassuming structure contrasts markedly with most mid-Victorian structures designed by professional architects. An outgrowth of the Gothic Revival and the vernacular tradition.

Old Swan House, London, England, by Richard Norman Shaw, 1876. This influential townhouse exhibits the pre-requisite characteristics of the so-called Queen Anne style popularized by Shaw in the 1870s and 1880s. It utilizes pseudo eighteenth-century elements, such as broken pediments and double-hung sash windows, with a delicacy and charm that represented a nostalgic refuge from the exigencies of modern living.

38-39 Cheyne Walk, London, England, by CR Ashbee, 1899. These two townhouses were designed to form a trio with Ashbee's Magpie and Stump House (1894). The rather fussy verticality of the latter, emphasized by a three-storey oriel window, contrasted with the relative horizontality of Nos 38 and 39.

or *Christian Architecture*, published in 1836 and 1841 respectively. Together with works by John Ruskin, such as *The Stones of Venice* and *The Seven Lamps of Architecture*, published a few years later, these books focused the attention of a generation not only upon the merits of the Gothic style, but also upon the artistic environment of the Middle Ages. It was in this atmosphere that Philip Webb and William Morris met in the office of GE Street, where they received their architectural training. Their awareness of the Middle Ages, strengthened by the university environment of Oxford and by their exposure to the Pre-Raphaelite Brotherhood, inspired the creation of Red House, which is regarded as the first example of arts-and-crafts architecture.

Red House reveals its connection with the Gothic Revival subtly by its overall verticality of form, its pointed arches and its simplified Gothic detailing. Through the collaborative process by which it was built and furnished, it recalls the spirit of artistic co-operation that flourished during the Middle Ages. It

also reflects a third, related influence that affected arts-and-crafts architects for the next 70 years, a growing appreciation of the unassuming rural dwellings built during previous generations by anonymous craftsmen.

It was this interest in vernacular sources that led to the English Domestic Revival Movement. One of its chief proponents was Richard Norman Shaw, an architect whose nostalgic Old English and Queen Anne structures evoke (with varying degrees of authenticity) the gentility of the past. The supporters of the revival admired early dwellings for their forthright construction, their timeless appearance and the unassuming ease with which they accommodated both the site and the user. To them, such structures exhibited an integrity that seemed lacking in the fashion-conscious, high-style designs of the nineteenth century.

Design reformers equated the modest exteriors of these unpretentious, anonymous dwellings with the homely virtues that the Arts and Crafts Movement sought to restore to daily life. They applauded the appropriateness of these vernacular models to their context or setting. By virtue of scale, materials and construction, each appeared comfortable in its surroundings, as if it had always been there.

Because of this sensitivity to context and appropriateness, arts-and-crafts architects regarded imported styles with scepticism. They believed that architecture should be regional in appearance, changing as necessary to reflect the climate, indigenous materials and local building traditions. They believed that it was no longer acceptable simply to re-create and apply historical styles indiscriminately. They preferred an approach which allowed for greater flexibility and which welcomed individual interpretation.

❧ ❧ ❧

The fundamental qualities

THUS FREED, they set out to explore architecture's expressive potential. They strove to design buildings that suggested by massing and elevation abstract qualities such as shelter and stability, or warmth and informality. They regarded these qualities as fundamental and universal, especially in residential design, and they evoked them, not by using superficial detail, but by exploiting the symbolic potential of volume, plane and line. They considered each element, including the roof, chimneys, elevations and overall massing. They also paid close attention to the scale, or relative size, of each part and to its proportional relationship to the whole.

Because of its size and expressive potential, the roof was a primary consideration. Many arts-and-crafts structures feature a roof that is massive and steeply pitched. It might vary in configuration from simple to complex, yet its purpose is the same: to establish the structure's characteristic silhouette, as it gathers plan and elevations within a comforting embrace. It defines the structure's personality, while expressing a sense of shelter and solidity.

The roof's form is often exaggerated to accentuate its protective function. It might rise two to three storeys in height, becoming itself as tall – or even taller – than the elevations below. Its massive contours overpower the façade, making it the predominant exterior element. At other times, the roof appears tautly stretched in all directions. It covers as many windows, chimneys, porches and dormers as possible, adjusting its slope as necessary. In his "Design for a Country Cottage", the Boston architect Ralph Adams Cram employs such an expansive roof to unify the conglomeration of exterior elements in one single comforting gesture.

Buildings by Frank Lloyd Wright or Greene & Greene demonstrate that shelter is expressed equally well by a roof that is horizontal and low. Instead of stressing verticality or mass, a low roof establishes a sheltering quality by means of broad, overhanging eaves which often extend well beyond the face of the wall, casting dark shadows on to the façade. The shadows obscure the clarity of each elevation and emphasize the weight of the roof, which, in turn, seems to flatten the bulk of the structure into the site.

Protection is expressed equally well by the appearance of the walls. Those that are punctured selectively by small windows and doors, as in Charles Rennie Mackintosh's Hill House, Glasgow, appear solid. If the windows and doors are deeply recessed, the impression of thickness and strength is amplified. In The Orchard, at Chorley Wood, Hertfordshire, Voysey uses walls which narrow towards the eaves from a broad base, like buttresses. They make the structure look firmly rooted to the site, braced for any assault by rain, wind or snow.

To accentuate the protective character of roof or walls, arts-and-crafts architects carefully manipulated each dimension and the relationship of each part to the whole. They exaggerated the height or the width of the roof to dwarf the supporting elevations. They designed chimneys that were unusually slender or elongated to contrast with the solid bulk or the horizontality of the roof. They reduced the size of doors,

333 Forest Avenue, Oak Park, Illinois, by Frank Lloyd Wright, c1889. Wright's early work was often derivative. Here, he provides an interpretation of Norman Shaw's Old English style, complete with steeply pitched roof, elongated ornamental chimneys, half-timbering and projecting windows. The historical detailing and symmetry would be abandoned by Wright later in his career.

Above. 428 Forest Avenue, Exterior, Oak Park, Illinois, by Frank Lloyd Wright, 1889. This structure served as Wright's residence and studio. Its balanced, geometric façade is related in colour and texture to the Shingle Style structures built along the New England coast in the 1880s.

Left. Perspective sketch for the FW Little Residence, Peoria, Illinois, by Frank Lloyd Wright, c1909. The relative symmetry of this structure is typical of Wright's early work, but its cruciform plan indicates the direction that he would pursue in later years. The low-slung horizontality of the mass reflects Wright's belief that "the horizontal line is the line of domesticity."

windows or trim to contrast with the broad expanse of thick walls. By manipulating scale and proportion in this way, they amplified the expressive character of each architectural element.

Voysey was particularly adept at applying these principles to residential designs. He calculated every dimension and every proportional relationship deliberately to contrast the small stature of the inhabitants with the mass of the dwelling. The recessed doors are low and broad. The little casement windows sparkle with tiny glittering panes. The smooth whitish facades are bright and welcoming. The moss-covered slate roofs extend almost to the ground. Together, these features give his dwellings the charming demeanour of an enchanted cottage in an illustration from a child's book. They appeal in a fundamental way to the child trapped inside every adult, satisfying the need for refuge and stability that persists even as one grows old.

Occasionally, architects exaggerated the scale of textures to make a massive form seem approachable. In his "Perspective Sketch of a Dwelling House", Cram's partner Bertram Grovenor Goodhue proceeds in a Voysean fashion. He manipulates each dimension and the parts within the whole to give the Old English cottage the engaging appearance of a doll's house. That impression is amplified by the scale of the random cut-stone and the half-timbering that embellish the facade: these materials seem overly large for the size of the elevations, making the facade appear diminutive by contrast.

In Bellesguard, a Barcelona hilltop retreat that resembles a medieval fortified house, Antonio Gaudi achieves the same effect by exaggerating the scale and quantity of certain structural details. He lines the roof with a host of toothy crenellations and pointed chimneys which protrude like sentries pikes, enlarging and multiplying them to emphasize their collective ferocity. He contradicts that impression, however, by punctuating the roof with angled dormers and the sheer walls with an over-abundance of windows. By doing so, he takes advantage of the hilltop site and its beautiful view, but in the process he makes the fanciful, roughly textured fortress seem no more imposing than a sand-castle. Like Bellesguard, many other arts-and-crafts structures convey a sense of shelter

Garden façade, The Orchard, Chorley Wood, Hertfordshire, England, by CFA Voysey, 1899-1900. Subtlty and understatement characterize the façade of this modest house designed by Voysey for himself and his family. It is a quintessential example of arts-and-crafts architecture, although Voysey vehemently denied allegiance to the Arts and Crafts (or any other) Movement.

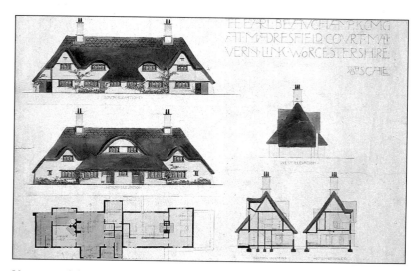

Unexecuted design for two cottages, Madresfield Court, Malvern Link, Worcestershire, England, by CFA Voysey, 1901. This design illustrates Voysey's virtuoso manipulation of form, detail, scale and proportion to achieve an enchanting result. The heavy, dark roof presses the bulk of the structure into the ground, making these diminutive cottages appear rooted to the site.

and protection, but do so in a manner that avoids intimidation. Most are designed to exude welcome and appear congenial. These qualities are conveyed by playful details and comforting proportions, together with a degree of informality.

Such informality is suggested by asymmetry of mass, plan and elevation. An asymmetrical mass accommodates the restrictions of the site, while an asymmetrical plan can be expanded as necessary, heedless of artificial restrictions. An asymmetrical elevation welcomes a random disposition of doors and windows of different sizes and shapes, their positions dictated by functional rather than cosmetic requirements. These openings express the character of the interior and elucidate the logic of the plan; they help the structure to strike a relaxed posture, embracing its surroundings, exposing its interior and extending a welcome to the passer-by.

Many arts-and-crafts architects, among them the German architect and art educator Hermann Muthesius, regarded windows as the structure's soul. They combined windows of various sizes and shapes at random to reveal the different functions of the interior. They utilized windows to demonstrate the sensitivity of structure to site, placing them as necessary to acknowledge impressive views, gardens or unusual features in the landscape. They grouped them in horizontal bands or vertical clusters on southern elevations to collect as much sunshine or daylight as possible. The window pattern revealed with candour the inner workings of the structure, while expressing a desire to maximize warmth and light.

If windows were regarded as the soul, the fireplace was deemed to be the dwelling's heart. A fireplace core was often the nucleus for the entire plan, positioned symbolically at the building's centre. Its functional and symbolic importance was stressed on the exterior by chimneys of exaggerated height or width, which served both as an anchor for the structure's mass and as a signpost of its most important interior element.

Although the shape of each exterior element was important for its symbolic connotations, form was by no means the sole determinant of a structure's character. Coloration and texture were equally expressive in conveying abstract qualities such as warmth and informality. They were chosen carefully not only for their aesthetic impact, but also to enhance the symbolic programme already established by the three-dimensional volume.

Coloration and texture were, of course, dictated by the materials used to clad the exterior. The choice reflected a conviction that was universal among arts-and-crafts architects: that each material must be better suited than any other to the

Bellesguard, Barcelona, Spain, by Antoni Gaudí, 1900-02. This expressionistic house postures with false bravado. It is a diminutive variation upon a theme established in other of Gaudí's structures, such as the Archbishop's Palace at Astorga (1887-93) or "Los Botines", a house designed in León (1891-94).

particular task at hand, and must be capable of ageing gracefully without losing either its visual or tactile appeal. Colours and textures were therefore chosen to be functional, not merely decorative – to have structural integrity or lasting beauty that was more than superficial.

Many architects made a point of using materials that were abundant in a particular area or characteristic of local architecture in order to guarantee that the building would appear integrated with its setting. The tawny Cotswold stone selected by Ernest Gimson, the weathered cedar shingles that were popular along the New England coast, the red brick used so eloquently by Hendrik Berlage and his Dutch colleagues were all chosen for their appropriateness to the climate and for

Right. Entrance, Watts Sherman House, Newport, Rhode Island, by Henry Hobson Richardson, 1874-76. This was the structure that introduced Norman Shaw's Old English style to the USA. The asymmetrical plan centres around an entry/stair hall that is dominated by a sculptural staircase. The exterior features the steeply pitched roof, elongated chimneys and multi-paned windows reminiscent of Shaw's Leyes Wood.

their contextuality.

Coloration and texture not only affected profoundly a structure's harmony with the site, but also its unity as a three-dimensional volume. A bold eclectic scheme, such as that illustrated by Shaw's Leys Wood in Sussex, Edward Ould's Wightwick Manor at Wolverhampton in the West Midlands, or Henry Hobson Richardson's Watts Sherman House at Newport, Rhode Island, might be used either to contrast a building with its surroundings, or to accentuate variations in the façade. On the other hand, a limited scheme of closely related hues and surfaces, as seen in Greene & Greene's Gamble House in Pasadena or McKim, Mead & White's Bell House at Newport, might serve to co-ordinate a structure with its natural backdrop, or to act as a foil for subtle details, ornamentation or construction features. Together, coloration and texture made the architecture of the Arts and Crafts Movement seem inviting. The russet brick of Red House, the tinted mortar that binds the ruddy brick and stone of the Watts Sherman House, the sage-green shingles and honey-coloured teak of the Gamble House evoke a kinaesthetic response, proclaiming on the outside that warmth and comfort lie within.

🌿 🌿 🌿

Construction techniques

PART OF THE APPEAL of arts-and-crafts architecture stems from its technical characteristics. How a structure is put together is often as important — if not more so — than how it looks. Most were designed to highlight construction techniques resurrected from the past, and thus to celebrate hand-craftsmanship. The architects were also dedicated to preserving and using the building methods of the past. But they were by no means consistent in their approach. In terms of construction, their designs are remarkable for their diversity. Some are built of masonry, while others are framed or clad in wood. Many use stucco or rough-cast on the outside, while a few are hung with terracotta tiles or made of rough-hewn logs. Many incorporate several different construction techniques.

This variety should not, however, suggest that decisions about modes of construction were arbitrary. An architect's first choice was always to use indigenous materials and a manner of building that reflected the local tradition. By using brick, for example, Berlage acknowledged its historical importance to Dutch architecture, as well as its appropriateness for the damp climate and urban context. By selecting rough-hewn logs for some sections of Hvittrask, Eliel Saarinen related his new home and studio to vernacular dwellings in the Karelia region of

Garden façade, Standen, Hollybush, East Grinstead, Sussex, England, by Philip Webb, 1891-94. This gracious country house reflects Webb's mature style and assumes a "cottagey" demeanour because of its irregular massing and varied coloration and texture. The prominent tower serves as a transition between a rambling service wing and a symmetrical main block.

Hvittrask, Kirkkonummi, Finland, by Eliel Saarinen, Armas Lindgren and Herman Gesellius, 1901-02. The structure, which contains three living units and a studio, is constructed from local materials — granite, logs, shingles and rough-cast — allowing it to blend sympathetically with the steep, wooded site.

Finland. Some architects or designers demonstrated their respect for the past by integrating old structures with new: Little Hyttnas, Carl Larsson's home and studio, incorporates a nineteenth-century log cottage of the Delecarlia region of Sweden. In this respect, it resembles Standen, which was designed by Philip Webb to accommodate the entirety of an early, tile-hung farmhouse that had stood on the site in Sussex for generations.

Appreciation for the time-honoured methods of the past often paralleled a retrospective attitude evident in other aspects of contemporary culture. The traditional log construction used

Above. Robert Bridge Residence, Marblehead, Massachusetts, by Bacon and Hill, c1880s-90s. This charming cottage incorporates a variety of Voysean traits, including the sleek, overhanging roof, rough-cast finish, random disposition of small-paned windows and semi-circular bay.

Right. Exterior detail, Laban Pratt Residence, Pope's Hill, Dorchester, Ma., by Cabot and Chandler, c1874-88. Japanesque whorls enliven the entrance of this house which is a marriage of Colonial Revival, Shingle Style and Queen Anne characteristics.

in building Hvittrask was influenced by National Romanticism, a movement that generated enthusiasm for all aspects of Finnish culture following the country's separation from Sweden at the turn of the century. Similarly, the coarse brick and stone that imbues Bellesguard with its rugged charm demonstrates Gaudi's application of traditional Catalan masonry techniques. The house is a testimony to the resurgence of interest in Catalan culture, which affected music, literature and the arts in northern Spain at the end of the nineteenth century.

These retrospective European movements were paralleled by the Colonial Revival in the United States, which was especially pronounced immediately after the 1876 Centennial Exposition in Philadelphia. In generating a nostalgia for American culture prior to the Industrial Revolution, it stimulated an interest in American architecture of the seventeenth and eighteenth centuries and was partially responsible for the abundance of shingle-clad cottages erected along the eastern seaboard in the 1880s and 1890s.

Although most arts-and-crafts structures incorporated building techniques characteristic of their regions, one form, elaborate half-timbering in the Elizabethan manner, became universally popular and often appeared where it was not entirely appropriate. Its quaint provincial character made it as popular in Germany or the eastern United States as it was in England. When used authentically, however, as in Leys Wood, Shaw's quintessential essay in the Old English style, it was functional as well as decorative, presenting a visible and forthright means of support while providing distinctive integrated colour, texture and pattern.

Although Leys Wood provides a gracious testimony to its merits, few interpretations of half-timbering are as exuberant, or as memorable, as that in Wightwick Manor. Here, the boldly patterned black-and-white elevations dazzle the eye. They utilize half-timbering enthusiastically, together with carving, ornamental brick chimneys and glittering multi-pane casement windows. These elevations tend to obscure the already complex form of the house, but they succeed, nevertheless, in setting the tone for the richly decorated and carefully crafted interiors.

The versatility of half-timbering is gloriously illustrated by the Regent Street building of Liberty & Co, which was designed in the 1920s by Edwin T and E Stanley Hall. The Elizabethan façade may have seemed somewhat out of place in its formal Regency setting, but it has a warmth and intimacy that was – and remains – attractive to the shop's fashionable clientele.

Liberty's exemplifies a commitment to handcraftsmanship

South front, Wightwick Manor, Staffordshire, England by Edward Ould, 1887. A superb example of the half-timbering, carving, ornamental brick chimneys and casement windows so beloved of the Arts and Crafts Movement.

that distinguishes arts-and-crafts architecture at its best. Its weathered oaken timbers, taken from the hulls of old ships, are carefully joined in the manner of an early housewright with mortise-and-tenon joints and exposed pegs. The half-timbering is complemented by chiselled masonry, handmade roof tiles and hand-painted leaded windows. The standard of craftsmanship on the outside is matched by that on the inside, where fittings and furnishings were executed by Liberty's own skilled, in-house craftsmen. The architecture reflects the aesthetic sensitivity and technical proficiency that had motivated the founder, Arthur Lasenby Liberty, when he set up his first shop in 1875.

Half-timbered façades evoke a tactile response. They appear to elucidate the process by which they were constructed, displaying joinery, finishes or trim. Other arts-and-crafts stuctures which exhibit a similar attention to detail prompt the same reaction: the cedar shingles joined together into a smooth, continuous skin; the borders of brick laid in subtle, decorative patterns; the timber framework carefully notched and pegged like fine cabinet-work.

41

Ornamentation

ARTS-AND-CRAFTS ARCHITECTS added variety to their buildings with structural coloration, eclectic textures and exposed construction techniques. They valued such elements both for their longevity and for their functional decorativeness, often relying upon them as the sole source of embellishment. Some of their colleagues, however, considered that buildings devoid of ornament were incomplete, and they developed an ornamental approach consistent with their own philosophy to complement each structure's particular character.

As a group, arts-and-crafts architects agreed that ornament must appear integrated rather than applied as a cosmetic afterthought. But they disagreed on its character and the extent to which it should be used. For the most part, they rejected embellishments that were either academic or historical, preferring them to be original and personal. They admired especially the generic simplicity of geometric motifs, or graceful, naturalistic forms derived from insects, flowers, foliage or trees.

Ironically, some of the greatest ornamentalists associated with arts-and-crafts architecture confined their decorative skills almost exclusively to the interior. The greyish bulk of Hill House, for example, provides little indication of the rich combination of chequers, grids and delicate Glasgow roses that Mackintosh used to enliven its interior surfaces. The blank façade of CR Ashbee's own house, the Magpie and Stump in Cheyne Walk, London, contradicts the elegant, abstract naturalism found on interior lighting fixtures, copper tiles, embroideries, murals and metalwork. The black and white rectangular block of the Palais Stoclet in Brussels belies the presence of its rich interior detail. Throughout the palatial town house, Hoffmann's characteristic patterns and motifs provide accents, floral and geometric.

Hill House, Helensburgh, Scotland, by Charles Rennie Mackintosh, 1902-04. This influential structure marries the integrity of vernacular architecture with the ornamental panache of Art Nouveau. The compartmentalized plan lacks the openness of American examples while including the prerequisite arts-and-crafts entry/stair hall, window bays with built-in furniture, and inglenook.

Some architects avoided ornamentation *per se*, preferring instead to treat architectural features as decoration. In his house at Darmstadt, Peter Behrens exploits the ornamental potential of every exterior architectural element. He uses dormers, windows, drip mouldings, chimneys and variations on quoins and pilasters as dark accents to contrast with the pale elevations. He groups them in asymmetrical compositions on each facade as the demands of plan and interior dictate. He designs four unmatched elevations with the intention of contradicting the overall symmetry of the cube-shaped house. Inside and out, he enlivens the structure with a complex interplay of angular and soft forms. He manipulates every element with skill and precision, demonstrating the graphic ability he learned from his early training as a painter.

Such exploitation of the decorative potential of architectural elements was not unique to Behrens. Voysey, Godwin and Mackintosh, among others, carefully considered the design and placement of every opening, chimney, moulding or piece of trim. They treated each elevation as a two-dimensional composition whose success depended upon a subtle juxtaposition of mass against void, light against dark, or hard-edge form against soft.

Some architects, in contrast, took a more overtly decorative approach, applying ornamental forms to the exterior that were better suited for textiles, furniture or decorative arts. In the diminutive Bahr House at Vienna, for example, Joseph Maria Olbrich achieves a surprising monumentality of form, but violates its strength with finicky, Jugendstil ornament. The sinuous, naturalistic applied wood trim appears arbitrary and artificial. Tree-like brackets run from foundation to eaves in a theatrical fashion, making them seem exasperatingly out of scale – too delicate to be functional, but too large to be purely

Palais Stoclet, Brussels, Belgium, by Josef Hoffmann, 1905-11. The starkness of Hoffmann's masterpiece is relieved by the ornamental tower and roof-top conservatory, but is sheer walls and bare windows must have seemed shocking in turn-of-the-century Brussels.

Palais Stoclet, Brussels, Belgium, by Josef Hoffmann, 1905-11. The starkness of Hoffmann's masterpiece is relieved by the ornamental tower and roof-top conservatory, but its sheer walls and bare windows must have seemed shocking in turn-of-the-century Brussels.

Peter Behrens' house, Darmstadt Artist's Colony, Darmstadt, Germany, 1901-02. The colony attracted design reformers from throughout Europe. Behrens designed this striking house for his family; it is resplendent, inside and out, with Jugendstil forms and ornament, evident even within a utilitarian space such as the kitchen.

Haus Freudenberg, Nikolassee, Germany, by Hermann Muthesius, 1907-08. Haus Freudenberg's steeply pitched roof, half-timbering and colourful, textured skin seem akin to Richard Norman Shaw's Old English style. But the symmetrical façade and formal plan are close in character to the work of Sir Edwin Lutyens.

43

Gluckert House, Darmstadt Artist's Colony, Darmstadt, Germany, by Joseph Maria Olbrich, c1898-1900. Like the Bahr house, this structure applies naturalist Jugendstil ornament to a softened, expressionistic form.

Entrance façade, Glasgow School of Art, Glasgow, Scotland, by Charles Rennie Mackintosh, 1897-99, 1907-09. This façade, a study in contrasts, established Mackintosh's international reputation. It juxtaposes hard line with soft, mass with void, complexity with simplicity, horizontality with verticality, symmetry with asymmetry. The mortar-board caps and cornices and zoomorphic metal trim are distinctive Mackintosh features.

decorative. The most satisfying ornamental element is a curvilinear wooden framework that surrounds three windows on the second storey. Flat and dark against a lighter background, it is distinctive while remaining subordinate to the wall surface.

Voysey, unlike Olbrich, is a master at combining monumental form with whimsical decoration. He enjoys his role as ornamentalist, and never hesitates to embellish exterior and interior with strategically placed vernacular elements. His decorative vocabulary includes timeless motifs drawn from Nature – birds, flowers, leaves and hearts – which, although born of the folk tradition, are reinterpreted in a highly original manner, consistent in their simplicity with the forthright character of his structures. Form and ornament together convey a sophisticated provincialism that is evident in all of Voysey's work, regardless of scale.

Many other arts-and-crafts architects also used natural forms for exterior ornamentation, experimenting freely and devising approaches that were both original and expressive. Some, such as Mackintosh, Hoffmann or Gaudi, developed systems of ornament which they repeated on structure after structure. Others, including Wright or Greene & Greene, evolved recognizable individual styles, but adapted the subject to suit the region. These aesthetic decisions, true to form, were governed by appropriateness and the desire to unify the structure with the surroundings.

❦ ❦ ❦

The structure and its site

THIS DESIRE prompted them also to consider the interrelationship between structure and site: a building must appear integrated with its surroundings and in harmony with its context, both externally and internally. To achieve this, they

Ward Willits House, Highland Park, Illinois, by Frank Lloyd Wright, 1902. The low-slung house is typical of Wright's Prairie Style approach. The strong light/dark contrast of the exterior is duplicated in the interior finishing. The innovative cruciform plan is organized around a central fireplace core.

deliberated over the shape of the roof, the fenestration and the colour and texture of each elevation, as well as the orientation of major interior spaces and the overall configuration of the plan.

Every location and every building type presented a different challenge. An urban structure, for instance, occupying a site of limited size in proximity to neighbouring buildings, was ringed round with more restrictions than was a country house, standing in relative isolation on an expansive property. Ultimately, the degree to which a structure was united with its setting depended upon the architect's concept, the client's requirements and the character of the particular site. As a reflection of such influences, buildings either maintained a sympathetic separateness, or blended into the background as if an extension of the landscape.

Those in the former category, such as Voysey's Broadleys at Gill Head, Windermere or Mackintosh's Hill House, establish a formal relationship with their surroundings. They harmonize with the site while remaining somewhat detached from it. They assert their separateness through introverted plans, contained massing or colouration and texture chosen to contrast with the natural backdrop. They utilize terraces, walkways or walls as borders to keep the landscape at bay. They survey water, lawns, gardens or orchards, but hold them at a distance.

Frank Lloyd Wright's Willits House in Highland Park, Illinois, is another example of such integrated separateness. Its horizontal mass and cruciform plan stretch to fill the flat midwestern site. But its reddish roof and crisp elevations of white stucco trimmed with dark wood contrast with the soft contours of nearby trees. Vine-laden planters and window boxes are strategically placed to soften the angularity of the façade. Yet the structure is raised upon a platform and is protected by low parapets – features which discourage, rather than invite, encroachment by surrounding vegetation.

Other arts-and-crafts buildings embrace the sites they occupy. In the picturesque tradition, they complement rather than contradict its predominant features. Their flexible plans accommodate its natural contours. Their massing replicates the jagged forms of hills and trees, or the flatness of a broad lawn.

Some, like the Gamble House, harmonize with the site to

such a degree that they appear almost subordinate to it. By virtue of its low-slung mass and dull sage-green colour, this house appears rooted to the site. Lush vines cover its foundation, suggesting that it is being reclaimed by the verdant landscape. Similarly, the weathered, shingled bulk of the Bell House nestles snugly into its wooded location. Its foundation is obscured by shrubbery; its irregular roofline and attenuated chimneys beckon toward the sky and the backdrop of sheltering trees, making it appear to be an outgrowth of the site, rather than an imposition upon it.

The relationship between structure and plan, or plan and site, was equally significant. Some of the most innovative plans to be developed by design reformers reflected the triadic interdependence of these elements. The best of these effortlessly accommodated the demands of the site and the requirements of the users, while accentuating the informality of the façade. The

Gamble House, Pasadena, California, by Charles Sumner Greene and Henry Mather Greene, 1908. The skeletal structure of this rambling house is frankly exposed, allowing framing members to be shaped and joined carefully, like fine cabinetry. Porches and terraces provide a transition between exterior and interior.

Entrance detail, Gamble House, Pasadena, California, by Charles Sumner Greene and Henry Mather Greene, 1908. The teak-framed entrance with its stained glass door, transoms and hovering light fixture reflect the exquisite attention to detail found within.

character of each plan was, to a certain extent, predetermined by such factors as setting and building type: an urban location, in this context also, imposed more restrictions than did a site in suburb or country. And, generally speaking, a commercial, institutional or ecclesiastical plan allowed for less experimentation than did its residential counterpart.

Arts-and-crafts architects were varied in their approach. Some took a relatively conservative posture, preferring plans that were compartmentalized. Others were more unconventional, striving to eliminate wherever possible traditional boundaries between individual rooms, interior and exterior, or exterior and site.

Residential planning provided great potential for experimentation in terms both of shape and of circulation pattern.

❦ ❦ ❦

A variety of plans

IN DESIGNING HIS HOUSE at Darmstadt, Behrens utilized a compact square which eliminated corridors, thus increasing efficiency. For The Orchard, Voysey selected a crisp contained rectangle, bisected into public and private zones by an entry/stairhall. For Red House and Standen, Webb chose a loose L shape, which was later used by Voysey in Broadleys and by Mackintosh in Hill House. The same flexible form served Carl Larsson when he was expanding Little Hyttnas over a ten-year period.

The L shape was universally popular, partly because it neatly segregated the structure into two distinct sections joined by a common core, separating service wing from main block, studio or workshop from residence, public areas from private. But its extended linearity had one disadvantage: rooms tended to be isolated from one another, connected only by a long corridor. The awkwardness of this arrangement prompted architects to explore ways to make the shape more efficient. For his home at Nikolassee, Muthesius utilized a precise V-shaped plan, which provided a compact disposition of rooms, eliminated the need for corridors and allowed major public spaces to interconnect conveniently.

In general, arts-and-crafts architects preferred asymmetrical plans that could be — or appeared to have been — expanded over time. These conveyed a sense of gracious informality, adjusting to the users' needs without compromising the integrity of the façade. They were also picturesque, appearing to be more in sympathy with the site than would a precise geometric form.

Whether compact outspread or wrapped round a central

courtyard (as in Leys Wood), the plans all combined distinct advantages with specific drawbacks. Each ultimately determined the responsiveness of the interior to the occupiers' needs. And each dictated, more than any other feature, the character of the structure as a whole.

One of the most outstanding residential plans of the late nineteenth century was developed by McKim, Mead & White for the Bell House. The asymmetrical plan revolves around a stairhall which serves as a nucleus for household activities. On the ground floor, the stairhall, dining-room, drawing-room and reception-room form a dynamic interconnected quartet; permitting movement from one to another in a circular fashion. They are joined by wide archways hung with sleek, panelled doors which slide along tracks like Japanese *shoji* screens. When the doors are open, the rooms become interdependent in a proto-modernistic fashion.

A cruciform plan, such as that used by Wright in the Willits House promoted better than any other type this interpenetration of interior spaces. The plan moves out from a central fireplace core, breaking free of the box form that had ensnared Western planning since the Renaissance. Such open plans diminish the need for corridors or separate circulation areas. Movement from room to room is facilitated by the lack of distinct interior partitions. The traditional boundaries are blurred; rooms are conceived as an ensemble, to be viewed collectively.

Dissolving boundaries, however, had one serious flaw: it tended to obliterate enclosed spaces that were needed for privacy and intimacy. The ubiquitous entry/stairhall may have constituted an efficient nucleus, but its multi-functional, often bustling, atmosphere discouraged quiet reflection or close conversation.

A congenial setting for such activities was provided by the inglenook, an element borrowed from early Anglo-Saxon buildings. Its evolution as a turn-of-the-century planning feature paralleled the development of openness, flexibility and efficient circulation. This small room-within-a-room became popular on both sides of the Atlantic, its inviting fireplace and built-in seating creating a cosy retreat. It was usually positioned at the side of a large open room, where it was tangent to, but slightly detached from, other activities. Its appearance varied according to the functional and aesthetic intentions of the architect, but most were showcases for custom-designed features that highlighted interior finishes and details.

In the dining-room of the Page residence in Boston, H Langford Warren incorporated a tiny version. Contained

within a bold brick arch, in the manner of HH Richardson, it serves both as a focus within the room and as a frame for an ornamental fireplace. In the entry/stairhall of the Bell House, the inglenook is large enough to accommodate movable furniture. A pair of high windows on either side of the fireplace provide daylight for reading and illuminate the japanesque roundels that ornament the dark wood panelling. A grander variation humanizes the Great Parlour in Wightwick Manor. Although it is large enough to house upholstered seating, small tables, oriental rugs and assorted bric-à-brac, it seems an intimate refuge by comparison with the cavernous scale of the Old English hall which it graces.

This opulent inglenook contrasts markedly with the sleek example designed by Greene & Greene for the Gamble House. Finely finished in oiled teak with articulated joinery, this is a serene extension of the sitting-room, with its autonomy subtly established by a low beam at frieze level supported by sculptural brackets. Built-in seating on either side of a low fireplace

Edward Robinson Residence, Manchester, Massachusetts, by Charles Howard Walker, 1888. Arts-and-crafts architecture in Boston tended to be less progressive than that produced elsewhere. Such conservatism was encouraged by Walker who was a highly influential educator, design critic and officer for The Society of Arts and Crafts in Boston.

Isaac Bell House, Newport, Rhode Island, by McKim, Mead and White, 1882-83. This influential Shingle Style structure nestles into the site, providing a noticeable contrast to its neighbours, monumental chateaux and palazzi in historical styles erected as summer retreats at the turn of the century.

Porch/verandah detail, Isaac Bell House, Newport, Rhode Island, by McKim, Mead and White, 1882-83. In a progressive fashion, the Bell House eliminates overt historical detailing. Instead, interest is created by the changing shapes of cut cedar shingles that constitute its soft, weathered skin, and the wrap-around porches supported by tapered, faux bamboo posts.

is illuminated by integrated lighting. It is cosy without being claustrophobic, informal while retaining a degree of elegant exclusivity.

Oriel or bay windows and structural furnishings built into cosy recesses also appear frequently in the arts-and-crafts plan. Like the ingle-nook, they provide a sense of enclosure, serving as intermediaries between the structure and its inhabitants. They reflect as well an awareness that the human spirit thrives in the presence of variety. Most arts-and-crafts structures were designed as carefully in section as in plan, in order to orchestrate satisfying changes in room dimension, ceiling height or floor level.

The Watts Sherman and Glessner houses (the latter built in Chicago) had already demonstrated HH Richardson's expert manipulation of interior space in this way. Sunlit stairwells ascend from halls panelled in dark wainscoting, the bright vertical thrust of the one contrasting with the sombre horizontality of the other. The airy atmosphere of the stairwells is accentuated by soaring ceilings and large windows, while in every hall, low, beamed or panelled ceilings provide a sense of enclosure. Mackintosh also was a master at the dramatic shaping of interior space, as is seen in the entry/stairhall at Hill House. And he too was gifted at selecting colours and textures which complemented a careful shaping of interior space.

In some arts-and-crafts interiors, stairwells are defined by screens of decorative verticals. These semi-transparent partitions provide a sense of enclosure while allowing a visual connection between the staircase and the entry hall or landing which it serves. Voysey defined the hall staircase in The Orchard, for example, by screens of densely packed, square-cut verticals which extend from tread to ceiling, instead of the traditional hand-rail. They give the staircase autonomy and definition, while at the same time enhancing the sculptural qualities of an otherwise utilitarian architectural feature. Similar partitions enclose stairwells in structures designed by Richardson, Mackintosh and McKim, Mead & White. Wright used them in combination with half-walls to enclose fireside seating, or to direct movement around the central

Charles J. Page House, Westland Avenue, Boston, Massachusetts, by Herbert Langford Warren, c1887-88, influenced by Henry Hobson Richardson.

fireplace core. These screens are an important feature in multi-functional rooms or open plans, providing "soft" edges to architectural features, and defining the boundaries of rooms discreetly.

Architects had always accepted responsibility for the design of major interior architectural elements such as fireplaces or staircases. But the design reformer went further, addressing every aspect of the structure from site and façade to furnishings and decorative arts. Many arts-and-crafts architects designed woodwork, fittings and stained glass as well as furniture, lighting fixtures and hardware. Some were so motivated by the desire to unite the structure from broadest concept to smallest detail that they even created patterns for textiles, wallpapers and ceramic tiles. They took full control in their determination to restore order to the chaotic atmosphere of the nineteenth-century interior.

This may explain their liking for built-in seating or storage and for decorative ledges and plate-rails. Such features ordained that there was a place for everything – that furniture and accessories were, in essence, an extension of the architecture. It was this strict co-ordination of parts which distinguished the architecture of the Arts and Crafts Movement at every scale: just as the furnishings were interrelated with the architecture, so too was the architecture interconnected with the site.

The Arts and Crafts Movement provided a means for developing an architecture of character. It challenged its supporters by establishing high ideals, but perplexed them by supplying no set rules. It freed design reformers from a slavish adherence to historical style, encouraging in its place the expression of fundamental values. Its emphasis upon appropriateness and contextuality ensured that arts-and-crafts architecture gained international acceptance. But, ironically, that very flexibility ultimately led to its decline. By the end of World War I, architecture was embracing a new idea, the concept of standardization. This was an approach that discouraged the regional or the personal in favour of the generic. As such, it was antithetical to the diversity that gave arts-and-crafts architecture its distinctive thrust.

Chapter Three

FURNITURE

THE GUILDS ◖ THE MOVEMENT IN SCANDINAVIA ◖ THE VIENNA SECESSION ◖ THE GERMAN WORKSHOPS ◖ FURNITURE MAKERS IN NORTH AMERICA

"I MUST NEEDS THINK of furniture as two kinds, one part of it being chairs, dining and working tables, and the like, the necessary workaday furniture in short, which should, of course be well made and well proportioned, but simple to the last degree..." wrote William Morris in *The Lesser Arts of Life*. "But besides this type of furniture, there is the kind I should call state furniture, which I think proper, even for a citizen: I mean sideboards, cabinets, and the like, which we have quite as much for beauty's sake as for use; we need not spare ornament on these, but make them as elegant and elaborate as we can with carving, inlaying, or painting: these are the blossoms of the art of furniture."

An ideal of furniture made "for beauty's sake" as much as for use unites arts-and-crafts achievement in this complex area. Architects, designers and craftsmen throughout Europe, as well as in the United States, were preoccupied with the production of furniture that would play both a symbolic and a practical role in the domestic environment. The resulting plurality of style and intention, which is of course characteristic of the whole range of arts-and-crafts production, defies simple definition. Furniture was made not only in response to changing values but also to specific needs, so that the work of Scandinavian designers, for example, is very different from that of their Viennese counterparts. Social concern could be described as one common factor, but there was no common consensus to show how that concern might be demonstrated in the design of tables and chairs, sideboards and settles. An ideal of the past and the significance of tradition also played an important role; but again we must ask ourselves, "Whose past, and what traditions were relevant to designers at the turn of the century?"

When William Morris invited his friend and colleague Philip Webb to design his first home, Red House, in 1859, the issues were more clear cut. Morris's youthful idealism had been determined by Romanticism in art and literature, and by the Gothic Revivalists' rejection of the Machine Age. John Ruskin had embarked on his crusade for humanism in design and architecture, rejecting mechanization, and all that mechanization implied in a rapidly industrializing society. Morris's decision to train as an architect when he left Oxford was his initial response to the Ruskinian ideal of commitment, and his determination to work as a "decorator" was also part of that response.

Describing this period in his life some years later, he wrote, "At this time the revival of Gothic architecture was making great progress in England...I threw myself into these movements with all my heart: got a friend to build me a house very mediaeval in spirit...and set myself to decorating it; we found, I and my friend the architect especially, that all the minor arts were in a state of complete degradation especially in England, and accordingly in 1861 with the conceited courage of a young man I set myself to reforming all that..." The furniture that Philip Webb and his colleagues designed for Red House represented, therefore, an early attempt to create "the blossoms of the art". As well as the magnificent painted cupboards and settles, Philip Webb produced solid tables in oak; and additional furniture was designed on commission by others in those early years. The medieval inspiration was lauded when the Morris exhibit was awarded two gold medals at the International Exhibition of 1862. The jury reported, "The general forms of the furniture...and the character of the details are satisfying to the archaeologist from the exactness of the imitation, at the same

Far right. Sideboard, in painted and ebonized wood, with painted and gilt leather panels, by Philip Webb, England, c.1862. One of the founder members of the Morris firm, Webb was the architect of Red House. These elaborate and costly designs are typical of Webb's early work in cabinet-making.

Right. Washstand, painted and gilt wood, by William Burges, for his own house, Tower House, London, c.1880. Burges was one of the first nineteenth-century British designers to produce painted furniture based on an interpretation of medieval precedents. This washstand, which is inscribed *Venez Lavez*, is typical of his flamboyant designs c.1880.

time that the general effect is excellent."

It is interesting that the first person who seems to have felt some concern about the cost and élitism of such commissions was not William Morris but Warington Taylor, the business manager of Morris & Co, referred to as "the Firm". Taylor, who was suffering from tuberculosis, conducted most of the business from Hastings, where he was hoping to recuperate, and it is through his letters that we can follow the day-to-day preoccupations of the Firm. In 1865 he is telling Webb, "It is hellish wickedness to spend more than 15/- on a chair when the poor are starving in the streets." What was needed, he wrote,

was "moveable furniture...something you can pull about with one hand. You can't stand fixtures now that there are no more castles." It is claimed that Warington Taylor introduced the now familiar rush-seated "Sussex" chair to the Firm, variants of which remained in production for many years. He also introduced the "Morris" easy chair with an adjustable back. It is significant that he had found examples of these in the workshop of a Sussex carpenter, for variants of vernacular or folk furniture were to form a major part of arts-and-crafts production, especially in Scandinavia, where the peasant dwelling rather than the medieval palace was to be the primary

White painted dresser, by Philip Webb, for Standen, Sussex, c1892. Webb was also the architect of Standen. Built 30 years after Red House, Standen is a large country house; its furniture and furnishings, however, are lighter than those produced in what Webb described as the Morris firm's "Gothic days".

One of the ranges of rush-seated chairs, by Morris, Marshall, Faulkner & Co., London, c1865. The chairs were based on a traditional Sussex design, and were produced cheaply for general sale, rather than on commission.

The Morris adjustable chair, in ebonized wood, upholstered with Morris's "Birds" double woven wool fabric (1878). Based on a Sussex carpenter's design (discovered by the Firm's business manager, Warington Taylor), the chair was produced from about 1865.

source of inspiration. Taylor, however, was not totally scathing about his employers' efforts; he approved of the fact that it had no style: "It is original, it has its own style: it is in fact Victorian."

As Morris became more preoccupied with wallpaper and textile design, he tended to delegate furniture commissions to his colleagues, and in the 1880s, when George Jack, Mervyn Macartney and WAS Benson were involved with this area of the firm's production, the furniture became more Georgian than Victorian, in keeping with the taste of their patrons, most of whom were drawn from the growing ranks of the upper middle classes. Ford Madox Brown, however, the Pre-Raphaelite painter who was one of the firm's founder members, produced a range of "working men's" bedroom furniture, designed so that it could be easily copied by local carpenters and artisans.

❧ ❧ ❧

The Guilds

FOLLOWING THE MORRIS PRECEDENT, several architect/designers set up their own enterprises in the 1860s and 70s. The architect Arthur Heygate Mackmurdo, for example, established his Century Guild in 1882, designing furniture as well as fabrics which were made for him by specialized firms. His furniture was eccentrically stylized, its essentially conventional forms frequently embellished with a fretwork motif of undulating lines, inspired perhaps by the work of the painter William Blake. His dining chair is his most familiar design, perhaps because it has been so frequently categorized – and illustrated – as proto-Art Nouveau. This is a claim which Mackmurdo himself would have rejected, Art Nouveau having been so thoroughly despised by British designers.

The Century Guild was disbanded in 1888, but an equally short-lived group was to lead to the establishment of a workshop which had a far more lasting influence on ideals for arts-and-crafts furniture. Kenton & Co was founded in 1890 when several young architects, including WR Lethaby, Ernest Gimson, Mervyn Macartney, Sidney Barnsley and Reginald Blomfield, set out, in the words of Blomfield, "to produce the best possible furniture of its time, with the best materials and the best workmanship". Although this enterprise was forced to close through lack of capital in 1892, Ernest Gimson and Sidney Barnsley went on to set up on their own in rural Gloucestershire, thus establishing a dynasty of designer/craftsmen in furniture, and proving against all odds that the English craft ideal could be reconciled with financial survival.

Ernest Gimson's furniture, in fact, epitomizes the craft ideal of "honest workmanship". He is perhaps best known for his rush-seated chairs, so similar to Shaker designs, which draw directly on a vernacular tradition. But he also produced "blossoms of the art of furniture", exquisite cabinets inlaid with mother-of-pearl, silver and ivory, made from native woods such as oak, elm, yew and walnut. This work, of course, replaced the earlier painted furniture of Webb and Morris and their colleagues; it was a tradition maintained by the Barnsley family, whose workshop survived at Sapperton, in Gloucestershire, until Edwin Barnsley's death in 1987.

Gimson and the Barnsleys are the best known of the British designer/craftsmen who specialized in furniture production. Most arts-and-crafts furniture was designed by architects, either to supplement their incomes, or to complement the houses they created. CFA Voysey, for example, conceived his houses as "total design", aiming to supervise or design every item

Bureau, by Ernest Gimson. Work such as this, demonstrating the designer's pre-occupation with simplicity and quality of workmanship, was intended to be "timeless". It appealed to affluent clients who aspired to the rural and vernacular associations of the simple life.

Walnut cabinet, with ebony base, by Ernest Gimson, England. A disciple of William Morris, Gimson produced furniture which is characteristic of the arts and crafts ideal. His cabinets, made in his own workshops, are exquisitely detailed and proportioned.

of their furnishing; his furniture, like his architecture, is deceptively simple and understated – "poor peoples' furniture for the rich", according to the claims of the more cynical. Edwin Lutyens and, above all, Baillie Scott designed or conceived furniture and interiors for "dream houses" which were internationally admired and emulated, representing an ideal of domesticity that struck a chord among the middle classes throughout Europe and the United States. In his book *A Small Country House* (1897), Baillie Scott described the home as an "enchanted realm". He wrote, "On crossing the threshold we pass into enchanted territory, where everything we possess shall be in harmony."

Thebes stool, with mahogany frame and leather seat, designed and made for Liberty & Co., London, 1884. Liberty was the first of several retailers to commission designs for an increasingly eclectic market who wanted "aesthetic" interiors.

Glass-fronted cabinet in satinwood, designed and made by Liberty & Co., c1905.

Piano, by MH Baillie Scott. For the architect Baillie Scott, the home was "an enchanted realm", and he designed domestic furniture to celebrate this ideal.

Round table in oak, by Heal and Sons, London. Heals retailed furniture and furnishings to the increasingly affluent middle classes, and from the 1890s its directors both commissioned and sold designs in keeping with the arts-and-crafts ideal of simplicity and sobriety.

The Movement in Scandinavia

THE HOME WAS ALSO the focus for an ideal of design and craftsmanship in Sweden at the turn of the century. Ellen Key, the Swedish sociologist and aesthetician, expounded the principle in her book, *Beauty for All*, in 1897: "...always, when we buy something for our homes, we should ask ourselves if it fulfils the most vital requirement – namely, that everything should answer the purpose it is intended for. A chair should be comfortable to sit on, a table comfortable to work or eat at, a bed good to sleep in. Uncomfortable chairs, rickety tables, and narrow beds are, therefore, automatically ugly. But it does not follow that comfortable chairs, steady tables and broad beds are beautiful. Things must, as everywhere in nature, fulfil their purpose in a simple and expressive manner, and without this they do not achieve beauty even if they satisfy practical requirements."

Sweden was the most industrialized of the Scandinavian countries in the nineteenth century and had promoted schemes for design reform since the 1840s, when the introduction of free trade together with economic depressions had threatened not only the stability of the country's traditional industries, but the development of new ones, as well. These reform schemes were co-ordinated by the Swedish Society for Craft and Design (Svenska Slojdforeningen), which was launched in 1845. With its motto, "Swedish handicraft is the father of Swedish independence", Svensk Form (as it is now known) concentrated on essentially practical programmes which encouraged self-sufficiency in local industries and enterprises.

In the early years it promoted evening training for workers and published patterns and prototypes for various products; throughout the century it organized exhibitions, especially in local workers' institutes, to disseminate its ideals. By the 1890s, when the "renaissance" associated with Art Nouveau as well as with the Arts and Crafts Movement was spreading throughout Europe, Sweden already had an established tradition of design reform on which to draw. It also, of course, had a surviving tradition of local or vernacular craftsmanship, especially in the textile and furniture industries, a tradition which was studied and preserved in museums and art schools. So far as the country's furniture production was concerned, local light industries, such as those in the province of Smaland, were able to maintain their output of low-cost and unpretentious designs for the domestic market.

One house in particular provided a focus for Swedish

domestic ideals in the 1890s, the country home of the painter Carl Larsson. His family spent their summers at Sundborn, and during one extremely wet summer when Larsson was unable to paint the surrounding landscape he painted his house and family instead. These water-colours were exhibited in the Industrial Exhibition in Stockholm in 1897, and aroused so much interest that they were published in book-form two years later. The book *Ett Hem (A Home)* set the style for a generation; it inspired the chapter on *Beauty in the Home* in Ellen Key's seminal book, and it demonstrated the survival of tradition in rooms that were meant to be lived in. Larsson's "best" furniture dates from the eighteenth century, whereas the work-

Brita's Forty Winks, illustration to *Ett Hem,* by Carl Larsson, 1899. When the Swedish painter Larsson published watercolours of the interiors of his house in *Ett Hem (A Home)* in 1899 he evoked a response in Swedish architects and designers, as well as the general public. For here was an ideal of domesticity that was both classless and timeless.

aday chairs and tables could have been produced on his own estate. It was these simpler objects which attracted the interest of Swedish furniture designers. Carl Westmann, for example, designed furniture in the spirit of *Ett Hem*, and like his contemporary, Eric Josephson, produced designs for "workers' furniture" to be displayed in the many exhibitions of household objects for "the less affluent" which were organized prior to World War I.

Westmann was one of the most prolific furniture designers during this period and, besides drawing on vernacular traditions, he was also obviously influenced by the work of the British, the Belgians and the Viennese. Like their British counterparts, Swedish designers were prolific in several media: Alf Wallender, for instance, is probably best known for his work in ceramics for Rorstrand, but he also designed simple furniture which was exhibited in workers' institutes, as well as more elaborate pieces for private commissions.

The most prestigious commissions in Sweden were associated with work for Stockholm Town Hall, which was designed by Ragnar Ostberg. Although not completed until

1923, work began on the scheme in 1909, and in 1916 Carl Malmsten won several prizes in a competition for furniture for the building. The son of a doctor, Malmsten had been trained for an academic career, but decided to become a craftsman instead and apprenticed himself to a carpenter. Following his success in the town-hall competition, he set up his own workshop and embarked on a prestigious and controversial career as a furniture designer. He was an educator, pioneering an ambitious programme of reform which began at primary-school level, and he was also an anti-modernist, upholding the value of tradition throughout his career. Unlike many designers of the following generation, he did not totally reject the values of an aristocratic or bourgeois culture, but aimed, rather, at maintaining what he felt to be universal standards of excellence and craftsmanship. He produced experimental pieces as well as luxurious inlaid cabinets, but he also concentrated on simple designs in the craft tradition, work which was celebrated in the 1950s when "Swedish Grace" enjoyed international prestige.

The Danes shared this prestige during the 1950s with their now classic designs for furniture. The foundations for their renaissance had, however, been laid in the period prior to World War I, when the country, slowly recovering from a long period of economic depression, was attempting to establish a sense of national identity in its design and architecture. Denmark's major "domestic" industries – ceramics, silverware and furniture – had developed under royal or aristocratic patronage in the seventeenth and eighteenth centuries. The furniture produced by the Royal Furniture Warehouse during this early period had been influenced by English design, but following Denmark's bankruptcy in 1819, the warehouse was dissolved, and most furniture was then made by individual craftsmen, or designed by architects and painters. The National Romantic Movement at the turn of the century had led to a preoccupation with peasant design and culture and to a revival of traditional craftsmanship. At the same time, the country's "neo-classical" past was not ignored, and the early work of Kaare Klint, one of Denmark's most prestigious furniture designers, is classical in inspiration. Although it might be difficult to relate Klint's first commission, the chairs he designed for the Faubourg Museum in 1914, to any ideal of the "simple life", these preoccupations with traditions of fine workmanship, as in the work of Malmsten, were to transform Danish conceptions of excellence in craftsmanship in the 1950s.

Within the context of Scandinavian developments, the Finnish interpretation – or appropriation – of arts-and-crafts idealism was unique. Finland had been part of the Swedish Empire until the beginning of the nineteenth century, when it came under the jurisdiction of Russia. Even though the country then began to enjoy some degree of autonomy, the majority of its artists and architects were trained abroad, either in Stockholm, St Petersburg or Paris. Towards the end of the nineteenth century, however, the Finns began to discover their own identity. The Friends of Finnish Handicraft was established in 1879 in order to "promote homecrafts in a patriotic and artistic spirit", and, more specifically, to study and preserve peasant traditions in embroidery and textiles. The country's architects and designers also looked to folk architecture for "ideas that could serve as the foundation of a distinctive Finnish style" as Yrjo Blomstedt, a leading architect, expressed it. The results of these endeavours achieved some degree of international recognition in 1900, when the Finnish Pavilion at the Paris World Fair was awarded several medals. The pavilion itself was designed by three young architects, Eliel Saarinen, Herman Gesellius and Armas Lindgren, and the display, designed by the Friends of Finnish Handicraft, included work by Louis Sparre and Axel Gallen. These five were

Above. Ship's dining saloon, by Sigurd Frosterus, Finland, 1907. Frosterus, who was a doctor of philosophy as well as architect, also wrote about aesthetics, and had studied with the Belgian architect and educator Henry van de Velde.

Left. Carved chair, by Eliel Saarinen for Hvittråsk, Finland, c1918. Like the studio house near Helsinki which Saarinen shared with his colleagues Armas Lindgren and Herman Gesellius and their families, the chair is inspired by an ideal of nationalism and the vernacular.

to contribute to the development of a national style in Finland, but a style which drew its inspiration from a range of sources in Britain, Austria, Germany and Belgium, as well as from Finnish folk traditions.

Louis Sparre was in fact Swedish, and he had met Axel Gallen when they were both studying painting in the Academie Julian in Paris. Gallen persuaded him to come on a painting holiday in Finland, and Sparre remained there for 20 years, with frequent tours of Europe. He was affluent and

Interior, by Louis Sparre, Finland, c1903. Sparre, an associate of Saarinen, Lindgren and Gesellius, set up the Iris Workshops in Finland in 1897 to produce furniture, ceramics and textiles in the "Finnish style".

cosmopolitan, and William Morris's Red House was included in his itineraries in 1894. Before working on the World Fair Pavilion, Sparre had produced designs for "Finnish-style dining-room furniture", and in 1897 he had set up the Iris Workshops in Porvoo, east of Helsinki, for the production of textiles, ceramics and furniture. Sparre designed the Iris furniture, which was marketed in Finland and in St Petersburg. Some of his interior schemes making use of these pieces have been preserved and demonstrate his affinities with the British designer Baillie Scott.

Most of the work produced in Finland before World War I was designed on special commission, mainly for houses built for artists and wealthy patrons of the national style. One of the most celebrated was Hvittrask, buildings by Saarinen, Gesellius and Lindgren and used as studios and homes for their families. Hvittrask, which is now preserved as a museum, is furnished throughout with designs by the trio and by Sparre. Saarinen designed all the furniture for the main building; the chairs in the living-room and the dining area are based on traditional prototypes, while the bedroom furniture was obviously inspired by the work of Charles Rennie Mackintosh, who had achieved international fame when his work was illustrated in *The Studio* in 1897, as well as in German and Austrian magazines of decorative art.

The Vienna Secession

THERE WAS LITTLE SYMPATHY for Mackintosh's work among arts-and-crafts circles in England: it demonstrated too much of the artifice and stylization associated with "that strange decorative disease", Art Nouveau. It caused a sensation, however, in Vienna, when it was exhibited in the Vienna Secession Exhibition of 1900. How far Vienna Secession furniture and design can be defined as "arts and crafts" is debatable. The impetus for the formation of the Wiener Werkstätte in 1903 was certainly based on English precedent, and on Josef Hoffmann's admiration for CR Ashbee's Guild of Handicraft. Hoffmann's "manifesto" for the workshops has a distinctly arts-and-crafts ring: "We want …to create good, simple articles of household use…Our point of departure is purpose; utility is our prime consideration."

One of the workshop's first commissions was to design and furnish a sanatorium at Puckersdorf, near Vienna, and the basic and functional furniture which Hoffmann and Koloman Moser designed for use throughout the building is certainly in keeping with the founding ideals. Luxury and prestige, however, tended to replace simplicity and utility when the workshops were inundated with commissions from wealthy, demanding and sophisticated patrons who had little interest in

Right. Dining chair, by Charles Rennie Mackintosh, Scotland, c1900. Sturdy rather than stylized, the design demonstrates the eclecticism, as well as the experimental nature of much of architect Mackintosh's work as a furniture designer.

Far right. White painted table, by Charles Rennie Mackintosh, Scotland. Elegant and innovatory designs such as these were highly acclaimed on the Continent (especially in Munich and Vienna); they were considered "decadent", however, by the traditionalists of the English Arts and Crafts Movement.

social priorities, craft traditions or vernacular culture.

Koloman Moser, for example, one of the co-founders of the workshops, who had trained as a painter and worked as an illustrator before experimenting with furniture, designed some of the most luxurious pieces associated with the group. His magnificent cabinets, with their elaborate veneers and inlays, would certainly qualify as "blossoms of the art of furniture"; they belong, like the work of Gimson and the Barnsleys, to the grand tradition of cabinet-making. His more starkly geometric designs, however, many of them in black and white, are innovative and iconoclastic, designed for clients more interested in "modernity" than tradition.

Adolf Loos, architect, designer and polemicist, loathed the élitism that came to be associated with Vienna Seccession work; the designs he respected were not the creations of what he called the "artist man", but those which had evolved through necessity and use. He had travelled in America and admired the products of mass production there. He also admired English design and maintained that since the English were engineers rather than artists, roast-beef eaters rather than pastry cooks, they were able to put quality and practicality before style, producing work that was timeless and universal. The furniture he designed, therefore, is unpretentious and functional, demonstrating his understanding of the nature of materials, and the relationship of material to form. These qualities can, of course, be related to machine as well as craft production, and it is significant that Loos used Thonet bentwood chairs in several of his commissions. One of the first of these was for the Café Museum in Vienna in 1899; the tables have solid bentwood bases and marble tops, in the Viennese café tradition; his billiard table has brass fittings, a device he frequently employed to protect chair legs, etc, and the chairs are standard designs by Thonet.

Thonet bentwood chairs had been in production since the 1840s, when Michael Thonet took out his first patents for bending and re-shaping strips of wood. In the 1850s, following the introduction of mechanization processes, the firm began to expand. By the end of the century, Thonet had become a household name; its familiar chairs were not only in cafés throughout Europe, but exported to the United States as well. It also figured in such prestigious commissions as the furnishing of the Liechtenstein Palace. The Vienna Secession designers had work produced by Thonet, and when Le Corbusier was equipping his Pavilion de l'Esprit Nouveau for the Paris Exhibition of 1925, he included Thonet dining chairs. Thonet relied on machine processes to produce furniture which achieved the egalitarian ideals of the craft tradition: it was simple, functional and unpretentious, and it was suitable for the cottage as well as the palace. Above all, the standard ranges were inexpensive, and therefore "available to all".

Stained oak buffet, by Josef Hoffmann for the Vienna Workshops Secession. Although the workshops were established to further social ideals in design, most of the work was produced for wealthy and *avant-garde* clients.

Oak hall clock, by Josef Hoffmann for the Vienna Secession. Such strongly rectilinear forms were typical of Hoffmann's work, and his subtly proportioned designs demonstrate an inventive, and iconoclastic juxtaposition of materials and textures.

The German Workshops

THE NEED FOR inexpensive machine-produced furniture which was expressive of craft values was also acknowledged in Germany. In 1907 an organization called the Deutsche Werkbund was established in Munich aimed at "the improvement of industrial products through the collaboration of art, industry and craft". Unlike the English guilds, the German organization included manufacturers among its members, and associated organizations such as the Dresden and Munich Werkstätte (Workshops), originally founded to promote British craft ideals, began to revise their attitudes towards machine production. In Dresden the Vereinigte Werkstätte für Kunst in Handwerk was founded in 1898 by Karl Schmidt, who had been trained as a carpenter.

Schmidt had travelled in England, and on his return had set up a successful furniture workshop at Hellerau, near Dresden. Among the designers working for him was Richard Riemerschmid, whose early furniture included cabinets and bureaux with elaborate veneers and inlays. In 1907, however, the workshops began to concentrate on serial or semi-mass production, and introduced ranges of *Typenmöbel* (type furniture) – chairs and cabinets made from standardized components. The financial success of these enabled the workshops to expand; they amalgamated with the Munich Workshops, and together built a so-called garden city based on British ideals at Hellerau. The furniture workshops remained the focus of the community; a training school was established, and the craftsmen and their families were provided with houses, schools, laundries, etc, as well as a theatre. This enterprise, ironically, was expanding at a time when British artist/craftsmen were struggling for survival. Its success was in part due to the use of machine production, and in part to the furniture's appeal to a growing middle-class market.

Bruno Paul, a founder member of the Munich Workshops, who was involved in the design and production of *Typenmöbel*, had trained as a painter and had worked as a cartoonist and an illustrator for the magazines *Jugend* and *Simplicissimus*. He conceived his first furniture for his own house, which led to commissions from private clients. In 1908, he began to design furniture which could be produced by semi-mass-production techniques, concentrating on a limited number of designs. The components of his chairs, tables and cabinets were standardized, but they were produced in different woods and finishes, so that a "unity of design" could be demonstrated throughout a house, from the kitchen to the nursery.

Left. Chair in oak, by Richard Riemerschmid, Germany, 1900. Riemerschmid, who trained as a painter, was to become a prolific designer; he later abandoned such experiments in eclecticism, and concentrated on furniture design for serial production, thus extending the arts-and-crafts ideal to a wider market.

Below. Dresser, by Peter Behrens, Germany, 1902. Like Richard Riemerschmid, Behrens trained as a painter, and was later to co-ordinate the design and architectural programme of AEG, the German electrical combine. In this capacity he designed furniture for workers' housing: less costly variants of this solid and unpretentious piece.

These experiments in standardization, although alien to the individualism associated with the Arts and Crafts Movement, succeeded in breaking the barrier of élitism. The simplicity intrinsic to the craft aesthetic survived, but this was no longer "poor people's furniture for the rich". Although only the middle classes could afford it in Germany, several large-scale industries such as Krupps and AEG furnished their workers' houses with designs based on similar principles.

❦ ❦ ❦

Furniture makers in North America

THE IMPACT OF British arts-and-crafts ideals for furniture on American designers is perhaps best epitomized by the work and philosophy of Gustav Stickley, editor of the magazine *The Craftsman* from 1901 to 1916. Although trained as a stonemason, Stickley began work in a relative's chair factory in 1875, and became its foreman in 1879. He had seen a display of Shaker furniture at the Philadelphia Centennial Exhibition in 1876, and when he set up his own workshops with his brothers at Binghamton, New York, it was Shaker simplicity that he tried to emulate. "We had no money to buy machinery," he wrote. "I went to a maker of broom handles who had a good turning lathe ...and with it blocked out the plainest parts of some very simple chairs after the 'Shaker' model." It was not until 1899, when he formed the Gustav Stickley Company in Eastwood, near Syracuse, New York, that he was able to consolidate his own ideas. He was already a convert to the ideals of Ruskin and Morris, having visited England that year, where he met Voysey and Lethaby, who was then involved with Kenton & Co (see above). Stickley is best known for his "Mission" furniture, strong sturdy designs, mainly in oak, which were intended to evoke the "simple life" of the early pioneers. The success of this furniture and its adaptability to machine production meant that he had many competitors, including two of his brothers who formed a rival company in 1902.

Nevertheless, he continued to pursue his own personal mission. In 1900 he had launched The United Crafts in the Craftsman Building in Syracuse; the workshops were reorganized on co-operative lines, although this was abandoned in 1904. It was during this period that Stickley launched his magazine, *The Craftsman*, which promoted his ideals for architecture as well as design, ideals that he was putting into practice in the Craftsman Workshops. Commercial success, however, encouraged him to over-extend his empire; in 1913 he opened a 12-storey Craftsman Building

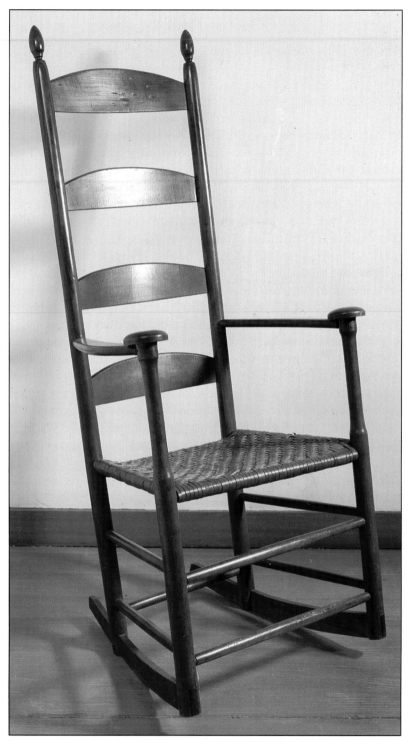

Shaker rocking chair, USA, nineteenth century. Shaker furniture, evoking a pre-industrial and vernacular craft tradition, possessed many of the qualities the British arts-and-crafts pioneers aspired to, and it was also a source of inspiration to the designers of the American Arts and Crafts Movement.

Sideboard, white oak and oak veneers, produced in Gustav Stickley's "Craftsman" workshops, New York, c1912. The hinges and handles are in hammered copper. Gustav Stickley's success in pioneering the craft ideal enabled him to launch the magazine *Craftsman* which survived until 1916.

Pages from the L & JG Stickley catalogue, 1922. L and JG Stickley, brothers of Gustav Stickley, had set up a rival enterprise in 1900, and by the 1920s their factory in Fayetteville was mass-marketing somewhat cruder variants of their brother's "citizens" furniture.

in New York City, a venture which bankrupted him. For by then "craft" furniture was being mass-produced by rival American entrepreneurs, and tastes were inevitably changing.

Stickley's constant aim had been to produce "democratic" furniture, and unlike his English counterparts, he used mass-marketing as well as mass-production techniques to promote his sales. His furniture, designed to be "durable, well-proportioned and as soundly put together as the best workmanship, tools and materials make possible", was sold

Armchair in oak, with leather sling seat, by Gustav Stickley, Eastwood, New York, c1900. Stickley had travelled in Europe in 1898, and was inspired by the work he saw there to extend the ideal of craftsmanship to a wider market.

throughout the United States. Also designing furniture during this period was Elbert Hubbard, who had also travelled to England in quest of Morris. Inspired by idealism as well as by entrepreneurship, he returned to establish his Roycroft venture in East Aurora, near Buffalo, New York. He began by setting up the Roycroft Press and in 1897 introduced a line of furniture very similar to Stickley's "Mission" range. He also combined his workshops with cultural enterprise, but his enthusiasm was condemned as naïvely populist; according to one critic, "He popularized Ruskin's and Morris's ideas to the point of boredom, the Arts and Crafts to the point of vulgarity."

The furniture made by another Buffalo craftsman at the turn of the century was more in keeping with the mainstream arts-and-crafts tradition. Charles Rohlfs was a friend of Hubbard, and his early pieces were also in the "Mission" style. Most of his work, however, is elaborately carved and pierced, and he was one of the few American furniture makers to use Art Nouveau ornamentation. Although his was only a small workshop which never employed more than eight people, he had a steady stream of commissions for office as well as domestic interiors, and his work was admired both in Europe and in the United States, mainly because of his contribution to exhibitions. His display at the Turin Exhibition in 1902, for example, led to his election to the Royal Society of Arts in London.

In keeping with the European tradition, American architects too made a significant contribution to arts-and-crafts furniture design. The Greene brothers' Gamble House, built in Pasadena, California, between 1908 and 1909, is an example of total

Tabourette, in American white oak, by Gustav Stickley and made in the United Crafts Workshops, c1901. The United Crafts was a short-lived co-operative venture, and the name was abandoned in 1904.

Music cabinet, in oak, with copper and pewter marquetry by Harvey Ellis, a distinguished craftsman who worked with Gustav Stickley for a brief period before he died in 1904. Ellis specialized in inlaid work, and this cabinet is typical of Ellis's work for Stickley.

Magazine rack, produced for Roycroft, East Aurora, New York, c1908-12. The Roycroft community and workshops had been founded by Elbert Hubbard in 1903 to popularize the ideals of William Morris.

Above. Waste paperbasket designed by Charles Rohlfs made of American white oak with an attached leather bag, c1910.

Desk, white oak with iron and brass fittings, by Charles Rohlfs, New York, c1898-1901. Rohlfs had a small workshop in Buffalo, and generally designed for private commissions. He was highly acclaimed for his work displayed at the 1902 Exhibition of Modern Decorative Arts in Turin.

Cabinet and chair, by the Greene brothers for the Charles M. Pratt house, Ojai Valley, California, c1909. The Pratt House, like the Greenes' earlier Gamble House, was used as a winter retreat, and the furniture was made by Peter Hall, a cabinet maker who worked with the brothers for several years.
Right. Chair, by Frank Lloyd Wright for Ward Willits house, Highland Park, Illinois, c1901. Furniture such as this recalls work of CR Mackintosh and, like that of the Greene Brothers, was designed to complement architectural space.

design, the clients having given their architects a free hand to create practically every detail of the interiors. Charles Sumner Greene, like so many of his contemporaries, had made the pilgrimage to England (for his honeymoon in 1901), and the furniture, like the architecture, that he and his brother Henry Mather Greene produced is a celebration of an ideal of the home. Like Mackintosh, the work of the Greene brothers displayed obvious Chinese influences, including the curved splats borrowed for the Chippendale style. But Japan, they felt, had transformed carpentry into art, and their furniture is distinguished by this high ideal. CR Ashbee was an admirer of the work of the Greene brothers, describing it as "tender, subtle, self-effacing and refined".

Ashbee first visited New York in 1896, and he was not impressed; he spent a day "going over works and workshops" and was "wearied with many hours of commercialism and shown endless symbols of waste and luxury". He attributed the failure of his own workshops in part to the fashion for spurious antiques "turned out in hundreds to the hum of the latest American machinery". In 1900 he went to Chicago, where he met Frank Lloyd Wright, "far and away the ablest man in our line of work that I have come across in Chicago, perhaps in America". Arts-and-crafts ideals were, of course, well known to Midwestern architects and designers at the turn of the century. "Good William Morris and John Ruskin were much in evidence in Chicago intellectual circles at the time," wrote Frank Lloyd Wright in his *A Testament.*

Frank Lloyd Wright, however, like Charles Rennie Mackintosh and the Greene brothers, designed furniture within an architectural context. When he conceived the Robie House and its furniture in 1908, the associations with the "Missions" and the early pioneers were abandoned, and traditions of the simple life, albeit expressed in sophisticated terms, no longer played a major part in his aesthetic. Wright's furniture is designed to complement architectual space, and to make a statement about the relationship of form to space. It is no coincidence, therefore, that the young Dutch designer, Gerrit Rietveld, who also trained in the craft tradition, was asked shortly before World War I to reproduce some of Wright's furniture for an avant-garde house in the Netherlands. Wright transformed the craft aesthetic to complement that "geometric sense of things" which is so characteristic of Modern Movement achievements.

TEXTILES AND WALLPAPER

🍃🍃🍃

MORRIS'S TAPESTRIES AND EMBROIDERIES ◖ THE SCOTTISH MOVEMENT ◖ CANDACE WHEELER ◖ ARTS & CRAFTS FARTHER AFIELD

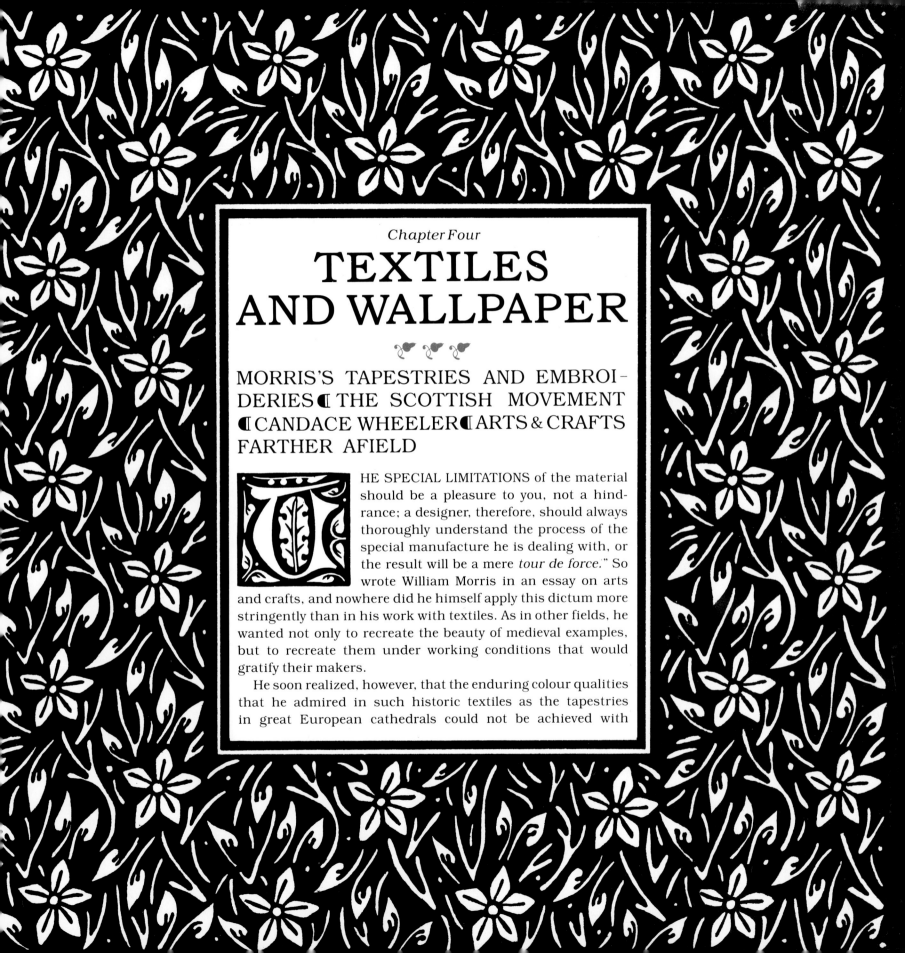

HE SPECIAL LIMITATIONS of the material should be a pleasure to you, not a hindrance; a designer, therefore, should always thoroughly understand the process of the special manufacture he is dealing with, or the result will be a mere *tour de force.*" So wrote William Morris in an essay on arts and crafts, and nowhere did he himself apply this dictum more stringently than in his work with textiles. As in other fields, he wanted not only to recreate the beauty of medieval examples, but to recreate them under working conditions that would gratify their makers.

He soon realized, however, that the enduring colour qualities that he admired in such historic textiles as the tapestries in great European cathedrals could not be achieved with commercial synthetic dyes. He therefore set about reviving the ancient techniques of vegetable dyeing, conducting his earliest experiments in 1865 on wool and silk embroidery yarns at the premises of Morris, Marshall, Faulkner & Co in Queen Square, London. These were, however, limited in scope, and in order to delve more deeply into the art he enlisted the aid of Thomas Wardle, a silk dyer and printer from Leek in Staffordshire. Their chief sources included early references such as John Gerard's *Herball* of 1597 and 1636, as well as contemporary practical manuals, of which *L'impression des Tissus*, by Persoz, published in Paris in 1846, appears to have been the most

"Sutherland," by Owen Jones, first woven as a silk tissue by Warner, Sillet & Ramm, London, England, 1872. The formal repeat is consistent with Jones's principles of design as stated in his *The Grammar of Ornament*.

useful. But it was not until 1881, when the firm acquired the Merton Abbey Tapestry Works, that he began to achieve truly successful dyes.

The works, which had been built in the eighteenth century as silk-weaving sheds and taken over by textile printers in the nineteenth, were well located on the banks of the River Wardle, which provided a constant water supply. Here, Morris installed the dye vats which enabled him to reinstate the ancient technique of indigo discharge printing. Indigo, along with woad, had been used for centuries to create deep and lasting blues, but the pigment could not be printed directly since it oxidized on contact with the air. The fabric had therefore to be dyed and the pattern afterwards discharged – or erased – with a bleaching agent. This laborious process had been superseded

Above. Plate LXIX, from Owen Jones's *The Grammar of Ornament*, London, England, 1856. The illustration showing stained glass from medieval cathedrals reveals Jones's commitment to the supremacy of architecture: "The Decorative Arts arise from, and should properly be attendant upon, Architecture."

Left. "Sultan" by Owen Jones, first woven as a silk tissue in four colours by Warners, Sillet & Co., 1870. The pattern illustrates Jones's principle, set out in *The Grammar of Ornament*, regarding the separation of contrasting colours with the lighter colour edged in gold, black or white.

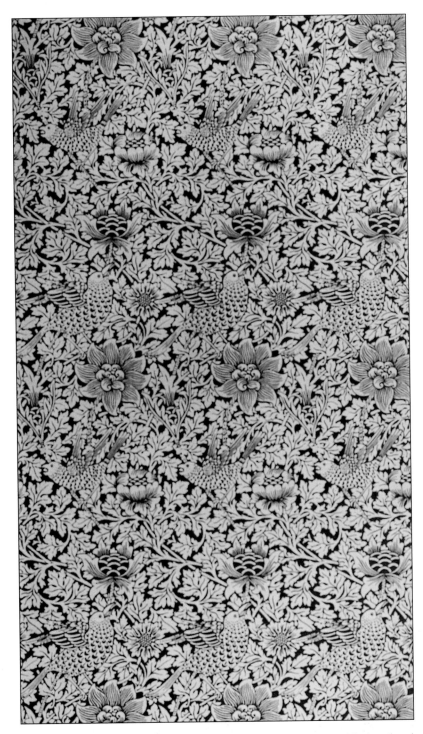

"Flowerpot," by William Morris, indigo discharge and colour overprinted at Merton Abbey, England, 1883. This is typical of the small net-type patterns designed between 1883 and 1885 as lining fabrics for Morris & Co.'s heavy woollen curtains (two widths of cotton were equivalent to the 54in (137cm) width of most wools). Repeat 4½×4½in (11.5cm×11.5cm); width 27in (68.5cm), later 36in (91.5cm).

for commercial printing by the introduction of the mineral Prussian Blue dye towards the end of the eighteenth century.

Morris, using the original indigo discharge system, created some of his most memorable narrative designs, among them, *Brother Rabbit, Bird and Anemone* and *Strawberry Thief*, for which Phillip Webb is believed to have drawn the birds. *Strawberry Thief* is one of several where additional colours were added by overprinting.

For all of these, as for his other Merton Abbey printed textiles, Morris used hand block-printing, the commercial application of which had fallen off considerably by the late nineteenth century, although it was still retained for some wallpaper and high-class furnishing and dress prints. The new and faster method of continuous printing using engraved cylinder machines had largely taken over.

Block-printing held many attractions for Morris. It provided job satisfaction for the worker, offered no limitations to the colour and scale of designs, and provided him with scope for further experiments in discharge printing. On the negative side were the comparative slowness and the high cost. Although neither deterred Morris, they did mean that the fabrics were too expensive for anyone except the relatively rich.

"Bird and Anemone", chintz, by William Morris, indigo discharge block-printed on fabric at Merton Abbey, England, 1882. The birds were probably drawn by Philip Webb who had drawn them in earlier designs. "Bird and Anemone" was also produced as a wallpaper at about the same time. Repeat 21¼in×9in (54cm×23cm); width 36in (91.5cm).

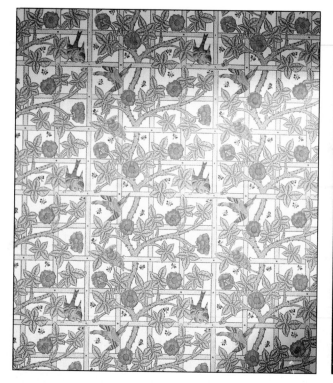

"Trellis", wallpaper, by William Morris, England, 1864. The pattern is said to be based on the rose trellises that bordered the central quadrangle at Red House. The birds were designed by Philip Webb who, at the time, was designing all the birds and animals for Morris & Co.'s stained glass. Repeat 21½in×21½in (53.25cm×53.25cm).

"Fruit," also known as "Pomegranate", wallpaper, by William Morris, England, 1864. One of the first three wallpapers designed by Morris (along with "Daisy" and "Trellis"), the square grid structure appeared unsophisticated to contemporary eyes and did not sell well. Morris did not design for wallpaper again until 1871. Repeat 21in×21in (53cm×53cm).

With this venture, nevertheless, he breathed new life into an old craft and paved the way for further development in the twentieth century.

His pattern designs both for textiles and wallpapers had more immediate impact on the retail trade. From the *naïveté* of such early wallpaper designs as *Daisy, Trellis* and *Fruit* (also known as *Pomegranate*), he soon advanced to the sophisticated complexity of overlaying "nets", or diapers, and diagonal "branches". These were often inspired by historic textiles, particularly Indian, Turkish, Persian and Italian. The Italian silk-cut velvets acquired by London's South Kensington (now Victoria and Albert) Museum in 1883, for instance, have long been associated with such later print designs as *Wey, Wandle* and *Kennet*. His woven textiles reflected the same resources.

Morris's involvement with weaving came later and brought him less personal gratification. Having mastered the principles by practising with a toy hand loom he acknowledged that the mechanical Jacquard loom could achieve the desired effects. Somewhat surprisingly, he regarded this method as an acceptable variant on hand-loom weaving. He had sufficient technical knowledge to produce the point papers, which guided the weavers, who were, for the most part, outside contractors engaged by the firm.

Historical models were, again, in weaving the chief source for Morris's designs. Mythical beasts, birds and dragons frequently appear, as do the familiar "turnover" or mirror-image effects. Some of his designs were indeed adapted directly from medieval Italian brocades and Spanish silks. His carpets, in turn, reveal strong links with their Eastern heritage.

He was more practical — realistic in terms of public needs and public purses — in his carpet production than in any of his other endeavours. He was less insistent for the general market on historical precedent, even going so far as to create one pattern, a composition of repeating African marigolds, that was produced on linoleum, as well as a number of striking designs for manufacture by machine. His most respected carpets, however, were hand-knotted, employing traditional techniques of the ancient oriental carpets of which he was both a student

"Bird," a woollen double cloth, by William Morris, originally hand-loom jacquard woven at Queen Square, London, England, 1878. Morris designed the cloth to hang on the walls of his drawing room at Kelmscott House, Hammersmith. It is reputed to be one of Morris's favourite patterns. Repeat 28½in×18½in (72.5cm×47cm); width 54in (137cm).

"Wild Tulip," wallpaper, by William Morris, England, 1884. Here, and in later papers, Morris makes extensive used of dots, produced by driving metal pins into the wood block, as shading on leaves and as background. Repeat 25½×10½in (65cm×25.6cm).

and a collector. In his own homes, he used them more often as wall hangings than as floor coverings.

He intended by no means to copy. He wrote, in a Morris & Co brochure:

> We people of the West must make our own hand-made Carpets, if we are to have any worth the labour and money such things cost: and that these, while they should equal the Eastern ones as nearly as may be in material and durability, should by no means imitate them in design, but show themselves obviously to be the outcome of modern Western ideas…

He and JH Dearle designed almost all the carpets hand-knotted at Merton Abbey.

Despite his innovative involvement in the craft of textile manufacture, Morris had little effect on either the production methods or the structure of the textile industry – nor even immediately on its appearance. The basic design vocabulary remained constant: florals still predominated in chintzes, with the occasional addition of animals, birds and figures. However, the patterns he introduced did lead to an entirely new treatment of these traditional forms. During the 1880s and 1890s, the previously conventional patterns of furnishing textiles and wallpaper became increasingly stylized, contributing profoundly to the development of Art Nouveau. And designers were becoming known as individuals. Manufacturers of British textiles had, in the past, insisted on anonymity, but by the end of the century they were revealing – even advertising – their designers' names. The example had been set by the Arts and Crafts Exhibition Society, which displayed both the name of the manufacturer and of the designer beside exhibits.

"Cherwell", by JH Dearle block-printed on to velveteen and cotton at Merton Abbey, England, 1887. The chrysanthemum closely resembles flowers used in earlier Morris designs, but the dark veining on the flowers and leaves are Dearle's innovation. From 1891 it was used for wallpaper as "Double Bough". Repeat 39⅓×25¾in (100×65.6cm); width 27in (68.5cm).

"La Margarete," wallpaper panel, by Walter Crane, printed by Jeffrey & Co, London, England, 1876. The design, which won an award at the 1876 Philadelphia Centennial Exhibition, was inspired by a poem of Chaucer's and owes an obvious debt to Morris's "Daisy". The frieze, Alcestis expands the daisy theme.

In the commercial textile trade, the patterns of Lewis F Day, Walter Crane and CFA Voysey had particular impact.

In 1881 Day was appointed art director of the Lancashire textile printers Turnbull and Stockdale. Although his floral designs for them often seem formal and derivative, they were important in conveying the new style to a wide public. Walter Crane's patterns, by contrast, reveal a well-developed skill in portraying birds, animals and the human form. He too designed a range of textiles and wrote and lectured about ornament and design. Both men also created wallpaper patterns for Jeffrey & Co, the high-class London hand-block printers. Voysey's work was more original than that of the other two. He produced a vast number of textile and wallpaper designs, all reflecting his conviction that simplicity in decoration should be recognized as a source of richness. Initial reference to historical patterns developed into clear, flat colours combined with florals, naïve figures and birds.

Unlike Morris, none of these men was involved in the production process, but they were dependent on the patronage of enlightened manufacturers to convey their designs to the public. Retailers also played a significant role in the process of dissemination, the leader among them, of course, having been Liberty & Co of London. In all of the many ways in which the shop translated the arts-and-crafts ideal into commercial reality, none was more far-reaching than its participation in this field of textiles. Many of Liberty's most characteristic fabrics, including its famous "Peacock Feather", originated in the remarkable London-based Silver Studio, which supplied the shop continuously until World War II. Founded in 1880 by the fabric designer, Arthur Silver, it was subsequently run by his two sons, Rex and Harry. Historic textiles provided the basis for

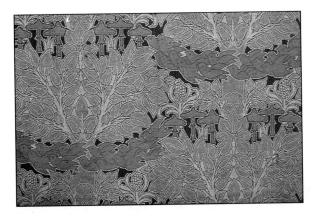

"The Fairyland," wallpaper, by CFA Voysey printed by Essex & Co., London, England, 1896. The bird motifs, with the heart, Voysey's trademark, demonstrate his ability to stylize while remaining faithful to natural forms. Also tapestry woven by Alexander Morton & Co., Carlisle, repeat 25in×27½in (63.5cm×69.8cm).

"Glade,' wallpaper block printed by Essex & Co, London, England, 1897. The original, showing stylized tulips, marigolds and butterflies printed in three colours on a buff ground, sold for two shillings and six a piece. Essex & Co was a leading wallpaper printer who specialized in hand printing and stencilled friezes. Repeat 24in×20½in (61cm×52cm).

"The Wykehamist," a machine-woven Axminster carpet, by CFA Voysey, produced by Tomkinson & Adam Ltd, Kidderminster, England 1897. The clear flat tones, outlined in darker colours, and the simple abstract forms which influenced continental designers, are typical. The same pattern was printed as a wallpaper by Essex & Co. Repeat 54in×27in (137.8cm×68.5cm).

Wallpaper frieze, by Rex Silver, produced by John Line & Sons, London, England, c1905. The stylized linear motifs, typical of the Silver Studio work between 1900 and 1910, replaced the full blown Art Nouveau of the late 1890s and influenced the development of French decorative art in the early 1920s. John Line & Sons was a major hand and machine wallpaper printer.

"The Orchard tapestry," by William Morris, woven at Merton Abbey for Jesus College Chapel, Cambridge, England 1890. This is taken from an 1866 Morris cartoon for a ceiling painting. The angels carrying a scroll, shown in the original, are replaced by female figures and an inscription from one of Morris's poems, with background details added by JH Dearle.

many of their patterns, and Arthur, a keen amateur photographer, produced a unique photographic record of historic textiles in the Victoria and Albert Museum, known as the Silvern Series, which were sold throughout the 1890s to progressive manufacturers. The studio was frequently required to adapt Morris patterns for machine production, which helped bring knowledge of his designs, if not his philosophy, to the cheaper end of the market. By the turn of the century, two Silver Studio designers, Harry Napper and John Illingworth Kay, were providing a strong stylistic impetus for Art Nouveau. Silver designs were sold to manufacturers in the United States and Europe as well as in Britain, the style-conscious French being among the most enthusiastic purchasers.

Morris's Tapestries and Embroideries

FOR MORRIS, TAPESTRY constituted "the noblest of the weaving arts". Since it could be produced only by hand, it remained for him the most philosophically and technically linked to its medieval roots. Although his deep admiration for tapestry stemmed from his formative visits to France in the 1850s with Edward Burne-Jones, it was not until 1879, that he set up his first experimental loom in his bedroom at Kelmscott House,

where he taught himself to weave with the help of eighteenth-century French manuals. After three months, he produced a stunningly intricate panel, *Acanthus and Vine* – more affectionately known as *Cabbage and Vine*, because of "the leaves' unruliness". It employed the "turnover" device, which he had already used to effect in his woven designs.

This success led him to establish a loom at Queen Square where he took on as an apprentice, JH Dearle who was to become one of the firm's leading designers in all its many disciplines. Dearle subsequently trained others in the high-warp, or vertical, tapestry technique which Morris used, and which differed considerably from the horizontal low-warp method of the only existing English producer, the Royal Windsor Tapestry Works. Production began on a large scale with the move to Merton Abbey, in 1881, where three looms could be accommodated, with as many as three weavers at a time working each, and capable of producing huge wall-sized tapestries.

The designs came mostly from Morris and Burne-Jones. The latter was responsible for virtually all of the Pre-Raphaelite figures, some of which were originally intended for stained glass. Morris designed only three complete tapestries, but provided much of the decorative detail for Burne-Jones's

"Artichoke," embroidered hanging, in crewel wools on a linen ground, by William Morris, for Smeaton Hall, Northallerton, Yorkshire, England 1877. This was part of a set designed for Ada Phoebe Godman. Mrs Godman was still working on the embroideries in 1900.

"The Vine," embroidered portière, by William Morris, England, 1878. The branch and tree form used in traditional crewel work was altered many times to suit clients; it was the basic pattern for later embroideries, including May Morris's "Acanthus" portière (c1912) and hangings by JH Dearle.

figures. Dearle also supplied background foliage and, eventually, complete schemes. Morris's involvement stimulated a revival in tapestry production which had been virtually moribund in Britain for a century. The Dovecot Studios, founded as the Edinburgh Tapestry Weaving Company in 1912 with weavers trained at Merton, was a direct outgrowth. The Merton Abbey Tapestry works continued to produce for private houses, churches and other large public places until World War II. In Britain, the standard of embroidery had declined both technically and artistically by the middle of the nineteenth century. Originality had been discouraged a century earlier, with the appearance of printed charts and patterns, and had by now been almost obliterated by the popularity of Berlin woolwork, where brightly coloured wools were applied to canvas in rigidly delineated floral or pictorial designs. The influence of Pugin, among others, had brought about a dramatic upgrading in church embroidery from the 1840s. The architect GE Street, in whose office Morris was briefly articled during 1856, had been a prime mover in this renaissance. Street, a confirmed medievalist long before the passion engulfed Morris, undoubtedly helped to shape the young man's ideas about the ancient art. Certainly, embroidery was the first textile technique with which Morris became personally involved. He studied early English embroideries – *opus angelicanum* – a celebration of English medieval ecclesiastical embroideries, but in his own early attempts he appears to have used wool yarn couched, or laid, on woollen fabric, rather than the metal threads associated with ecclesiastical work.

His first known embroidery, repeatedly incorporating the words *If I Can*, was worked in aniline-dyed crewel wools with irregular long and short stitches, which created a heavy, tapestry-like piece. Having accomplished this, Morris embroidered no more, but, acting as teacher, passed the production on to others. He designed several friezes and panels for Red House, which were embroidered by his bride, Jane, and her sister, Elizabeth Burden. With the founding of Morris, Marshall, Faulkner & Co in 1861, both domestic and ecclesiastical embroideries were undertaken, with the firm's participating members all contributing designs and the work performed only with yarns dyed to their specifications in their own premises.

In 1885, Morris's daughter May, who had grown up in the business, took control of the embroidery section. A skilled craftswoman, she herself became an influential figure, the author of a definitive book, *Decorative Needlework*, and a teacher in major arts-and-crafts schools, both in Britain and in the United States. These included the prestigious Royal School of Art Needlework in London, for which Morris and Burne-Jones had produced designs in its fledgling days. Founded in 1872 under the patronage of Queen Victoria's daughter, Princess Christian of Schleswig-Holstein, the school was dedicated to the restoration of "Ornamental Needlework for secular purposes to the high place it once held among decorative arts". It provided training and employment for educated young women, and encouraged them to reproduce the best examples of old English needlework. Its goal was the perfection of practical skills, rather than of creativity, which seems an ironic contradiction of arts-and-crafts ideals. Designs were provided in the form of sketches by leading artists

"Fruit Garden," portière, an unfinished embroidery designed as a kit, by May Morris, England, c1892. It is worked on "Oak", a green woven silk damask designed by William Morris in 1881, with an inscription from his poem *The Flowering Orchard*. Kits enabled a wider public to buy Morris & Co. designs and work them at home; it is thought that only three of this one were ever sold.

and designers – Selwyn Image, GF Bodley, Walter Crane – some, including Morris patterns, are still available today.

Other similar organizations grew up elsewhere. The Leek Embroidery Society, in Staffordshire, was begun in 1879 by Elizabeth Wardle, the wife of the silk weaver Thomas Wardle (later Sir Thomas) who had helped Morris with his early dyeing experiments. The Society gained a reputation for ecclesiastical work heavily applying silk and gold threads to plain and printed tussore silk, brocades, velvets and velveteens. They also used Thomas Wardle's silks, some of which were printed with Morris designs. In the south of England, at Haslemere, Surrey, Godfrey Blount established in 1896 the Peasant Art Society as part of a working community of artists and craftspeople, known as Peasant Industries, which looked to peasant crafts as a source of design. They created hangings made of hand-woven linen, vegetable-dyed and appliquéd. With flat unshaded areas and strong outlines, they achieved an effect that suggested stained glass windows. Liberty & Co, already known as a supplier of "art" fabrics, were also instrumental in reinstating embroidery as a creative activity. The opening of their costume department in 1884 reinforced the importance of historical models as a source of visual and practical reference. Traditional crafts were also influential, and smocking became a speciality.

The Scottish Movement

IN SCOTLAND, new ideas in embroidery were disseminated through educational institutions and exhibitions, the major contributors and innovators being women. Phoebe Traquair, one of the most talented, was skilled as a muralist, bookbinder and enameller, as well as an embroiderer. Her most ambitious piece of needlework, the "Denys" series, consisted of four screens depicting allegorical figures and was extravagantly wrought in gold and silk thread on linen. This was displayed by the Arts and Crafts Exhibition Society in 1903, and other pieces of her work were exhibited regularly in Europe and America. At the same time, the Glasgow School of Art was becoming a focus for a special form of creative activity in which art embroidery played a pronounced role.

Leadership came first from Jessie Newbery, a teacher at the school, and later from three of her students, the Macdonald sisters, Frances and Margaret, and especially Ann Macbeth, who produced needlework in what became known as the "Glasgow Style". This evolved by way of the techniques developed by Morris and the Royal School of Art Needlework into something distinctive and recognizable, involving the use of

Embroidered panel depicting St Elizabeth, by Ann Macbeth, worked by Elizabeth Jackson on cream stain in floss silks in green, grey, mauve, pink, purple and blue, Glasgow, Scotland, c1912. This is one of Ann Macbeth's many figure designs. They were highly regarded and frequently shown at major exhibitions throughout Europe. Dimensions 16¼in×8¼in (41cm×21cm).

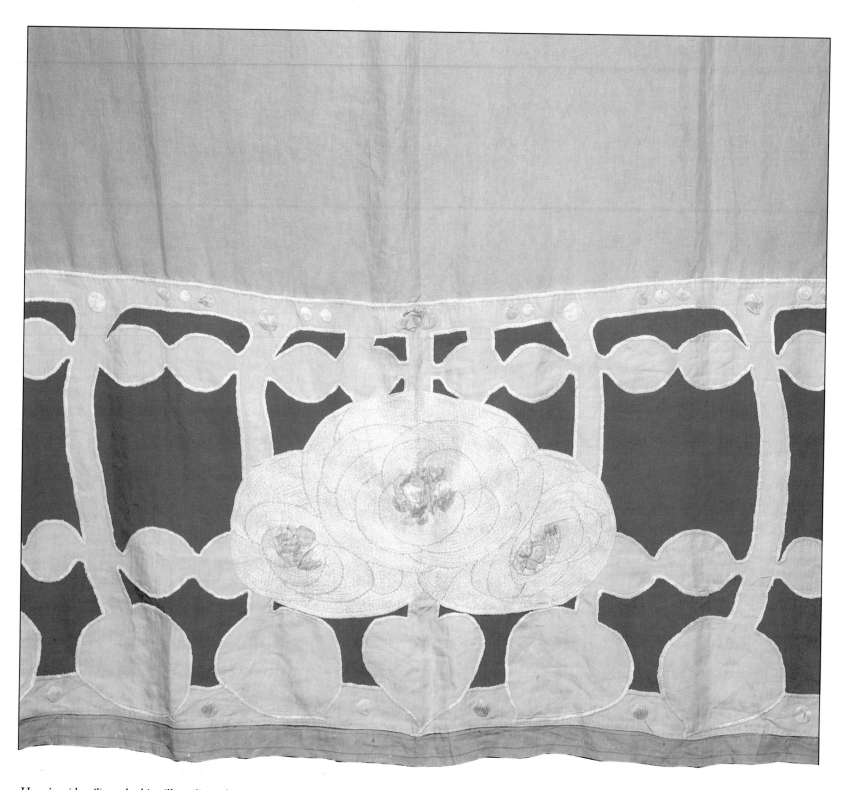

Hanging (detail) worked in silk on linen, by Ann Macbeth, Glasgow, Scotland, c1900. This early piece shows how appliqué was developed to significant effect by Macbeth, following the example of Jessie Newbery.

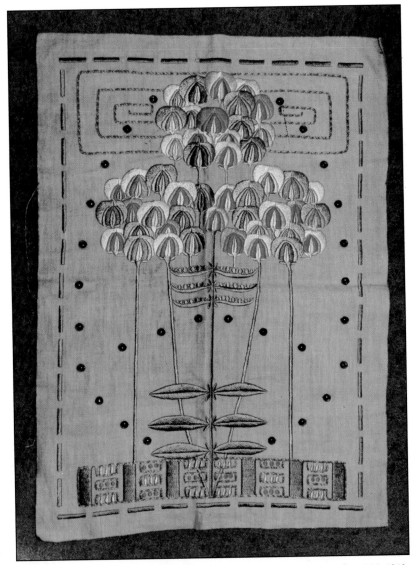

Embroidery, attributed to Anne Knox-Arthur, Glasgow, Scotaland, c1900-1910. Knox-Arthur taught in the embroidery department of the Glasgow School of Art, taking charge when Ann Macbeth retired in 1920. The delicate colours and abstract motifs worked on coarse fabric are characteristic of the Glasgow style.

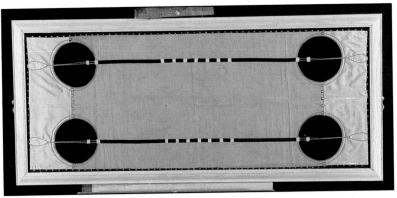

Table runner in embroidered linen and silk with appliqué cotton and cotton braid, attributed to Charles Rennie Mackintosh, Glasgow, Scotland, c1900-1906. This piece was worked by Margaret Macdonald Mackintosh for the Mackintoshes' apartment at 120 Main Street, Glasgow, where they lived from their marriage in 1900 until 1906.

appliqué, minimal amounts of stitching and needle-weaving on homely fabrics such as hessian, unbleached calico, flannel and linen. The purposes were practical – cushion covers, bags, belts, collars – and individual creativity was encouraged. The decorative techniques were bold and simple, but they were wrought with perfection.

The style was characterized by soft tones of silver, pearl grey, pink and lilac, usually set off by heavily embroidered lines, and often including lettering. The motifs were more conven-tionalized than those typically associated with the Arts and Crafts Movement. Florals and vegetation were common features, and the stylized "Glasgow rose", which was probably invented by Jessie Newbery, appeared frequently.

Candace Wheeler

IN THE UNITED STATES, when needlework skills had languished after the Civil War, new impetus was provided by the display of London's Royal School of Art Needlework at the 1876 Philadelphia Centennial Exhibition. So impressed was Can-dace Wheeler, a prosperous, artistically influential woman, that she was prompted in 1877 to found the New York Society of Decorative Art, which she envisaged as an "American Kensington School", with the objective of providing women with the opportunity to produce high-quality work that would not only be valued by society, but would also be both re-creational and profit-making. Its scope was wider than that of the Royal School, but art needlework was its chief focus. English women crossed the Atlantic to teach technique and design to this society and to others which it generated in major cities. Output included lace, ecclesiastical embroidery, hangings and tapestries, as well as sculpture, painting, wood-carving and pottery.

Candace Wheeler herself moved dramatically into commerce when in 1879 she entered into partnership with LC Tiffany to form the Associated Artists, which rapidly became one of New York's leading interior-decorating firms. Also involved were the textile designer and colourist, Samuel Colman, and the

83

"Consider the Lilies of the Field," one of a pair of portières, by Candace Wheeler, for Mark Twain's house, Hartford, Connecticut, USA. The body is of lilies and reeds on muslin, embroidered in outline and seed-stitched with painted highlights. The inclusion of the motto at the top resembles the device used on Morris & Co. embroidery. Dimensions 73in× 41½in (185cm×105cm).

ornamental woodcarver, Lockwood de Forest, who worked as a team from their Fourth-Avenue atelier, much in the spirit of Morris & Co.

The textiles designed and produced by Associated Artists included luxurious curtains, portières and wall coverings which made use of embroidery, needle-woven tapestry and loom weaving. The studios undertook commissions on the highest levels, from decorating the White House in Washington for President Chester Arthur to creating opulent bed hangings for the London home of Lillie Langtry which were embroidered in silk with "sunset coloured" roses.

Candace Wheeler was the prime mover in initiating "genuine" American designs, turning for inspiration to traditional patchwork, indigenous floral and fauna, and events from American history and from literature. These were pro-duced commercially for her by, among others, the Con-necticut silk manufacturers, Cheney Brothers. She was also personally involved with tapestries and patented a method of weaving in which a needle, rather than a shuttle, carried a soft weft across a durable silk canvas especially made for her by Cheney Brothers. Although the process was too costly to be financially viable, Associated Artists produced several major pieces: *The Miraculous Draught of Fishes* based on the Raphael cartoon in the Victoria and Albert Museum; and *the Hiawatha Tapestry*, based on Henry Wadsworth Longfellow's poem.

The last decades of the nineteenth century witnessed the formation of numerous American societies and schools which stimulated interest in textile arts and crafts and promoted the use of old techniques, such as netting and candlewick. Native American arts – particularly Navajo weaves – came to be prized

Navajo blanket, USA, late nineteenth century. This hand-woven Navajo saddle blanket is typical of those admired and col-lected by followers of the Arts and Crafts Move-ment in America. The severe formality of the patterns influenced the design of rugs by Gustav Stickley among others. Dimensions 32in×30in (81cm×76cm).

Portière, by George W Mahler and Louis J Millet, for the James A Patten House, Evanston, Illinois, USA, 1901. Made in cotton and silk velvet, the design was appliqued in cotton damask and embroidered in silk. The thistle is used as a decorative motif to unify the various materials used in the building. Dimensions 80¼in× 47⁷⁄₁₀in (204cm×121cm).

Drawing room, by Associated Artists, Mark Twain's house, Hartford, Connecticut, USA. The textiles, wallpaper and carpets show how Associated Artists successfully developed their own arts-and-crafts style of interior decoration from historical influences to create an atmosphere of restrained elegance.

and emulated for their striking patterns and simplicity of production on basic hand looms. Similarly functional rag rugs, which had originally been made from used fabric, were now created from new materials, thus ensuring control of the designs. By the turn of the twentieth century the influence of the British Arts and Crafts Movement had subsided. The United States had succeeded in evolving original designs and techniques by looking at its own heritage.

Arts and Crafts farther afield

THE REVERBERATIONS of the Arts and Crafts Movement continued to resonate strongly elsewhere in the world, but almost everywhere it was usually distinguished by strong national identification. In Scandinavia, for instance, guilds and societies along Morrisian lines were formed to preserve traditional craft skills, and to stimulate fresh interpretation of them.

Schools of arts and crafts were opened in Stockholm and in Helsinki and the public were encouraged to open weaving studios and to create work of their own. Design inspiration came initially from folk patterns, but the re-awakened artistic spirit soon led to the emergence of new forms. In Finland, Axel Gallen-Kallela, employed brilliant flame-like motifs in his textiles. He produced as bed-covers, hand-knotted shaggy-pile *ryijy* rugs of the type originally made by peasants to put on the floor. Gabriel Engberg, with her bold geometrics also contributed decisively to the revival of the *ryijy*.

Following the lead given by the Paris Exposition Universelle of 1900, which demonstrated how effectively influences from abroad could be united with native techniques, the Norwegians turned to eighteenth-century tapestries for a lead. They coupled stylized biblical motifs with the heroic dragon found in their own Norse legends to achieve striking results. This can be seen most markedly in the work of the painter, Gerard Munthe, who led a tapestry revival that parallels William Morris's activities at Merton Abbey. Munthe's *The Three Suitors*, woven for the 1900 Paris exhibition, reveals the successful amalgamation of medieval tradition with his contemporarily flattened linear style.

Frida Hansen, another of Norway's most important weavers, was also initially influenced by a combination of tradition and the new styles she encountered on a visit to Paris in 1895. In 1897 she founded the Norwegian Tapestry weaving studio in Oslo, where she devised a method of "transparent" weaving in which areas of the warp were left exposed to contrast with large stylized floral motifs in bright colours. In Sweden, the Friends

Carpet, Eliel Saarinen, hand-woven, Finland, 1904. The Museum of Applied Arts, Helsinki holds an original watercolour working drawing of the carpet designed by the architect. Dimensions c12ft×5½ft (3.66m×1.65m).

of Textile Art Association (*Handarbetetsvanner*) was founded to help give women independence and to revive old textile techniques. The Swedish craft heritage was re-examined under the influence of the writings of Morris and Walter Crane. New designs were devised which enhanced old techniques, and craft and home *slojd* exhibitions were held regularly throughout the country.

A similar arts-and-crafts reawakening was taking place in Eastern Europe, with traditional folk-art techniques providing sources for woven textiles and lace. In Hungary, geometric folk weaves revealed a combination of peasant art with a distinguishable Scandinavian influence. In Czechoslovakia the painter, designer, and weaver Rudolf Schlattauer founded a tapestry factory which aroused nationwide interest in textile art. This was evidenced in the relocation of Slovak arts and crafts from rural peasant villages to professional urban centers. Polish tapestry weaving remained a part of that country's folk culture until the early twentieth century, when it also became subject to a more professional approach. For the Russians, cottage industries also persisted, especially in the more remote areas. Women spun, wove, and vegetable-dyed linen and wool for garments which they embellished with drawn-thread work, and other forms of embroidery, using designs handed down through the generations. These were gradually taken up by Moscow artists such as Nathalie Davidoff and Victor Vasnietzoff who wanted to help preserve the village crafts. They, in turn, designed embroideries for execution by peasant women, often based on local legends and fairytales. Even here, there were arts-and-crafts overtones. Ruskin and Morris had left their mark.

Tapestry-woven carpet attributed to the Arts and Crafts School of Breaza, Muntenia, East Wallachia, Romania c1920-1930. The carpet is woven in red, blues, olive green and mustard with a white knotted border. Dimensions 182in×118in (4.6m×3m).

Chapter Five

GLASS

TECHNICAL ADVANCES ❧ STAINED GLASS ❧ INTERCHANGE OF INFLUENCE ❧ INTERNATIONAL SPREAD OF IDEAS

OHN RUSKIN, in berating Victorian craftsmanship declared that cut glass is barbarous. He preferred blown glass because he liked its plasticity, and since plasticity was a property of glass (which is, after all, a "liquid") and since Ruskin believed in the honest use of materials, then it has to follow that cut glass is dishonest. He and his followers conflated good design with morality in design.

They evolved a doctrine which stated that one should go for best structures and forms and truth to materials; then, as such phrases were less clear than they sound. For example, if we agree that the properties of glass are that it is (a) transparent and (b) essentially a liquid, then if follows (c) that forms should reflect these qualities. But the moral imperative is really arbitrary. Ruskin and William Morris, together with the men and women who followed in their wake, persisted with philosophical error which confused the properties of a material with its qualities. The material has certain properties – glass has ductility, for example. But we provide the qualities: we say whether a form is sinuous or hard, cruel or soft – or barbarous. True there are always connections to be argued between properties and qualities, but these are not as binding as those who argue for "truth to materials" like to maintain.

Of course, Ruskin and Morris used morality as an issue in design in another way, which is to say from the viewpoint of the craftsman. And here Ruskin had a point in his attack on cut glass.

The glass industry was one of the toughest because, even though it was not transformed by mechanization like textile, garment and metal manufacture, the work was dangerous. The risk of burns was high, and inhalation of acid fumes and contact with poisons added to the health risks. Children, who were employed to feed putty powder on to the polishing wheels during the process of polishing cut glass were at particular risk: the powder contained a mixture of lead and tin oxides and was breathed into the lungs because ventilation was poor. And so, in so far as we are willing to dismiss an exquisite item of beauty because of its cruel manufacture (which we probably ought to do), then we can see that Ruskin, viewing the cut glass as a symbol of unnecessary pain, had a right to condemn it. The perfection wrought was, in Ruskin's eye, wrought not from glass, but from human pain.

The art-and-crafts solution to the unethical work of industry was to put the craftsman in charge of a project from beginning to end by giving him and his team creative autonomy and responsibility for getting the job done in a manner that was both fair to the client and to the craftsman. This, however, is an expensive approach when the trade thrives on competition through price cutting. The Arts and Crafts Movement was always a luxury movement.

What made the combination of moral and aesthetic judgement so vigorous as an approach to design in the Vic-

Cameo glass vase with engraved birds and palms, by George Woodall for Richardson & Sons, Staffordshire, England, c1890. Cameo glassware was enormously popular but the clean cut and engraved glass was rejected by William Morris for its close resemblance to machined production ware.

Vase, by James Powell and Sons, England, 1913. The acid-etched vase shows an arts-and-crafts regard for "honesty", yet is modernist in design and capable of mass-production.

torian age was, obviously, the need to impose patterns of order over a situation that was beginning to dazzle and perplex the participants: the sheer variety of things that the nineteenth century could produce, the increase in possibilities for manufacture, and the rapidity with which living conditions could change made for variety, unease and conflicts of taste.

❦ ❦ ❦

Technical advances

TECHNICALLY THE NINETEENTH CENTURY was a period of improvements in manufacturing processes in glass. But the most important feature of the age, to which both the Aesthetic Movement and the Arts and Crafts Movement contributed, was the range of decorative methods: apart from cutting and engraving glass, new Victorian techniques included those of cased glass, and acid etching. There were important revivals too, including those of cameo glass and Venetian filigree glass.

Especially in Britain and the United States, there was a great expansion in consumerism because there were more things available for a lot more people to buy. And what makes things attractive to buy? Colour. Roger Dodsworth, glass historian, notes that by the time of the 1851 Great Exhibition, many of the English factories were showing glassworks in a range of colours – oriental blue, rose, ruby, cornelian and pearl opal. Moreover the American and English factories developed glass in which one colour would shade into another. Naturally these colours were given creamy, consumer-orientated names – "Burmese", "Peach Bloom", "Amberina".

Glass has also been a significant decorative art form in the United States for nearly 200 years. In the 1820s the Americans invented press moulding in which glass is pressed into a patterned mould; this process was swiftly developed as a method for producing a wide range of glass artefacts. These were cheap and imitated quite well the more expensive cut-glass wares. And then, in 1864, William Leighton developed soda-lime glass which was clear, like lead glass, but again much cheaper. The combination of soda glass and press moulding made the cheap imitation of cut-glass ware even easier and the cut-glass craft companies fought back by making their patterns so complicated that they could not be imitated. And so by the 1880s America, in particular, was producing cut-glass ware of fantastic elaboration.

The advance (or retreat) into elaboration is one of the few ways in which handcrafts can compete with mechanical competition: it is all a matter of building in added value to convince a customer that the price differential is worth paying. As industrial processes become ever more sophisticated in their pastiches of craftware, the true craftspeople (like Morris) are forced into ever more virtuoso complexity. In this way decoration becomes an end in itself. In fact, whatever arts-and-crafts practitioners have said about "truth to materials" and "essential ornament", a lot of arts-and-crafts designs show elaborate, unnecessary and therefore "dishonest" ornamentation.

As we know, William Morris set up in business with Edward Burne-Jones, Philip Webb and others in 1861. Earlier Philip Webb had, together with Morris, started designing glass for the Whitefriars glass house. This company had begun in the late seventeenth-century and in 1835 it was taken over by James Powell. Around 1860 the company began producing the elegant, plain, well-proportioned glass wares of Webb's designs. These were, naturally, "hand" blown. It is also worth noting that James Powell and his son did their own designs; some were based on Venetian patterns and as the century progressed there was an Art Nouveau influence. In the archives of the company there are botanical and herbal works. Plants – indeed empirical natural science in general – were a major influence on progressive decorative design in the nineteenth century.

The influence and ideas of the Pre-Raphaelites is important in its effect on the later style of arts-and-crafts glass. (One of the continuous difficulties about the arts-and-crafts period is that, although it is located in the last two decades of the nineteenth century, its roots are at least 40 years long.) The Pre-Raphaelite Brotherhood of painters, of whom Dante Gabriel Rossetti was one of the core members, were committed to a close study of nature and they evolved techniques to present clear, sharply focused images.

The emphasis upon the science and observation of nature is the spirit of the Victorian age. Charles Darwin had expounded on natural selection in *On The Origin of Species* published in 1859; Ruskin himself had a serious interest in geology; and Morris had turned to the natural world, especially plant forms, to provide himself with a decorative vocabulary. Then there were the empirical observations of Karl Marx which generated the socialism which sustained Morris.

❦ ❦ ❦

Stained Glass

ROSSETTI, OF COURSE, influenced Morris's close friend Edward Burne-Jones, who painted some of the earlier Morris furniture. In 1857 he designed his first stained-glass panel for the Powells at Whitefriars and he was involved in the first stained-glass commission of Morris, Faulkner & Marshall. Ironically according to Martin Harrison's research, Rossetti did not much care for the medium. He said to Ford Madox Brown, "Anything will do for stained glass."

As Burne-Jones developed his artistic skills, he grew further away from the close observation of the Pre-Raphaelites and his figures became more expressive, although they showed some of the odd rubbery languid quality that characterized Rossetti's painting. Good examples of Burne-Jones's later work are to be found in the stained glass windows he designed for Birmingham Cathedral. In 1897 he was made an honorary member of the Vienna Secessionist school.

The company of Morris, Faulkner & Marshall produced a large number of stained-glass windows between 1861 and 1875. The general approach of the firm during this period, as described by Painton Cowen in *A Guide to Stained Glass*, was to allocate the main design of each commission to one of the central designers, with Morris and Webb adding in the decorative background. Morris designed some windows himself. Rossetti did 36, Ford Madox Brown about 130, and the rest were done by Burne-Jones. Stained glass was big business.

Martin Harrison has described the basic tenet of the Arts and Crafts Movement as far as stained glass was concerned as being to break with the factory-like production lines which the Victorian companies had evolved. The designer was to make or supervise the making of each stage. The other characteristics are: a predeliction for Pre-Raphaelite figures that combine monumentality with languidness; and plant-form backgrounds from Ruskin and Morris.

Many nineteenth-century artists were influenced by the Pre-Raphaelites, and many were swayed by Ruskin and Morris; yet among them were those who had reservations about Morris's commitment to the designs of the medieval craftsmen. One of those was Henry Holiday.

He studied at the Royal Academy Schools, was influenced by the Pre-Raphaelite painters, and worked with the architect and designer William Burges. He took over from Burne-Jones at Whitefriars then started his own stained-glass studio in 1891.

Twenty years before, Holiday had argued strongly that artists, designers and architects had to acknowledge that the times they were living in. Modernism – above all science – would not go away, however much one longed for the security of medieval order. He said, "We cannot put on thirteenth-century sentiment…When a medieval artist drew the Creator standing upon the earth planting the sun and moon in the heavens, one with each hand, the conception was colossal. But we

Wedding of St George and the Princess by Dante Gabriel Rossetti, c1870; in the Victoria and Albert Museum. Rossetti was a brilliant draughtsman and his renderings of medieval subjects are an important part of the Victorian re-invention of history. These are the images upon which we base Hollywood films.

Stained glass window, Christ Church Cathedral, Oxford, England, by Sir Edward Burne-Jones, 1871. The window commemorating the death of four undergraduates who died in Greece, shows the four evangelists, with related scenes below.

Stained glass window of St Philip, St Michael's Church, Waterford, Hertfordshire, England, by Philip Webb, c1876. Webb worked extensively for Morris & Co, as well as James Powell and Sons.

Detail from *Weep Not* by Walter Crane, c1891. Crane was one of the main propagandists of the British Arts and Crafts Movement. His clearly delineated designs have a little of the stridency of the propagandist together with the insistence upon facts of the Victorian.

Stained glass panel, for Castell Coch, Wales, by William Burges, 1875. Burges was an architect working in the Gothic style and is famous for the pleasure he took in intense colour. His masterpiece is the elaborately decorated Tower House, London.

Stained glass window *Two Angels with the Ascended Christ,* St Michael's Church, Waterford, Hertfordshire, England, by Sir Edward Burne-Jones, 1896. The use of a simplified foliage design as a background is a characteristic arts-and-crafts recipe. The overall effect is conducive to solace but the figures exhibit pre-Raphaelite languor.

Doors to the Willows Tea Room, Glasgow, Scotland, by Charles Rennie Mackintosh, 1898. Although Mackintosh has some of his roots in the Arts and Crafts Movement and also, clearly, in Art Nouveau, he was very much his own man. He cared less than Morris and his acolytes for nature and fine workmanship.

A pair of leaded skylights in the B. Harley Bradley House, Kanakee, Illinois, USA, by Frank Lloyd Wright, 1900. Wright's work in stained glass has much in common with Mackintosh's. It is interesting to note the use of stylized Native American motifs.

cannot do this now. Our heads are full of diagrams of the solar system… our work is to discover that which is truest and best in our age…" Holiday thus had grasped what Morris had put to one side: the need to find an aesthetic and a *content* that was appropriate to modern times. Establishing that content is the hardest part, however; it eludes designers of decorative art even now, especially in glass.

One of the most active propagandists of the Arts and Crafts Movement was Walter Crane, the first president of the Arts and Crafts Exhibition Society founded in 1888. Crane, like Morris, was an active socialist and did some stained-glass work. One acerbic assessment of his work is that he was a wispy follower of Morris tinged with Art Nouveau.

According to students of the period, however, the leader of the Arts and Crafts Movement, as far as stained glass is concerned, was Christopher Whall who began as a painter; in his first ventures into stained glass in 1879, Whall was appalled by the way his designs were translated for the medium. He set up a small workshop of his own in which he trained a number of other important artist/designers such as Louis Davis and Reginald Hallward. He also lectured on stained glass at the

Central School of Arts and Crafts and wrote what was considered until recently to be the standard text on the subject: *Stained Glass Work.*

In accordance with the empirical spirit of the times, Whall urged designers to draw from life and from the model. He was highly critical of stylized figures and critical also of the practice (adopted by many arts-and-crafts people) of using the same cartoon over and over again in one design after another.

With a few exceptions, arts-and-crafts decorated glass, especially stained glass, did not find a modern voice in Britain. Two of these exceptions were Christopher Dresser and Charles Rennie Mackintosh. Mackintosh, who trained as an architect, was attracted to Art Nouveau decoration which he developed into a particularly abstract form. Indeed his abstraction was criticized when he showed some of his designs at the fifth exhibition of the Arts and Crafts Exhibition Society in 1896.

The rectilinear style developed by Mackintosh in company with the designers HJ MacNair, and Margaret and Frances Macdonald, proved influential, especially in Austria. There was also a reciprocity of aesthetics between Mackintosh's glass designs (as seen in the Willow Tea Rooms in Glasgow) and the contemporary work Frank Lloyd Wright.

❦ ❦ ❦
Interchange of influence

THE MOST DIRECT interchange of influence, however, was between Mackintosh and Vienna: designers such as Koloman Moser and Josef Hoffmann were much impressed by what was happening in Glasgow. The strands of the Arts and Crafts Movement entwine even tighter as we see that CR Ashbee and Walter Crane became honorary members of the Vienna Secession, that Mackintosh exhibited with the Secessionists in 1900, and that Crane was a friend of and "propagandist" for Wright.

At the turn of the century the Vienna Secession, the group of Austrian artists and architects who had broken away from the established academy to found their own organization, began exhibiting their own work and that of foreigners such as Mackintosh. The writ of Ruskin and Morris held firm for Seccessionists such as Josef Hoffmann, who, with Koloman Moser, had helped to establish the art-craft workshop cooperative, the Wiener Werkstätte. Hoffmann stated that the aim of those associated with the workshop was to re-establish good (but simple) craftsmanship and refined but not elaborate design. The Wiener Werkstätte produced glass which was manufactured by glass companies in Bohemia. As the twentieth century progressed the Secessionist glass designs became more and more geometric and architectural in their form.

"Architectural" is an adjective which can be applied to some of Christopher Dresser's work, which was also known to the Secessionists. Dresser began lecturing on botany in 1854 and in 1857–8 published an essay called "Botany as Adapted to the Arts and Art Manufacturers" in the *Art Journal*. He became a designer and in 1876 set up Dresser and Holme, a company importing oriental wares. In the 1890s, having by then been design director for the Linthorpe Pottery as well a designer for Mintons and the author of, among other works, *Modern Ornamentation*, he designed glass for James Couper & Sons of Glasgow. He too moralized against dishonesty in aesthetics. His simple, relatively plain glass volumes are functionalist and modern (they anticipate the Bauhaus aesthetic); their geometry is tempered with a grace which comes from the very thing Ruskin had urged – an understanding of the fluid nature of glass. Stylistically, Simon Jarvis, design historian, says Dresser practised an extreme version of the High Victorian geometric.

Dresser, whose importance to the design of metal wares is indisputable, made a vital contribution to design in glassware partly because he was not hemmed in by an ideology that was frightened of the machine or machine production. In glass, as in much else, he provided an intelligent, modern bridge between the enlightened historicism of Morris and the New Age. He designed

Bowl, by Josef Hoffmann, manufactured by J. and L. Lobmeyr, Austria, 1915. Hoffmann, a pioneer of functionalism, was a founder of the Vienna Secession, and the Wiener Werkstätte.

with modern production methods in mind, which meant acknowledging the division of labour within a framework of pre-determined production sequences.

Morris, on the other hand, sought to allow production to spring up from the creative work of one guiding craftsman. Of course, he occasionally failed, and Martin Harrison notes that Morris & Co had had to streamline production methods in spite of their ideology. What Morris initially failed to realize and what continues to dog not only glass but other media practised as a craft activity is that the concept is commercially peripheral. Craft processes are, in the modern world, inherently uncompetitive; the logical route for those who wish to practise any manufacturing activity on a craft rather than a modern production basis is to pursue it on a semi-amateur footing.

Paradoxically, for Ruskin the aesthetic which resulted from Dresser's approach is every bit as honest and as beautiful as any which comes through Morris & Co. The issue which so troubled Ruskin and Morris as to the nature of the work and the pleasure it gave to the people doing it, was, and remains, in the modern age a separate issue from the beauty, the truthfulness and the quality of the end product.

Above. Vase, by Christopher Dresser, manufactured by James Couper and Sons, Glasgow, Scotland, c1880. This piece can be seen in the Victoria and Albert Museum, London.

Right. Vase, by Christopher Dresser, manufactured by James Couper and Sons, Glasgow, Scotland, c 1880. In his glassware Dresser, known for his geometrical designs for metalware, betrays his training and studies as a botanist. The subtlety of colour which distinguishes this vase shows Dresser's debt to the craftsman who actually produced the piece.

🐦 🐦 🐦

International spread of ideas

THE NINETEENTH CENTURY, dominated as it was by trade, saw an increase in the number of international exhibitions which, together with magazines, spread ideas from one country to another rapidly. American technology was soon superior to European technology, but the styles were Eurocentric, partly because so many immigrants were European and also because travel, especially by the children of the new Americans back to Europe was popular.

With regard to the influence of the Arts and Crafts Movement upon American design, it must first be noted that America had developed one "tradition" of its own in design – that of the Shakers. The Shakers were a communal religious sect and although their expertise was in furniture, not glass, the aesthetic they promulgated (which was a by-product of their Christian beliefs) parallels and anticipates Morris and, indeed, Dresser.

One of the American glass painters who was initially close to the British Arts and Crafts Movement was John La Farge, who, as well as being taught by his father, a fresco painter, studied in Paris. He was for a while influenced by the Pre-Raphaelites but was especially impressed by the flat pattern-making approach to decoration developed by Morris. However, during the 1890s

"Lily Lamp", by Louis Comfort Tiffany, USA, c1900. Eighteen lamp shades create the overall effect of pond lilies on a bronze base. This lovely piece avoids being kitsch thanks to the quality of the observation which informs the design and colouring.

A selection of cameo glass pieces, by Frederick Carder, USA. The Anglo-American glass designer was manager of the Steuben Glass Works (1903) and inventor of a production process for the manufacture of cameo glass.

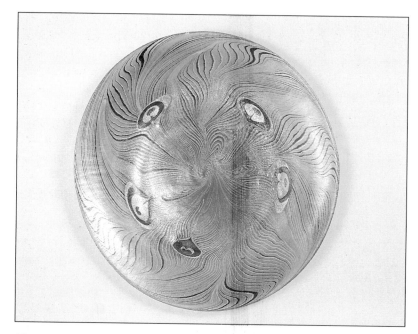

Glass plate, by Louis Comfort Tiffany, USA, 1902. This is an example of the hand-made iridescent glass which Tiffany called *favrile*. Such iridescent glass is made by exposing the molten glass to the gases of vaporized metals.

he developed a much more figurative and naturalistic content.

La Farge patented a method for producing opalescent glass in 1880. LC Tiffany also developed a similar process independently in 1881. La Farge had a number of major clients, including millionaire families such as the Vanderbilts and the Whitneys.

British arts and crafts were shown at the Centennial Exposition in Philadelphia in 1876 and the work displayed included items from William Morris, Walter Crane and Fairfax Murray. Later in the century both Crane and Ashbee began to visit and lecture throughout America and both became friends of Frank Lloyd Wright, himself a founder member of the Chicago Arts and Crafts Society set up in 1897.

Wright admired both Ruskin and Morris but made it clear that he was not antagonistic towards the machine. Indeed, his rectilinear designs for glass, like those of his slab designs for his metal furniture of 1903, show an imagination which sees the machine and its precision and rationality as sources for metaphor and symbolism and, unlike Morris's antipathy, as a cause for celebration. Wright's imagination was, even more than Dresser's, a natural conduit between arts-and-crafts design and the machine age. His aesthetic began with organic or botanical forms but moved towards a geometric order. His leaded glass, as seen in Darwin D Martin's house in Buffalo, for example, shows an aesthetic which has turned the attenuations of Art Nouveau line into a formal arrangement of squares and rectangles.

With regard to Art Nouveau and arts and crafts in American glass, the most notable practitioner is LC Tiffany, who claimed to be influenced by William Morris. He had the splended idea of running a quasi-Italian renaissance workshop: he would be the master with a plenitude of assistants, and his ambition was to improve industrial design by injecting art into it; he also wanted to raise the standards of design as used in the home. These aims paralleled Morris's.

He parallels Morris in another way. Morris had a genius for pattern and, in particular, for making decorative use of flowers and plants, but on flat, two-dimensional surfaces. Tiffany shared the same ability to compose with nature, but he could do it three-dimensionally like a sculptor. He made the glass and his metalware mimic the plasticity of drooping plants and entwining tendrils.

Tiffany was an eclectic: he had travelled in Spain and North Africa, he was excited by the exotic, and his personal triumph was the patenting of handmade iridescent glass which he called Favrile. It proved immensely popular. The exotic, warm-coloured lamps he produced were high-

Cypriote vase by Louis Comfort Tiffany, USA, 1892. This is another example of iridescent glass. Tiffany was interested in and influenced by Roman glass, and appears to have simulated the beautiful changes that time brings to glass. His recipes have done time's work for it, but better.

ly successful and the Tiffany style, a golden or red-blood, womb-like excess has continued to appeal to Western consumers and has been much copied. He had started in stained glass in the early 1870s and founded the Tiffany Furnaces in 1892. In 1895 he showed a collection of stained-glass windows which had been designed by a number of French painters – Pierre Bonnard, Edouard Vuillard, and Henri de Toulouse Lautrec.

Tiffany had rivals. One of the fiercest was Frederick Carder who worked first in England (he was born in Staffordshire) and left in 1903 to found the Steuben Glass works in Corning, New York. Carder was the designer and he developed a range of iridescent and metalicized glassware to compete with Tiffany's.

Elsewhere in the world, in Scandinavia and Sweden especially, the British Arts and Crafts Movement was particularly influential. There, a writer called Ellen Key published a book called *Beauty for All* inspired by William Morris's writings. The emphasis upon social democracy in Sweden and the interest in creating a humane environment in sympathy both with nature and the need to make life comfortable made the arts-and-crafts ideology with its concentration upon the home an appropriate one.

The Scandinavians were not swamped by the ideology of "the machine"; none of the nations underwent an industrial revolution that was remotely equivalent to those seen in Britain, the United States or Germany. Whereas the industrial landscape of Britain

Boudoir lamp, by Frederick Carder, USA, 1916. Carder used 'Aurene' glass which he invented shortly before World War I. A lustre glass, it was a rival to Tiffany's similar range; indeed, Tiffany sued Carder for breach of patent rights.

Above A selection of work, by Frederick Carder, for the Steuben Glass Works (1903-18) and the Steuben Division of Corning Glass Works (1918-33). Carder designed in a variety of styles and although here the strongest influence is Art Nouveau there is more than a nod towards the Tiffany workshops.

Left. A range of blown drinking glasses, by the Steuben Glass Works, Corning, USA, c1920. Left row: Verre de Soire glass. Middle row: Rosaline and Alabaster glass. Right row: Oriental Poppy and Oriental Jade.

had led British designers and craftsmen to take an elaborate and forced view of natural decoration in their work in order to emphasize their ideological embrace of nature and their rejection of the machine, in Sweden the tension between industry and nature was nothing like so acute. For one thing the natural landscape was intact.

Take, for example, the work of Anna Boberg, Sweden, Reijmyre Glassworks, wife of the architect and designer Ferdinand Boberg. The characteristic of her work was the juxtaposition of abstract and natural designs, a balancing of nature and art which captures the essence of the Swedish landscape well. The incorporation of abstract marks into natural imagery characterizes much of Scandinavian design and handicrafts to this day.

Although he is known primarily as a ceramics designer, Gunnar Wennerberg was one of the best Swedish glass designers. He did much of his work for the Kosta factory and created overlay glass inspired by Emile Gallé, the highly talented French glass-maker and the doyen of Art Nouveau. Overlay glass consists of a core covered with one or more layers of glass in different colours, wheel-cut or etched through these layers to produce a raised pattern of a colour that contrasts with the ground. Wennerberg was also interested in the render-ing of surfaces to make compositions of different textures.

By the end of the nineteenth century one of the virtues of Art Nouveau from the arts-and-crafts point of view was that it appeared to put craftsmanship and decorative art on a footing with other arts. In fact the craftsmen were fooling themselves: the avant-garde in painting and sculpture was already, via Impressionism and Post-Impressionism, in the act of de-skilling itself. This rejection of skill has continued throughout this century. Moreover, while the craft revival in design held strong to some degree until World War I, it had little or no rapport with the important developments in fine arts as practised by Braque and Picasso, for example. There is no common ground between Pablo Picasso's *Les Demoiselles d'Avignon*, one of the first major Cubist works painted in 1907, and arts-and-crafts ideology. The very concept of arts-and-crafts beauty was smashed to pieces by the painters.

Nevertheless, the middle classes, in so far as they take an interest in the visual arts, have remained loyal to Morris & Co. They have consistently, in Britain at any rate, preferred the bourgeois decorative arts to the full blooded imagery of Modernism. Glass in particular has remained a minor, although delightful, art reflecting middlebrow sensibilities, whatever its form or setting.

Vase "The Eternal Debate", by Emile Gallé, France, c1889. Gallé was a leading glassmaker with many imitators and at the forefront of the Art Nouveau move-ment. His designs were sometimes embellished with poetry by Baudelaire.

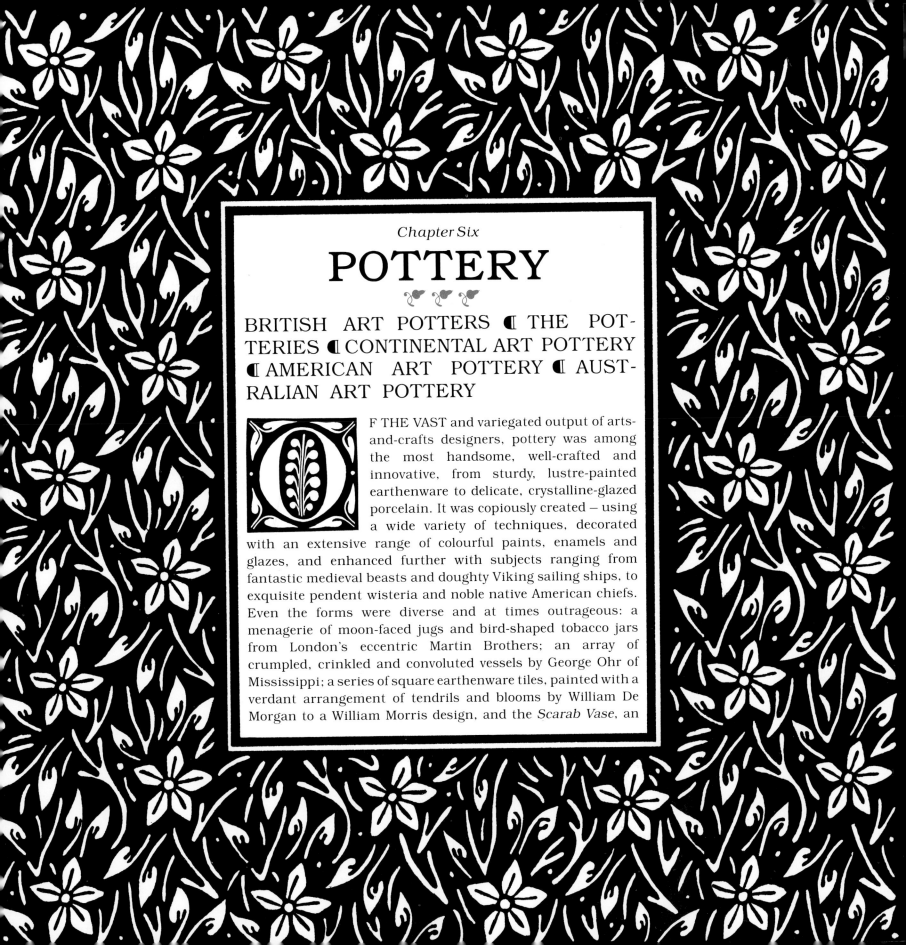

Chapter Six

POTTERY

BRITISH ART POTTERS ◖ THE POT-
TERIES ◖ CONTINENTAL ART POTTERY
◖ AMERICAN ART POTTERY ◖ AUST-
RALIAN ART POTTERY

O F THE VAST and variegated output of arts-and-crafts designers, pottery was among the most handsome, well-crafted and innovative, from sturdy, lustre-painted earthenware to delicate, crystalline-glazed porcelain. It was copiously created – using a wide variety of techniques, decorated with an extensive range of colourful paints, enamels and glazes, and enhanced further with subjects ranging from fantastic medieval beasts and doughty Viking sailing ships, to exquisite pendent wisteria and noble native American chiefs. Even the forms were diverse and at times outrageous: a menagerie of moon-faced jugs and bird-shaped tobacco jars from London's eccentric Martin Brothers; an array of crumpled, crinkled and convoluted vessels by George Ohr of Mississippi; a series of square earthenware tiles, painted with a verdant arrangement of tendrils and blooms by William De Morgan to a William Morris design, and the *Scarab Vase*, an award-winning, massive, lattice-worked extravagance from the American, Adelaide Alsop Robineau.

The making of pottery and porcelain had long been an important enterprise in Britain – Staffordshire and Derbyshire, especially so it is only natural that arts-and-crafts potters built on, and greatly added to, this firm foundation. Many of the techniques used by mid-nineteenth-century British potteries were not at all shoddy or second-rate, as in other mass-production mediums, and their products proved both influential and attractive to other British potters, as well as to Americans. There was also a growing interest in older production and decoration methods, many of these allowing individuals within large studio situations to design, throw, fire and paint their wares – that is, control the entire creative process from start to finish, as does the studio potter of today. At the same time, there was an increase in creative teamwork, in keeping with arts-and-crafts tenets, whereby, for instance, a vase or charger came to exist through the joint efforts of a skilled potter, who threw and fired the vessel, and an equally talented painter, who decorated it, according to the design of still a third person, perhaps a well-known illustrator.

In the United States, the most far-flung and successful vehicle promoting the aims of the English Arts and Crafts Movement was that of art pottery, which more than in Britain became the rich domain of gifted women – enterprising businesswomen-cum-designers, as well as "Sunday painters", college students seeking artistic careers, disadvantaged young women being offered respectable opportunities, or sickly ones therapy.

The growth of art pottery in both Britain and America was stupendous: not only were newly founded potteries creating outstanding and popular vessels, but long-established factories either started creative art-pottery divisions producing lovely works in small quantities, or else marketed wares designed by prominent craft-revival artist designers.

🌷 🌷 🌷
British Art Potters

LONDON-BORN WILLIAM FREND DE MORGAN was associated with William Morris's firm from 1863 designing both tiles and stained glass, and in 1872 he founded his own pottery and showroom in Chelsea. At first he painted ready-made blank tiles and vessels, primarily utilizing two techniques, lustre and enamel. In the early Chelsea period, from 1872 to 1882, his subject matter was rather eclectic: tiles and dishes decorated with somewhat laboured neo-classical designs, such as putti,

scrolls and palmettes; with Morris-inspired stylized blossoms and tendrils, or with a bestiary-full of creatures, both playful and monstrous, often executed in shimmering lustre tones of red, yellow, pink, silver and gold. The metallic film decorating these lustre pieces was much used on the designs of two De Morgan employees, Charles and Frederick Passenger, and also sparked their imitation by other potteries. They were created in part because of De Morgan's admiration of Italian maiolica from Gubbio, the ruby lustreware of which was especially vibrant. But De Morgan expanded his palette further, around 1875, adding to his repertory the so-called "Persian" colours – rich deep shades of turquoise and royal blue, red, yellow, violet and green (often with black on white slip grounds).

Between 1882 and 1888, De Morgan flourished at a new

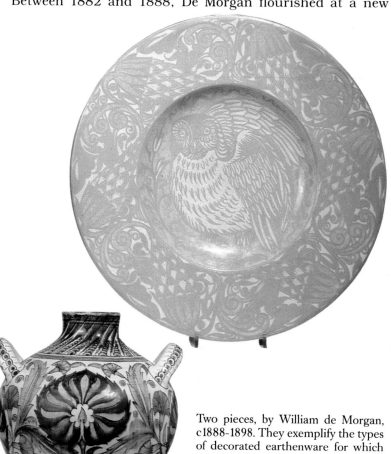

Two pieces, by William de Morgan, c1888-1898. They exemplify the types of decorated earthenware for which this London potter was renowned. The lug-handled baluster vase is painted with stylized motifs in the so-called Persian colours. The owl-centred charger with its florid border is a stunning example of his metallic lustreware — not in the usual ruby hues, but in yellow and ochre pigments.

purpose-built pottery in Merton Abbey, close to Morris's works; the two sometimes collaborated on tile projects, Morris doing the designing, De Morgan producing and decorating. In 1888, he set up a new factory in Sands End, Fulham, with Halsey Ricardo, an architect, as partner. The pair worked together until 1898, a decade considered to be De Morgan's richest and most successful period. Because of failing health, De Morgan had begun to spend time in Italy, where he established a studio in Florence, providing designs for his own firm and for the Italian pottery Cantagalli. In 1898, the two Passenger brothers, Charles and Frederick, became partners, as did also his kilnmaster, Frank Iles. De Morgan himself stopped producing pottery in 1907 and turned to a new career, that of novelist, but his three partners kept the firm running until 1911.

Along with the Passengers and a talented artist, Joe Juster, among others, De Morgan had produced lustred and enamelled earthenware of increasing beauty and technical virtuosity, especially in the early Fulham years. He made his own blanks at Merton Abbey — tiles as well as dishes, bowls, vases and bottles — and some of their forms, clearly oriental in inspiration, were especially attractive. Besides the plant, flower and animal designs which his wares featured, De Morgan also favoured a beloved arts-and-crafts motif: the sturdy Viking sailing ship, usually a richly ornamented galleon on a glittering sea of stylized waves. Individual art tiles and panels were always a mainstay of De Morgan's production. His botanical, zoological and maritime designs were presented alone, in pairs or even as parts of "four-square" designs on single tiles; sometimes they formed a running design or a large pictorial composition. From the kilns of the four eccentric Martin brothers — Robert Wallace, Charles Douglas, Walter Frazier and Edwin Bruce — came some of the most renowned and unusual art pottery of all: salt-glazed stoneware which, among other creatures, took the

Three pieces, by Martin Brothers, of London and Southall. The two-handled vase (1886) features a charming design of daisies and foxgloves against a buff background. The bird-jars, both with detachable heads, are prime specimens from the Martins' stoneware aviary; the leering creature, *left*, dates from 1891, the hook-beaked flyer is dated 1905.

forms of chubby-jowled, wide-nosed, two-faced jugs and leering or sneering anthropomorphic bird-jars. Robert Wallace had studied sculpture, exhibiting from around 1863, but by 1871 he had turned to creating stoneware, first working with Jean-Charles Cazin at the Fulham Pottery, and two years later setting up a studio with his brothers in the King's Road, Fulham. Charles Martin handled the financial and retail ends of the business (a shop near High Holborn was opened in 1879), while Robert Wallace was the modeller, Walter the chief thrower and firer, and Edwin the chief painter and decorator.

In 1877, the partnership moved to Southall, Middlesex, and until 1914 the three creative Martins produced an extensive body of functional and/or decorative pieces, from stoneware vases and jugs, to toothpick holders and spoon-warmers. Salt-glazed in shades of cream, brown, grey, blue and green for the most part, quintessential Martin-ware took the form of semi-real or wholly imaginary bipeds or quadrupeds, but they also made conventionally shaped vessels: tiny vases whose textured, earth-toned glazes simulated snakeskin, sea-urchin shell and tree bark; larger jugs or vases sporting incised and painted organic or animal motifs; still others in the shapes of gourds. The most interesting Martinware pieces were their grotesques, including hybrid-creature jugs with gaping mouths that served as spouts and curling tails as handles; Heckle-and-Jeckle-like birds whose facial expressions ran the gamut of human emotion and whose postures expressed the full range of "body language"; and two-faced globular "Janus jugs", some with barrister wigs and sly knowing smiles, others with droll man-in-the-moon grins and sneers.

The inspiration for these unique, one-off creatures was partly Darwinian, partly Japanese, partly Victorian Gothic, but always elaborated by the creative, somewhat disturbed, minds of the brothers. Despite a variety of physical and emotional catastrophes that plagued their ill-starred lives, the prolific, immensely talented Martins produced their wares for over 30 years, garnering praise from clients who ranged from Dante Gabriel Rossetti to Queen Victoria. And although they were not strict adherents to an arts-and-crafts philosophy—they lived and worked in an isolated, eccentric world of their own — their stoneware vessels and sculptures have become among the most valued and admired of art pottery. Some of the Martin brothers' animal-shaped vessels were faintly echoed in wares created by Sir Edmund Elton at his Sunflower Pottery, which was located on the family's Somerset estate, Clevedon Court. A self-educated artist potter, the gifted amateur produced his "Elton ware" from about 1879, boldly shaped earthenware jugs, jars, bowls and vases made from local clays, often decorated with applied avian and floral motifs of medieval inspiration. By the early 1900s, Elton was sheathing his vessels with handsome metallic glazes, his most distinctive bearing a glistening *craquelé* surface, attained by firing a layer of liquid gold over one of liquid platinum. Some Elton vases sported several applied handles, and one jug features crackled glaze, a spout in the shape of an open-jawed serpent's head and a tail-like handle.

The botanist, designer and author Christopher Dresser created some outstanding vessels for several pottery firms, mostly in the 1880s and 1890s. Like other well-known artists of the time, he attached himself to small firms, thus giving them credibility, and to large companies such as Wedgwood and Minton, further enhancing their reputations. The Glasgow-born, London-educated Dresser was the main impetus behind the short-lived Linthorpe Pottery in Yorkshire, which he founded in 1879 with the wealthy landowner John Harrison. Linthorpe was managed by Henry Tooth who, in 1882, established the Bretby Art Pottery in Derbyshire with William Ault. Ault in turn started his own eponymously named company in 1887, for which Dresser designed in the 1890s.

Dresser's designs for Linthorpe were influenced largely by various Oriental and ancient motifs. Their glazes were generally dark brown with green, or else solid yellow, blue or green, their forms often of Middle and Far Eastern inspiration. Interestingly, Burmantofts Faience of Leeds, which was opened in 1882 by Messrs Wilcox and Co, employed several ex-Linthorpe employees; not only did Burmantofts produce a range reminiscent of Dresser's solid-coloured *Japoniste* vases for Linthorpe, but also "Isnik" pieces clearly inspired by William De Morgan's "Persian" wares.

Some of Dresser's creations for Ault are among his best-known designs in any medium. One vase, available with either

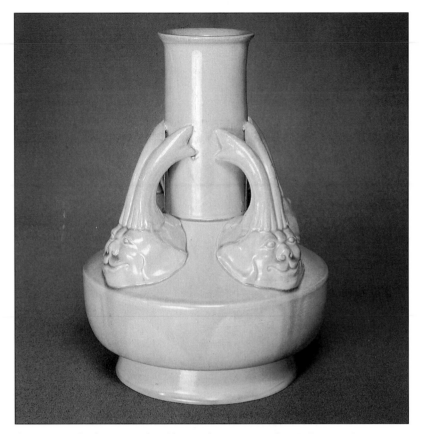

Grotesque "Gothic" vase, by Christopher Dresser, for William Ault's pottery, Derbyshire c1892. It is covered all over with a buttercup-yellow glaze, sports four "handles", and is among Dresser's best-known pottery designs.

Earthenware pot pourri and cover, one of a pair, by Christopher Dresser for Linthorpe Pottery, Yorkshire, c1879-1881. The pot was decorated by Clara Pringle. Its spherical shape, amber glaze and floral motif are reminscent of oriental pottery, whereas the Greek key motif at the upper rim of the jar has classical roots.

a buttercup-yellow or deep-turquoise glaze, sports four handles which are fierce monster heads, from which protrude pairs of inward-curving horns. Another has a double-gourd form with four applied handles shaped as goats' heads. Dresser's designs for Minton and Wedgwood were executed in the 1860s and 1870s, and for the most part consist of traditionally shaped vessels with oriental or other exotic motifs. From the late 1860s, the Liverpool-born artist and designer Walter Crane designed both tiles and pottery for several major firms, including Wedgwood, Minton and Pilkington. For Maw & Co in Shropshire, a tile manufacturer, he designed hand-coloured, transfer-printed tiles, and for Pilkington's so-called Lancastrian Ware he created vases, chargers and plaques in the early 1900s, which were painted by Richard Joyce with rich medieval motifs, such as a jousting knight in silver lustre. Another of his designs for Pilkington is a series of six tiles known as "Flora's Train", each depicting a charming "flower-fairy", clad in a flowing gown and wearing a petalled hat that echo the form and hue of the blossoms gently entwining each of them. Examples of the *cuenca* technique, these moulded earthenware tiles are filled in with colourful glazes, almost like *cloisonné* enamel.

A lustre charger by Walter Crane for Pilkington's Tile and Pottery Co., Clifton Junction, Lancashire. Painted in gold resist on a petrol-blue ground it features a peacock in all its full-feathered glory; the border comprises a repeating pattern of stylized anthemion-like motifs. Pilkington began to produce its lustre-ware around 1906, under the art direction of Gordon Forsyth. The shimmering platter was decorated by Charles Cundall, who worked for Pilkington from 1907 to 1914; later he was a portrait painter in London.

Vase, by Sir Edmund Elton for the Sunflower Pottery, Somerset, 1882. Elton's output of earthenware ranged from crackle-glazed jugs with zoomorphic spouts and handles to lovely vases such as this one, which features an applied-blossom design. He used local clays for his wares, and was essentially a self-taught amateur turned successful artist-potter.

The British Potteries

THE MAJOR BRITISH POTTERIES hopped on the bandwagon and set up departments or studios devoted to producing wares in the arts-and-crafts manner. Doulton & Co, established in 1815 by John Doulton and located from 1826 in Lambeth, South London, employed craftrevival designers and painters of note, many connected with the Lambeth School of Art. The firm was a keen employer of women (over 200 by the early 1880s), not only as anonymous decorators, but as major designers and painters, among them Hannah Barlow and Eliza Simmance. Until the 1860s, Doulton manufactured decorative bottles and flasks and ordinary household jugs and jars, as well as stoneware drainpipes and conduits, but the alliance with the Lambeth School, under its headmaster, John Sparkes, led to the production of more sophisticated decorated pottery, including porcelain and earthenware. The latter was made at facilities in Burslem, Stoke-on-Trent, where various new glazes were introduced, some imitative of oriental techniques, and others of French crystalline surfaces.

Numerous arts-and-crafts motifs worked their way into the design repertory of both the Burslem and Lambeth works. Out of Lambeth came a wide variety of decorative pieces. At first these were rather heavy-handed historicizing vases and plaques, but later saltglazed and faience wares appeared which were highly inventive in terms both of modelling and the manner and subject matter of their decoration. Hannah Barlow and Mary Mitchell produced wares with handsome incised decorations, and Eliza Simmance and Florence Barlow (Hannah's younger sister) perfected the *pâte-sur-pâte* technique, in which a bas-relief design is affected by applying several layers of slip. Advances in modelling were made by Mark V Marshall and George Tinworth, with handsome applied elements – lizards, frogs and blossoms, clinging to vases and jugs in a naturalistic manner.

The *oeuvre* of Hannah Barlow, the first woman artist to work for Doulton, constitutes a rich, highly distinctive body of stone-ware. While a teenager, Hannah began designing for

Vase by Hannah Barlow, for Doulton's, London, 1895. Barlow was one of Doulton's best-known decorators in the arts-and-crafts period. Her incised stoneware vessels comprise a veritable menagerie of domestic and wild animals: this large vase features a frieze of goats, filled with blue and brown slip on a white ground. Frank Butler's borders are shades of green and blue, with floral and foliate forms and, on the neck, impressed pomegranates.

the art pottery studios of Doulton & Co. She had always enjoyed sketching animals and this untrained youthful talent blossomed at Doulton, where, from the early 1870s, her charming, well-executed floral, bird and animal designs found their way on to vases, jugs, tankards and decorative panels. In time she became the best known of Doulton's women artist decorators, and her pieces were shown at various galleries throughout Britain as well as at international expositions. Through the 1880s and 1890s and until her retirement in 1913, she executed more than 1,000 animal designs a year.

Minton's Stoke-on-Trent pottery and porcelain works was another long-established firm which embraced the studio art movement. Founded in 1793 by Thomas Minton, the Staffordshire company opened Minton's Art-Pottery Studios in South Kensington in 1871, which existed only until 1875. Wares with an arts-and-crafts bent, however, were produced up to about 1895 at the Staffordshire factory.

Two other solid old firms, Josiah Wedgwood & Sons (established in 1759 in Burslem) and Pilkington's Tile & Pottery Co (founded in Lancashire in 1892) produced arts-and-crafts-style wares. Pilkington made tiles to designs by Walter Crane, CFA Voysey and Lewis F Day, and in 1902 they added lustreware known as "Royal Lancastrian" to their extensive output. Rich arts-and-crafts motifs such as knights fighting dragons and proud peacocks figured on this line, and among their gifted painters were Gordon M Forsyth, Gwladys Rogers and Richard Joyce. Wedgwood, in 1903, forged a 30-year-long relationship with the designer/decorator Alfred H Powell, who had exhibited at the Arts and Crafts Exhibition Society with his wife, Louise. The couple also produced painted earthenware at their own potteries. One of Alfred's most handsome vases for Wedgwood, made in 1920, is covered with a brightly painted medieval landscape on a cream-coloured earthenware ground. Although its date is somewhat late, its motif and sentiment clearly and lovingly hark back to the 1860s and 1870s. There existed in Great Britain dozens of smaller firms who also created wares in the arts-and-crafts manner. Some rigidly followed the example of William

Baluster vase, by Mark V Marshall (d1912), for Doulton, London, c1910. Although Marshall is best known for his stoneware vessels featuring earthy toned floral, foliate and reptilian motifs, he also designed delicate-hued, distinctly "pretty" pieces, such as this vase.

Morris and the writings of Ruskin in terms of designs and techniques; others merely put a foot on the bandwagon, hoping to benefit financially from the craze for lustreware and art tiles by producing second-rate goods, still others fell somewhere between the two.

Many of these wares were sold at Liberty's, the London retail emporium, which offered well-crafted, but generally mass-produced objects to an eager public. Arthur Lasenby Liberty in effect watered down the arts-and-crafts ideal and made it palatable, affordable and attractive to his customers. He put many guild members out of their jobs as a result, but at the same time he gave numerous potteries a taste of success. And a good deal of this pottery *was* hand-decorated, if not totally handmade, in small factories whose operations in many ways resembled guild settings. Among the various art-pottery lines that Liberty stocked were Burmantofts Faience, Barum Ware, Pilkington's Royal Lancastrian, William Moorcroft's Florian Ware, Royal Doulton, and the designs of the Bretby, Aller Vale, Foley, Poole, Farnham and Della Robbia potteries.

After William De Morgan's firm, the one organized most strictly along arts-and-crafts guidelines was the Della Robbia Pottery, established in Birkenhead, on the banks of the Mersey, in 1894. Its co-founders were the painter and poet Harold Rathbone and Conrad Dressler, a sculptor who was largely responsible for Della Robbia's architectural commissions. The company was formed to produce architectural decorations, but colourful and attractive utilitarian pieces soon formed a significant part of its output, along with ecclesiastical wares, mosaics and metalwork.

Rathbone was strongly averse to repetition and perfection in his works, preferring each piece to be judged on its own. He was equally determined that his employees use their talents to the fullest, expressing their own ideas and enjoying their work. In the 12 years of its existence, the Della Robbia Pottery produced a diverse body of functional and decorative hollow-ware and architectural elements. Various decorating methods were employed, among them painting, applied relief and moulding, but a conventional maiolica technique was the most common, i.e. lead glazes applied over a white slip. Rathbone further demanded that an incised (or *sgraffito*) outline be scratched into each piece to delineate which sections were to receive the glaze. Colours were rich and lustrous, a pale blue-green being the predominant hue, with bright yellows, reds and oranges, black, cream and other shades of blue and green common. Decorative motifs included Renaissance-style portraits, Celtic interlace, Islamic and heraldic patterns, floral and foliate designs, even grotesque creatures; forms ranged from traditional round plaques and platters, to rectangular clock cases, to a fish-shaped spoon-warmer.

Despite all this, Della Robbia was not notably profitable, and in 1900 Rathbone merged another ecclesiastical and architectural works hoping for more church-related commissions. This firm

Vase, by Burmantofts Faience, c1880-1891. The vase is distinguished for its rich yellow-to-green feldspathic glaze, and for its applied dragon, curling around the shoulder and neck of the gourd form. Motifs such as the incised eight-pointed star on the upper section often figured on Burmantofts' Eastern-inspired vessels.

existed for six years, but lack of commercial success forced it into voluntary liquidation.

A far more successful venture was begun in 1913 by William A Moorcroft, a Staffordshire potter, who had been associated with James A Macintyre & Co at Burslem from 1897 until he started his own pottery at Cobridge. His art pottery line for Macintyre, Florian Ware (introduced in 1898 and made until around 1904), proved highly successful, and provided the basis of many of his own later Cobridge designs.

Moorcroft's wares were very much his personal product; he developed them, designed their shapes and decorations, and oversaw those who actually worked with the clay and paint. Although he believed, like Dresser, in the superiority of form and that ornament should be subservient, his name is today most identified with the handsome, distinctive designs that cover his expertly shaped pieces. From early wares with a high-relief slip outline to later works with smooth, shiny surfaces, his firm designing hand can be clearly discerned. The floral patterns – poppies, lilacs, cornflowers, violets – adorning Florian Ware were sometimes busy and over-stylized, but after 1904 the blossoms became more softly muted, more at one with their backgrounds, whether white or coloured. Among the non-floral designs, the stylized peacock-feather was especially attractive. One of Moorcroft's best-known patterns, the Hazledene tall-trees-in-a-landscape, was introduced in 1902 and remained popular through the 1920s. Two other of his famous patterns, Claremont, with its bold, colourful toadstools, and Pomegranate, originated in the late Macintyre period and were produced into the 1930s when the Moorcroft palette (which now included rich *flambé* glazes) was rife with lustrous greens,

Seven pieces, by Della Robbia Pottery, Birkenhead, England. Della Robbia's varied output was among the most handsome English arts-and-crafts pottery. These pieces share decorative elements and, but for the aqua-glazed covered bottle, are united by their use of rich cream-, yellow- and gold-toned glazes.

reds, oranges and yellows, often against a characteristic deep-blue ground. Moorcroft's forms ranged from baluster and waisted vases and classically shaped ewers and tazzas to elaborate lidded *bonbonnières* and architectonic clock cases.

The wares of several South Devon potteries producing so-called "Torquay Pottery" from around 1870 were handmade from local clay in the arts-and-crafts manner and decorated with paints and glazes also made locally, if not on the premises. These included the Watcombe Pottery, the Aller Vale Pottery and the Longpark Pottery.

A smaller firm, the Ruskin Pottery, which always maintained the highest standards, was established in 1898 in Birmingham by Edward Richard Taylor and his son, William Howson Taylor, whose output was acclaimed for its extensive range of handsome *flambé* glazes. Fired at extremely high temperatures, the vessels often gleamed with breathtaking combinations of mottled hues, both strong and muted, these enhanced by stunning stippled effects resulting from the use of copper salts;

lustre glazes too were employed. Another master technician among arts-and-crafts potters was Bernard Moore, who specialized in *flambé* and lustre glazes, many covering vessels of Far Eastern inspiration.

From 1879, the Barnstaple, North Devon, pottery of Charles H Brannum produced a line of art pottery known as "Barum Ware" – simply shaped vases and jugs decorated with flowers, animals and other devices in coloured slip on white ground; later pieces were moulded in avian and other creatures' shapes. Barum Ware was sold through Liberty, as were vessels made by the Foley Pottery, a Staffordshire porcelain manufacturer. In the 1930s Foley commissioned designs from painters such as Duncan Grant and Vanessa Bell, whose own Omega Workshops created distinctive art pottery. The Workshops' director Roger Fry and his colleagues were determined to show the public the advantages of the decoration by artists of quotidian objects, including pottery vessels, most of which were made at Harold Stabler's Poole Pottery in Dorset.

"Barum Ware", blue-glazed earthenware jug in the shape of a bird, by Charles H. Brannum, Barnstaple, North Devon, c1879. Prior to this art-pottery line Brannum made ovens and kitchenware.

Nine pieces, by the Ruskin Pottery, Birmingham, England. The pottery was renowned for its *flambé* glazes, fired on to vessels at a high temperature. This group shows the variety of colours and shapes, most of the latter of oriental inspiration.

Vase, by William Moorcroft, Cobridge, Staffordshire, c1916. Moorcroft produced this popular pattern for years, ever brightening its palette and smoothing down its surface. The toadstool motif appeared on Moorcroft's wares until the 1930s.

"Florian ware", vase, by William Moorcroft, for James A Macintyre, Burslem, England, c1902. In strong and muted shades of blue on a white ground, the vase features a lovely landscape, outlined in high-relief slip.

Continental Art Pottery

MOST OF THE POTTERY being made in France, Belgium, Germany, Scandinavia and elsewhere on the Continent was in the Art Nouveau vein. More akin to arts and crafts was the homely, tin-glazed earthenware made by the Zuidhollandsche firm at Gouda in the Netherlands, which was sold by Liberty & Co, and ceramics by Hungary's Zsolnay Ceramic Works at Pécs, renowned for its iridescent lustre glazes, especially its dark greens, blues and reds.

Of the French art factory potters, several directly influenced or even taught art potters in Britain and the United States, among them Jean-Charles Cazin, who worked in London from 1871, and Taxile Doat, the Sèvres potter who, in 1909, worked at University City Pottery in St Louis, Missouri. Auguste Delaherche, who designed for Haviland, produced pieces which relate to many examples of American art pottery. There is a relationship, too, between Clément Massier's lustred earthenware vases and bowls, produced at his atelier in Golfe-Juan – particularly in their experimental spirit – with De Morgan's pieces (a Massier employee, Jacques Sicard, was later a designer for S A Weller in Zanesville, Ohio).

In Belgium, Alfred William Finch, who was of English extraction, designed earthenware at Boch Frères' Keramis workshop. His work was sold through Henri van de Velde, the influential Belgian architect/designer who was devoted to the ideas of Ruskin and Morris. Even more directly influenced by arts-and-crafts ideals was the Wiener Werkstätte, founded in 1903 by Koloman Moser and Josef Hoffmann and modelled on CR Ashbee's Guild of Handicraft. Although the pottery produced by Wiener Keramik for the Werkstätte was clearly in the modernist vein, with a preponderance of geometric and other stylized motifs, the foundation on which the Viennese association was based was as idealistic as that of the Della Robbia Pottery.

American Art Pottery

IN THE UNITED STATES, the halcyon days of art pottery encompassed the period from approximately 1870 to 1930. Not only were vessels such as vases, cups, bowls, chargers and jardinières produced in endless varieties and huge quantities, but there was also a boom in art-tile production. These objects were at times more sophisticated and innovative in style, technique and decoration than their European counterparts, although they were of course greatly indebted to them.

While some American potteries found success in a matter of years, others failed in just as brief a time or were taken over by other firms, only a handful lasted more than a decade or two. The history begins in Cincinnati, in the Midwestern state of Ohio, where in 1873 Mary Louise McLaughlin, a daughter of that city's foremost architect, took a popular class in china painting at the local school of design. By 1876, she was exhibiting her overglaze-decorated wares at the Centennial Exposition in Philadelphia, and in 1879 she organized the Cincinnati Pottery Club (sometimes called the Women's Pottery Club). One of the local women she invited to join her group was

Maria Longworth Nichols, who apparently never received the invitation, for in 1880 she started her own pottery. Called Rookwood, after her family's estate, it was to become America's foremost maker of art pottery.

McLaughlin's career, which lasted only until about 1904, was neither as long nor as commercially successful as Nichols', but her contribution to the creative atmosphere that enveloped china-mad Cincinnati cannot be overemphasized. Although her underglaze-slip wares, called "Cincinnati Limoges" because of their resemblance to the French porcelain, were expertly executed and attractively decorated with lush floral

Two earthenware vessels, by Ruth Erickson for Grueby Faience Company, Boston, c1900. These vessels are relief-moulded with leaves; the cylindrical vessel also features bas-relief flowers touched with yellow glaze. The dark-green matte glaze was a signature of sorts of Grueby, and soon came to be one of the most popular shades in American art pottery.

scenes, they were, ultimately, derivative and sold less well than Rookwood's later wares. In the early 1880s McLaughlin decorated some Rookwood-thrown and -fired pieces in underglaze paint, but in 1883, unable any longer to use Rookwood's facilities, she became involved instead in illustrating, lace-making and embroidery, among other pursuits. In 1898, however, she returned to pottery-making, working at a kiln in her backyard – Sèvres formula in hand – and experimenting with hard-paste porcelains she called "Losanti Ware", in honour of Cincinnati's old name, L'Osantiville. At first she painted decorations on these pieces and later turned to carved floriate and foliate motifs, which had pale glaze colours in the Art Nouveau vein. McLaughlin received many professional accolades and awards, and, although her career was far from the financial success that Nichols' was, of the two she remained the experimenter, the risk-taker and the stalwart individual artist potter.

Maria Longworth Nichols (later Storer) first came into contact with pottery via Karl Langenbeck, a ceramics chemist, with whom she carried on china-painting experiments in 1871. Highly ambitious, she turned what had started out as a mere hobby into a thriving business. Soon after establishing her Rookwood Pottery, she was employing a talented group of men (who did throwing and firing as well as decorating) and women (decorators in the main) and producing a line of handsome glazed wares. One employee, Laura A Fry, is credited with inventing an ingenious atomizer method for spraying coloured slips on to the green, wet clay body, achieving a smooth surface on which several colours could be laid and relief-slip design applied. Fry's technique was used for the so-called "Standard" glaze Rookwood pieces, which often featured *Japoniste* floral and insect designs on green, yellow, amber and taupe grounds.

Various other glazes and lines were introduced in subsequent years – the cool "Sea Green", the pastel-dominated "Iris" and several matte types (among the latter was "Vellum", by far the most popular of its kind, with its misty, ethereal qualities). Besides classically shaped vessels, Rookwood produced pieces which bore a resemblance to such organic forms as gourds and the lotus. Another speciality was a flat rectangular plaque, usually painted with a Vellum-glaze landscape, a hazily impressionistic mountain scene perhaps or a grey-green Tonalist river view. In addition to highly popular depictions of nature – floral sprays, landscapes, fish, birds and even bats in flight – there were also vases painted with portraits of noble Native Americans, these for the most part by one of Rookwood's finest decorators, Matthew A Daly, in sombre tones

against an amber standard glaze. Other decorators included Albert R Valentien, Carl Schmidt, Kataro Shirayamadani, Harriet E Wilcox and Artus Van Briggle, who later started his own pottery in Colorado Springs.

Rookwood pieces were occasionaly embellished further with silver: a mug of 1898 was painted with brown-green hops by Sara Sax and capped with a silver collar by Reed & Barton of Taunton, Massachusetts, and an elaborate trumpet-necked vase was overlaid with a chased silver floral mount by Gorham Manufacturing Co of Providence, Rhode Island. Many pieces made between 1905 and 1915 were decorated with monochromatic, earth-toned matte glazes. Stylized floral forms and common arts-and-crafts motifs such as the peacock feather were used on these decidedly solid, handsome wares.

Earthenware vase, decorated by Harriet E Wilcox for Rookwood pottery, Cincinnati, Ohio, c1900. The design of freesias is underglaze-painted against a lustrous "Standard" Rookwood glaze, the earthy tones were called 'Rembrandtesque'.

Other potteries sprouted in and around Cincinnati during Rookwood's heyday. These included: the Avon Pottery (begun by Nichols' former employee, Karl Langenbeck which lasted only a year; TJ Wheatley and Co; and William A Long's Lonhuda Pottery, opened in 1892 in Steubenville, Ohio, which produced pieces with underglaze designs imitating Rookwood's. In 1896 Samuel A Weller, who ran a commercial ceramics factory in Zanesville, Ohio, bought Lonhuda. As the Weller Pottery, it became a significant force in American art pottery, as did Zanesville itself, which nurtured so many art potters, ersatz and authentic, that it was nicknamed Clay City. In addition to producing traditionally shaped wares with painted underglaze decoration, Weller moulded some of his pots with leaf and insect designs, covering the whole piece in solid green, blue or brown matte glaze. He also hired Jacques Sicard, and the talented Frenchman's Sicardo ware, lovely lustre floral designs on iridescent grounds of amber, green and aubergine, transformed standard Weller vessels into shimmering confections. Frederick Hurten Rhead, a British-born ceramics designer, worked for Weller from 1902 to 1904 creating several lines characterized by stylized natural forms. Rhead also taught at University City Pottery and was head of the Arequipa Pottery in Fairfax, California (set up at a sanatorium for tubercular girls), but his best-known undertaking was the art directorship of Zanesville's Roseville Pottery, established by George F Young in 1892. The company's first art pottery line, known as Rozane, was hand-painted on slip on a dark ground and then brightly glazed; later wares were covered with matte glazes and often featured moulded floral and leaf decorations. Immensely prolific, though not necessarily maintaining the highest standards, Roseville managed to produce its popular, relatively inexpensive wares until 1954.

From 1896, William A Long, late of Lonhuda Pottery, worked for JB Owens, who first sold art pottery named Utopian, and later added other lines to his diverse production. Some were decorated with mission scenes, others with foliage designs under parchment-like glaze. Owens discontinued his art pottery around 1907, turning instead to making colourful art tiles, which were popular both for inside and outside decoration. A major manufactory, the Mosaic Tile Company, was founded in Zanesville by Karl Langenbeck shortly after the demise of his Avon Pottery in partnership with Herman Carl Mueller and William Shinnick. Both Langenbeck and Mueller, a German émigré, had formerly worked for the American Encaustic Tiling Company, where they created handsome terracotta plaques and tiled relief panels, often depicting neo-classical figures.

Tile, by Arthur Osborne, for the Low Art Tile Works of Chelsea, Massachusetts, c1880. Osborne designed this long vertical tile of a shepherd and his dog and flock, using the clouded, or pooled, glaze effect characteristic of many Low tiles; it was obtained by allowing the glaze to collect in the tile's crevices.

Bowl, by Frederick Hurten Rhead at Rhead Pottery, Santa Barbara, California, c1915. He used an inlaid process, and Egyptian scarab motif, an unusual one for art pottery although Egyptomania was an ever-recurring trend in design.

American Encaustic, which produced both floor and wall tiles, also employed the talented brothers, Albert and Léon V Solon, the latter of whom was once chief designer at Minton. Rookwood also produced tiles, or architectural faience, as they termed them, from around 1904. Some were covered with matte glazes, some tin-glazed, many made for fireplaces and walls and depicting animals, plants and fruits.

Other Midwestern potteries included the Overbeck Pottery in Indiana, begun by the four Overbeck sisters, and Pewabic in Detroit, Michigan, which was founded by Mary Chase Perry and was best known for its rich blue, gold, green and iridescent glazes, covering simply shaped vessels and square tiles. In the Chicago area, the Gates Potteries of Terra Cotta, Illinois, produced a line of green-glazed art pottery from 1900 called Teco, which was often designed by sculptors and architects (including at least one by Frank Lloyd Wright). The sculptor Fritz Albert designed several Teco vases, distinguished for their pierced decoration as well as for their unusual, organic forms. Around 1903 the architect Hugh MG Garden designed an ovoid vase with four sets of fluted bands and concentric circles at the gently tapering top. Its matte-green glaze, similar to that of Grueby Faience, of Boston, was one of the most popular shades of art pottery of the time. Other Teco green glazes were more crystalline, but this design element was incidental, since it was the form and not the decoration of Gates vessels that was considered all-important. In line with Wright's approbation of the machine, Gates pieces were made from moulds, not thrown by hand, which would have been anathema to early British arts-and-crafts artisans. Wright, however, was not defying his predecessors' ideals, but adapting them to the industry-bound present. The Boston area was especially rich in potteries, the Grueby Faience Co being its most prominent. William H Grueby had worked at the tile-maker J and JG Low, in Chelsea, Massachusetts, before establishing his own firm in East

Boston in 1894. From around 1898, the majority of his vessels and tiles were covered with distinctive glazes; they came in shades of yellow, blue, mauve and brown, but the dark green hue, with a mottled effect like that on water-melon rind, was by far the best known — and soon the most imitated. Grueby's glazes were thought to have been influenced by the vessels of the French art potters, Auguste Delaherche and Ernst Chaplet, whose works he had seen at the 1893 Chicago World's Fair. The thick-walled, faintly organic vessels — highlighted with moulded veining and floral and foliate elements, sometimes in another colour — were beautifully proportioned, simply decorated and subtly hued master-works. Most were designed by George P Kendrick (a Grueby director until 1901, thrown at a wheel, and finally decorated by one of a number of talented women painters including Ruth Erickson and Lillian Newman.

Tile, by Grueby Faience Company, Boston, c1905. Grueby created hand-decorated tiles, like this square featuring a vintage galleon.

Grueby also manufactured architectural tiles. Mostly hand-decorated, these tiles — sometimes single, sometimes in series — bore floral, landscape, animal and maritime motifs. They were first shown, together with Egyptian-inspired scarab paper-weights, at the 1904 St Louis World's Fair, and were marketed by the Grueby Faience Company. In 1907 Grueby Pottery Company was set up to produce only art-pottery. In 1913, however, it was dissolved. A new firm, Grueby Faience and Tile Company, was then established, which produced tiles only. It was in turn bought in 1919 by the C Pardee Works of New Jersey, which moved the operations to its own tile factory in Perth Amboy, New Jersey.

An earlier firm in the Boston area was Chelsea Keramic Art Works, which had begun to produce art pottery in the town of Chelsea in 1872. Three brothers, Alexander W, Hugh C and George W Robertson, together with their father, James, at first produced mostly historicizing, elaborately decorated vessels. However, spurred by the 1876 Centennial Exposition in Philadephia, Hugh began to create underglaze-decorated wares, similar to Limoges, which he called "Bourg-la-Reine", and to experiment with new Eastern-inspired glazes and shapes inspired by Oriental pottery on show. By 1884, the partnership had been dissolved and Hugh ran the firm alone. He became so obsessed with obtaining *sang-de-boeuf* (oxblood-coloured) glaze that his company steadily declined, and finally closed in 1889. Three years later, however, he became manager of a new firm called Chelsea Pottery, where he succeeded in reproducing the Oriental *craquelé* glaze. This lovely crackled surface covered most of Chelsea Pottery's vessels, as well as many of those made by the Dedham Pottery. In 1896 the Chelsea Pottery moved to Dedham. Dedham also produced stoneware vessels, awash with multi-hued glazes, some even iridescent, that achieved dripping, bleeding or splashed effects.

The J and JG Low Art Tiles Works in Chelsea, founded in 1878 by a father and son both named John, produced European-style, high-gloss, solid-coloured tiles, as architectural elements and also as examples of fine art. Floral-design and animal and figural reliefs dominated their output; among the latter were handsome bas-relief profiles and genre scenes, known as "plastic sketches", modelled by Arthur Osborne. These were produced as artistic entities and were sold in fancy metal frames. A "natural process" of tile embellishment was also developed by Low, in which tiles were ingeniously adorned with impressions of actual grasses or leaves by carefully pressing the plant forms into the clay. The Low factory closed down in the early 1900s.

In the early years of the twentieth century, two Massachusetts potteries were founded as community-minded, social endeavours. The Marblehead Pottery was established with the purpose of providing occupational therapy for "nervously worn-out patients" at Dr Herbert J Hall's sanatorium, and Arthur E Baggs, a teacher of distinction, was put in charge of the workshops. Marblehead's first products were unveiled to the public around 1908 and displayed simple shades, subtle matte glazes and stylized organic, animal and maritime motifs, sometimes painted directly on a piece, sometimes lightly incised into it. The designs were often so conventionalized as to appear semi-abstract; straightforward geometric patterns were used as well. "Marblehead blue" was its best-known matte glaze, but grey, brown, red, yellow and green also appeared, sometimes three or four at a time on the earthenware bodies; tin-enamel glaze was used later on. Marblehead was always a very small enterprise, even at its peak in the 1910s, when it added maiolica to its output; operations ceased in 1937.

Boston's Paul Revere Pottery was founded around 1906 in order to teach young disadvantaged girls, mainly from immigrant families, a craft which was both enjoyable and remunerative. Under the direction of Edith Brown and Edith Guerrier, The Saturday Evening Girls' Club, as it was known (despite the fact that the girls worked regular eight-hour days), flourished and soon moved to larger premises in nearby Brighton in 1915. The earthenware products they produced were colourful, matte-glazed useful wares — breakfast bowls, pitchers, tea tiles and nursery sets — their floral, animal and sailing-ship designs often outlined in black. One of the luminaries of American art pottery was Adelaide Alsop Robineau, who, although born in Connecticut, spent most of her adult life in Syracuse, New York. A bright, resourceful child, she taught herself to paint on china and later became a teacher of the art. In the 1890s, she studied painting in New York with the American Impressionist, William Merritt Chase, and exhibited her watercolours and miniature paintings; but she essentially made her living as a china decorator. She married the French-born Samuel E Robineau in 1899, and the pair, together with George Clark, bought the journal *China*

Vase, semi-matt glaze, by Paul Revere Pottery, Boston, c1910. This handsome vase has a incised and painted daffodil design on its upper border.

Two pieces, by Adelaide Alsop Robineau, Syracuse, New York, c1920. Robineau was a master potter and teacher, who created some of the loveliest examples of American art pottery over a long, successful career and covered a wide range of techniques. The "Fox and Grapes" lidded vase *(left)*, evokes stylized, medieval designs as well as the curvilinear aspects of Art Nouveau. The tall, crystalline-glazed vase *(above)*, on the other hand, recalls Robineau's earlier thin-walled porcelain vessels, also covered with exquisite crystalline glazes, resembling coloured blossoms of frost on pale, speckled grounds.

Low-relief moulded tile, by Rookwood Pottery, 1911. Rookwood's extensive range of pottery comprised not only utilitarian vessels, but also landscape plaques and, from 1902, art tiles. This one, featuring a pair of rabbits flanking a tulip tree, is covered with a high-gloss glaze rather than the matt glaze generally employed by Rookwood.

Decorator, the name of which they changed to *Keramic Studio*. Under Adelaide's editorship, the magazine, which was dedicated to the dissemination of good ceramic design, became a great success.

In 1903, Robineau herself began to experiment with various pottery techniques and glazes, at first adhering to the conventional Beaux-Arts style with its dependence on historical and naturalistic sources. She later became taken with Art Nouveau, however, and less traditional, more curvilinear and highly dramatic designs began to creep into her work and on to the pages of *Keramic Studio*, but it also introduced her to the making of porcelain: this came about through her readings of articles by the Sèvres artist/designer, Taxile Doat.

She later studied with Charles F Binns at Alfred University, in Alfred, New York, and was soon creating delicate, thin-walled pieces of porcelain with exquisite crystalline qualities, like blossoms of frost on pale-coloured grounds. The Robineaus tried to mass-produce her designs, but the fragile creations did not translate well into large quantities. She turned her attention once again to individually crafted pieces and these one-off masterworks sold at exclusive outlets such as Tiffany & Co in New York, and won awards at many major world-wide exhibitions. She captured the grand prize at the 1911 International Exposition of Decorative Art in Turin, Italy, for a body of works which included her "Scarab Vase", a tall, leanly ovoid vase decorated overall with stylized scarab beetles on a lustrous white body. Her later works consisted less of highly decorative subjects and patterns and more of simpler oriental and Mayan motifs.

L C Tiffany was renowned more for his Favrile and stained glass than for his pottery. He had been producing his glittering, technicoloured vases, windows and lamps (some with Grueby Faience bases) for over a decade before the first examples of art pottery emerged from his Corona, Long Island studio. He had actually begun experimenting with pottery as early as 1898, but it was not until 1905 that he offered any for sale. The shapes, both hand-thrown and pulled from a mould, were usually naturalistic in shape, deriving, for instance, from gourds and giant blossoms. In the main, delicate white semi-porcelain clay bodies were covered with rich coloured glazes of oriental inspiration, the two most preferred being a mottled creamy yellow shading to black termed "old ivory" and a blotchy green suggestive of moss. Glazes would sometimes "pool" in the relief, resulting in a rich effect that was pleasing to Tiffany.

Theophilus A Brouwer Jr's Middle Lane Pottery in Easthampton, Long Island, was a far cry from Tiffany's

Mushroom lamp, by the Fulper Pottery Company, Flemington, New Jersey, c1910-15. The openwork pottery shade is inset with pieces of red and green leaded glass. The glossy glaze, in shades of green, is often called *verte antique*. Fulper's "Vase-Kraft" pottery was considered an ideal accompaniment to the sturdy arts-and-crafts furniture manufactured by Gustav Stickley's Craftsman shops.

large-scale operation. In 1893 he set up his atelier, experimenting with various lustre glazes and with the use of gold leaf under those glazes, methods that produced opulent, glowing effects. His iridescent glazes, used initially to enhance decorations of flora and fauna, were eventually allowed to stand on their own in a brilliant style he called "Fire Painting". Essentially a self-taught potter, whose methods included the unorthodox transferral of vessels from one hot kiln to another, Brouwer gave up pottery for sculpture in about 1910.

Working in Rochester, New York, was Frederick E Walrath, another of the talented practitioners who studied ceramics at Alfred University with Charles F Binns. Walrath usually created conventionally formed vessels painted with flat, stylized floral and foliate forms, although he made some sculptural figures as well. His glazes were sometimes crystalline but usually matte and grainy-looking, and his rich palette ranged from yellow, orange and green to blue, brown and purple. In Doylestown, Pennsylvania, Dr Henry C Mercer, an archaeologist and antiquarian, set up the Moravian Pottery and Tile Works in 1900. He employed various glazing and decorating techniques, most resulting in an antique, hand-hewn look. Local Pennsylvania Dutch designs and, later, classical and medieval motifs covered his relief and intaglio tiles, many of which were copied from old British specimens in such locales as Margam Abbey in Wales and Castle Acre Priory in Norfolk.

There has been speculation that some tiles attributed to Mercer were in fact made by his rival Herman Carl Mueller, whose initials he shared, and who had come to America as a fledgeling sculptor in 1878. He designed and produced tiles and plaques for American Encaustic and for the Mosaic Tile Co, among others, and in 1908 set up his own company in Trenton, New Jersey. Mueller Mosaic, created tile designs for the New York City subway system, as well as massive tile murals for such clients as the Walker-Gordon Dairy in Plainsboro, New Jersey.

Charles Volkmar was a New Jersey art potter much influenced by French painting and underglaze decoration, having studied the former in Paris in the 1860s and learned the latter at the Theodore Deck and Haviland factories. On his return from France he set up a number of potteries, the first in Greenpoint, New York, the last, with his son, Leon, in Metuchen, New Jersey. His style changed markedly in the 25 years between the two. From landscapes inspired by the Barbizon School, and painted in underglaze slip on red earthenware vases, he advanced to matte-glazed landscapes in the style of Rookwood. There were also unusually textured vessels, vases and bowls whose glazes simulated crackled, parched earth.

The Fulper Pottery had the longest life of all the American art potteries. Established around 1815 (as the Samuel Hill Pottery) in Flemington, New Jersey, it first produced industrial drainpipes and tiles, later including domestic pottery. In 1909 the founder's grandson, William Hill Fulper, Jnr. added art pottery called "vase-kraft" to its line. With its sometimes monumental, oriental-inspired shapes, the range proved extremely popular, and its ingenious lamps, whose mushroom-shaped shades bore openwork designs filled in with stained glass, were especially admired. Although Fulper's forms were sometimes considered too clumsy, there was no disagreement on the beauty and variety of its glazes – matte, lustre, *flambé*, crystalline, spotted – which were given such fanciful names on their paper labels as "Leopard Skin", "Cucumber Green"

Vase, by George Ohr, Biloxi, Mississippi, c1900. Ohr created bizarre vessels whose crinkled, crumpled and collapsing shapes seemed to defy all conventions of pottery-making. The two handles on this vase seem to wriggle against the vessel's sides, while the neck has been twisted. Despite its unconventionality, it was expertly thrown and glazed by a consummate master – and showman.

and "Mission Matte". In New Orleans, a pottery department was established in 1895 at the Sophie Newcomb College for Women (founded in 1886 as the Women's arm of Tulane University) which developed into the source of some of America's loveliest art pottery. Its director was Ellsworth Woodward, whose brother William taught art at Tulane and was also head of New Orleans' Baronne Street Pottery, and Mary G Sheerer, a china painter who had trained with Rookwood, was instructor of design. A true arts-and-crafts spirit inbued the group, which soon evolved from a clutch of enthusiastic amateurs working with limited equipment into an organized, quasi-professional community of talented experts.

A distinctive Newcomb style resulted, whose guidelines were simplicity, sensibility and individuality. A strong sense of regionalism prevailed as well, and the flora and fauna depicted on Newcomb's lovely, useful wares were indigenous to the area. There grew up too a characteristic Newcomb palette: soft blues, greens, pink, yellows and creams. At first the simply shaped, low-fired bisque vessels were underglaze-painted with stylized floral motifs, their outlines often previously incised. The early glossier wares later gave way to popular matte-glazed under the influence of Paul Cox, who had also studied with Binns at Alfred University. His more muted glazes led to an overall softening of the pastel colours, as well as to less conventionalized decorations.

The vases of Sadie Irvine, a gifted student who later ran the

Vessels, by the Newcomb College Pottery, New Orleans. The vessels were known for their pastel glazes and their organic subject matter. Pictured are a covered pot and vase: the pot's upper border and lid are decorated with incised and painted wild tomatoes; its glossy glaze dates it to c1900-10. The daffodil- and leaf-decorated vase, from after 1910, is covered with a matt glaze. These later vessels also assumed the softer pastel colours for which Newcomb is best known, and were often moulded in low relief, rather than incised.

pottery department, were some of Newcomb's finest. Her most famous design, a vase featuring a dreamy landscape of moss-covered live oaks, a pale yellow moon peeping from behind the pendent moss, appeared in various permutations on many Newcomb vases.

George Ohr, who worked at Newcomb College for a short time, was noted for his strangely shaped, highly experimental pots. Covered with varicoloured glazes, alone or in mottled or spotted combinations, these pieces featured such humorous elements as folded necks, crinkled ears, pinched sides or compressed rims. One even took the shape of a crushed top hat.

Ohr worked in Biloxi, Mississippi, the coastal site of some especially desirable clays, where he perfected a method of throwing earthenware vessels whose walls were as delicately thin as those of porcelain. A consummate showman, he grew a long handlebar moustache which he gathered and tied around his ears while at the potter's wheel. He also proclaimed himself the world's greatest potter, but in 1909 he suddenly forsook his art and opened a Cadillac dealership in Biloxi. As refined and sophisticated as George Ohr's pots were bizarre, were the vases of Artus Van Briggle's pottery (bearing the same name) in Colorado Springs, Colorado. Ohio-born Van Briggle worked for Rookwood from around 1887, and Maria Longworth Nichols, was so impressed by paintings he exhibited at the 1893 Chicago World's Fair, that she sent him to Paris to study at the Académie Julian. There, he enrolled in sculpture classes as well as painting, and his modelling in clay stood him in good stead not only at Rookwood, but at his own small pottery.

Van Briggle's first wares in Colorado were produced in 1901, and their deeply sculptural qualities placed them firmly in the Art Nouveau vein. The matte glazes he had been working to perfect at Rookwood were present as well, sometimes in two tones. Floral and human forms figured heavily on his wares, perhaps his best-known piece being the vase sometimes called

"Lorelei", with the long tresses and arm of a languorous woman curving around the neck of the blue-green, matte-glazed vessel, and the rest of her robed body draping around the sides. Unfortunately, Van Briggle, who received many medals for his work at the 1904 St Louis World's Fair, died earlier that same year. His designs continued to be produced by his wife, and they proved so popular that a new, enlarged facility was built in 1907.

A creative potter who worked on the West Coast was Ernest A Batchelder. He was also a devoted admirer of the British Arts and Crafts Movement, having studied at the Birmingham School of Arts and Crafts and visited CR Ashbee's Guild of Handicraft. Batchelder was interested in oriental and Native American art, as well as in the medieval designs which inspired his British counterparts. After teaching at schools in Massachusetts, Missouri and elsewhere, he set up his own craft school in 1909 in Pasadena, California. Although he is best known for his striking medievalizing tile designs – cast, usually monchromatic squares featuring distinctive conventionalized plants and animals – there were also tile series carved with landscapes that included local flora. He also produced vessesls such as jardinières bearing bestial and avian motifs, as well as florid designs of intertwining leaves or *Japoniste* branches and trees.

Australian Art Pottery

EVEN AS FAR AFIELD as Australia, an art pottery movement was taking root. Around the turn of the century various arts-and-crafts societies sprouted in the major cities. It was not easy, however, for individual potters to acquire equipment and supplies and most early commercial art pottery was therefore hand-painted. Even when they had kilns, potters were often forced to dig their own clay. As a result, members of the societies tended to pool their resources and purchase shared equipment.

The best-known art potter was Merric Boyd, who became interested in the craft around 1908. His first studio, at Murrumbeena, Victoria, was set up in 1911, and he exhibited a year later. He did wartime service in Europe, and was then employed in Staffordshire potteries, including Wedgwood, and studied at the Stoke-on-Trent Technical School. He returned to Australia in 1919, and within a decade his work had become highly respected. His sculptural approach to his medium resulted in handsome earthenware and stoneware vessels, some with organic incised or underglaze decoration, often of indigenous animals, trees and plants.

Hexagonal advertising tile, by Ernest A Batchelder, California. Batchelder was highly admired for his medievalizing sand-pressed tiles, and was a devotee – indeed product – of the British Arts and Crafts Movement: he studied at the Birmingham School of Art and visited CR Ashbee's Guild of Handicraft in 1905.

The pottery of the Arts and Crafts Movement covered a wide range of different techniques and traditions. Although there was no definitive style or method in arts-and-crafts pottery there was a huge amount of both beautiful and striking pottery produced both from individual potters and large factories. In Britain the pieces produced varied from the grotesque productions of the Martin Brothers to the Near Eastern and Renaissance influenced work of William De Morgan. The Arts and Craft Movement also marked a democratisation in the manufacture of pottery. In certain cases the designer and the potter worked closely together to produce work that reflected the ideals set forward by William Morris. Also the larger potteries started to produce arts-and-craft ware and employed distinguished painters.

Although the Arts and Crafts Movement did not influence continental pottery in the same way as it did in Britain and America; it was more influenced by Art Nouveau forms. A number of potters worked both in Britain and America and took with them the traditions of fine continental work.

In America the pottery scene was extraordinarily diverse with small companies setting up and fading away and the larger companies producing work that attempted to jump on the arts-and-crafts bandwagon. American pottery covered the whole gamut of pieces from domestic pottery through to high art pottery and a renaissance in the production of decorative tiles. Both in Britain and America the Arts and Crafts Movement stimulated a huge development in art pottery which may be seen as advancing the interest in craft pottery whch exists today.

Chapter Seven

GRAPHICS

SPREAD OF THE IDEAL ❦ THE COM-
MERCIAL HOUSES ❦ LITERARY HOUSES
❦ THE PRIVATE PRESSES

OWARDS THE END OF THE NINETEENTH century, technological advances made it possible for publishers to meet the reading needs of a rapidly growing literate public. Fast new power presses, automatic type-casting and typesetting machines, plus cheap and plentiful paper enabled them to produce increasingly large numbers of books and magazines. Quality was sacrificed to speed and quantity, with little or no thought for aesthetics. A few companies, however, maintained the tradition of fine printing. The Chiswick Press and T & A Constable in England, Theodore De Vinne and Taylor and Taylor in America, all produced books that were still carefully designed and printed. A renewed interest in medieval illumi-nated manuscripts revived the idea of the book as a carefully crafted object reflecting the hand and the soul of its maker.

The reaction against the shoddiness in the printing and graphic arts began to gain momentum in the 1880s under the influence of William Morris and the Arts and Crafts Movement.

Medieval illuminated manuscripts and early printed books were the perfect embodiment of Morris's ideals; these "pocket cathedrals", as he called them, were to him glorious examplars of the handcraftman's work. Surprisingly, although his contributions to the printing and graphic arts probably eclipse his contributions to all the other crafts, he did not found his Kelmscott Press until 1891, when he was 57. But his admiration for all things medieval had led him to try his hand at calligraphy and illumination much earlier. The results are extraordinary manuscripts of his own works, such as *The Story of Sigurd the Volsung and the Fall of the Niblungs*, and his calligraphic rendering of Virgil's *Aeneid*. They are neither copies nor imitations, but homages to the very essence of the Gothic.

During the first Arts and Crafts Exhibition Society in 1888, Morris spoke on tapestry and carpet weaving, Walter Crane on design, and Emery Walker on printing. Walker's lecture was accompanied by lantern slides of fifteenth-century typefaces which were a revelation to Morris, who determined to create a face that would have the same perfect proportions and beauty.

Morris had already become involved with the typography of his own commercially published books at the Chiswick Press. Consulting with Charles Jacobi, Chiswick's manager, he had chosen old-style faces such as Caslon and Basle, and the books were elegantly designed, reflecting his study of *incunabula*. Even so, none of them had been of high enough quality to be included in the first Arts and Crafts Exhibition. This, together with the low standard of contemporary books in general, spurred him to create the Kelmscott Press – named after his home in Hammersmith – with the close collaboration of Walker. As Will Ransom, the chronicler of the privatepress movement said, the revival of fine printing would have occurred without Morris, but his charisma speeded the process and helped spread the ideas far and wide.

The Kelmscott books reflect Morris's concern for craftsmanship and his conviction that a book can be a work of art, with all the components united in a harmonious whole: "A book quite unornamented can be positively beautiful, not merely un-ugly if it be, so to speak, architecturally sound; the page must be easy to read, the type must be well designed and the margins in due proportion to the size of the letters." For Morris the placement of text is paramount, and the double page forms a unit. He hated greyness, and his pages are tightly set, with little space between letters and no leading between the lines. The type is small, boldly black and in keeping with the content of the text. Woodcut ornaments and decorations of medieval inspiration contribute to the solid black appearance

of the page. The paper is handmade, by the firm of Joseph Batchelor, and is thick and very white to contrast with the densely rich black ink that was made in Germany to Morris's specifications. He often used a second colour, usually red, for the shoulder notes and running titles. The binding is either thick boards with cloth spine or vellum with silk ties.

He enlisted the help of skilled artisans. Walker provided his enormous technical proficiency and artistic talents. Edward Prince superbly cut the type. William Bowden, a retired master

William Morris *A Note* ... published by Kelmscott Press, 1898; one of 525 copies. Published posthumously under the direction of Sidney Cockerell, this slim book contains and exemplifies Morris's credo on bookmaking and displays the three typefaces he designed. The frontispiece is by Edward Burne-Jones.

printer, supervised the presses. William H Hooper, who had engraved the drawings of Tenniel, Millais and Leighton for *Punch* and the *Illustrated London News*, engraved the decorations and illustrations. Morris restricted himself to designing the ornaments, borders and initials, and commissioned major artists to create the illustrations.

Chief among these was the Pre-Raphaelite painter, Edward Burne-Jones, with whom Morris produced the Kelmscott *Chaucer*. The 87 illustrations are admirably suited to the text and, combined with the type and decorative borders, fulfil Morris's ideal of the book as the perfect embodiment of the mind, soul and hand of the craftsman at work towards a common goal. Arthur Gaskin's illustrations for *The Shepheardes Calender* were also brilliantly successful – so much so that Morris let them fill the page without the addition of borders. Walter Crane, on the other hand, illustrated the first Kelmscott book, *The Story of the Glittering Plain*, with designs too fussy to harmonize with the sharp and bold typography.

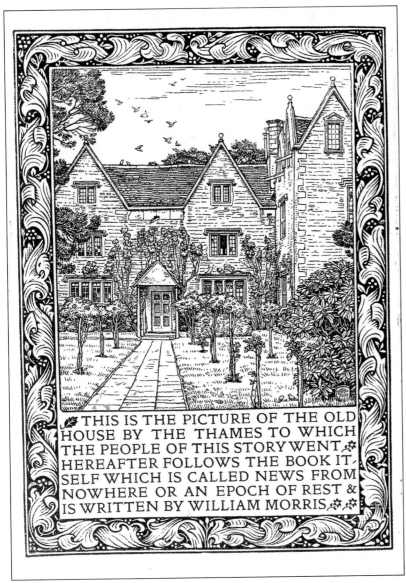

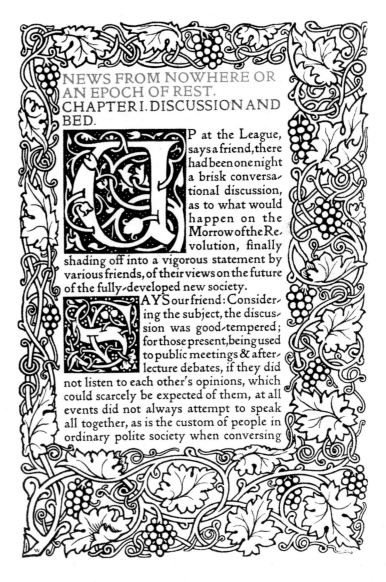

William Morris *News from Nowhere,* published by Kelmscott Press, 1892; one of 300 copies. Decorations are by Morris, frontispiece by CM Gere, engraved by WH Hooper. The type, Golden, is Morris's first as is the novel, a Utopian story, set in the future.

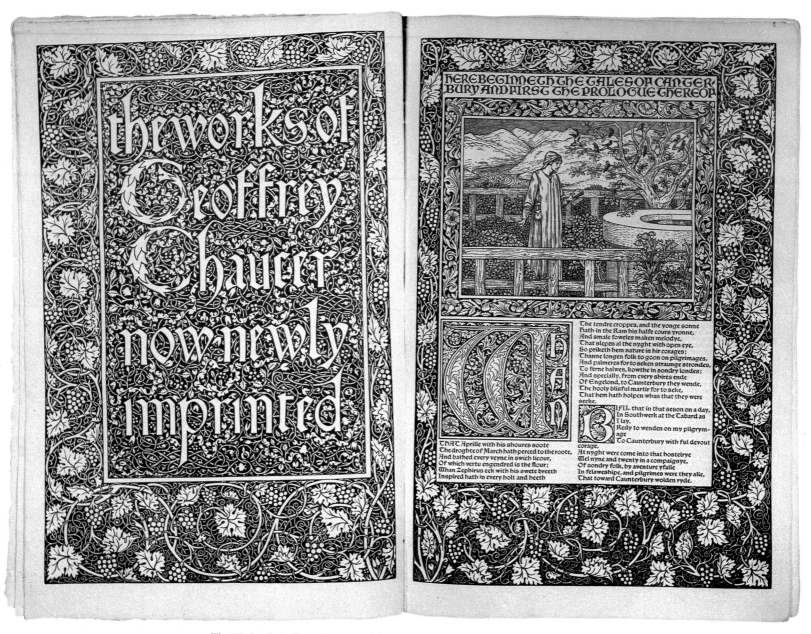

The Works of Geoffrey Chaucer, published by Kelmscott Press, 1896; one of 425 copies; 87 illustrations by Edward Burne-Jones; Chaucer type for the text, Troy for display. Begun in 1891 and completed in 1896, five months before Morris's death, the magnificent Chaucer is the "pocket cathedral" which Morris intended a book to be.

The Kelmscott Press produced a total of 53 titles in 66 volumes, ten of these titles were produced after Morris's death in 1896. Two years later, the assets were sold off. The typefaces were made public, but, on Morris's instructions, the wood-blocks of the ornaments that he had designed – over 600 – were donated to the British Museum with the proviso that they be kept out of circulation for 100 years.

Morris's concepts of good design and good typography had far greater influence than did the Kelmscott books themselves, which were often criticized for demanding to be looked at rather than read. Yet they demonstrated by comparison how inferior contemporary typefaces and designs were and how much better they could be. More important, they proved that a book can be a work of art through which design, and printer breathe physical beauty into a writer's creation.

Arts-and-crafts graphic design is less a unified style than a commonality of attitudes in which the art of the book is seen as a collaborative effort between writer, designer, decorator and printer. It is an approach that affected both commercial and private presses, and their products share many attributes, chief among them – as with Kelmscott – a concern for design in which all the elements are harmoniously integrated and through which the author's voice is given an attractive physical body.

Books were produced chiefly in two styles, "arts and crafts" and "aesthetic". Although they appeared quite differed, they had much in common: thoughtful design; the use of vellum or fine handmade paper with deckle edges; and a deep respect for the relationship between the object and its contents. While the arts-and-crafts book is of medieval inspiration, on the Morris model, the aesthetic is classical in its inspiration. The format is usually small – "dainty" – the margins wide and the whiteness of the paper emphasized. The type is old-style, as in arts and crafts, but far lighter. Ornaments, mostly inspired by Renaissance designs, and sometimes by Art Nouveau, usually appear only in initials and head and tail pieces. The general feeling is one of airiness.

Since the bright morn, they led her to the gate,
Where she beheld a golden litter wait,
Whereby the King stood, aged and bent to earth,
The flute-players with faces void of mirth,
The down-cast bearers of the ivory wands,
The maiden torch-bearers' unhappy bands.

So then was Psyche taken to the hill,
And through the town the streets were void and still;
For in their houses all the people stayed,
Of that most mournful music sore afraid.
But on the way a marvel did they see,
For, passing by, where wrought of ivory,
There stood the Goddess of the flowery isle,
All folk could see the carven image smile.
But when anigh the hill's bare top they came,
Where Psyche must be left to meet her shame,
They set the litter down, and drew aside

11

The Story of Cupid and Psyche from *The Earthly Paradise* published by Kelmscott Press in 1896 with illustrations by Burne-Jones.

Spread of the ideal

MAGAZINES DEMONSTRATING ARTS-AND-CRAFTS ideals flourished on both sides of the Atlantic, reaching out to audiences of young designers, artists and printers who were eager to explore new avenues. Among the earliest was the quarterly, *The Hobby Horse*, which was published in 1884 by the Century Guild. In the mainstream of the movement, it was originated by John Ruskin's disciple, George Allen; excellently printed at the Chiswick Press, and decorated with handsome woodcuts, chiefly by Selwyn Image and Herbert Horne. And it stood as proof that form could be as important as content.

The Dial, which was established five years later by Charles Ricketts and Charles Shannon, was largely a vehicle for Ricketts' innovative design ideas. These in turn had been stimulated by the painter James McNeill Whistler, who, in designing his own books, had introduced asymmetrical title-pages and made spare use of ornament. The *Dial* offered literary contributions by Ricketts, Shannon, T Sturge Moore, John Gray and Laurence Housman, as well as woodcuts, etchings and lithographs by Shannon, Ricketts, Sturge Moore and Lucien Pissarro.

In the United States, the *Knight Errant*, which survived barely more than a year, was the direct heir of *The Hobby Horse*. Produced in Boston, Massachusetts, by an enthusiastic group of publishers, designers, poets and architects, it paid obeisance to Kelmscott in its first issue with praise for the Press's book, *Poems by the Way*, and in its second with a long article on the typography of Morris.

The *Studio*, published both in England and in the United States, was the major source of information on developments in the arts. It contributed greatly to public awareness of the design revolution, not only through its articles, but through design competitions which provided recognition for established artists and opportunity for new ones. A second specialist magazine, *Modern Art*, was founded in Indianapolis, Indiana, in 1893 by Joseph Bowles who later founded the magazine *Art and Life*, was one of the most literate voices of the Arts and Crafts Movement. Designed by Bruce Rogers, who was to become one of the towering figures in the art of the book, it was devoted almost entirely to the printing and graphic arts.

The magazines most responsible, however, for spreading the news of the Morrisian revolution in the United States were two industry periodicals, the *American Printer*, published in New York, and the *Inland Printer*, in Chicago. The *Inland Printer*,

The Century Guild. *The Hobby Horse.* The lavishly produced Hobby Horse was one of the most important journals of the Arts and Crafts Movement.

the first to call attention to Kelmscott Press books with articles and illustrations, was also among the first major publications to commission original covers and posters for every issue. This move opened an entire new field for promising young designers such as Will Bradley and Frank Hazenplug.

Perhaps the most ardent American gospeller of all for the Movement was the furniture maker, Gustav Stickley, through his magazine, *The Craftsman*. Although an impassioned Morris admirer and a staunch advocate of factory reform, Stickley was neither a book designer nor a printer, and his Kelmscott-inspired publication was clumsy. Although in later years, both typography and layout shed their early medievalizing in favour of a more modern style, the importance of *The Craftsman* resides more in its content than in its appearance.

The influence of these specialist publications soon also embraced American general interest magazines such as *Harper's*, *Lippincott's* and *Century*. Not only did they experiment with the new graphic ideas, they were among the first to make bold use of the poster, which had by then in France already become both a powerful advertising medium and an accepted art form. Among its most brilliant practitioners were Jules Chéret, Pierre Bonnard and Henri de Toulouse-Lautrec. Chéret was the first to recognize that the poster could be more than a bludgeoning advertising tool and that text and illustration could be artfully combined to create designs that were strong and attractive in their own right.

The effects of Japonisme and Art Nouveau, with their heavy

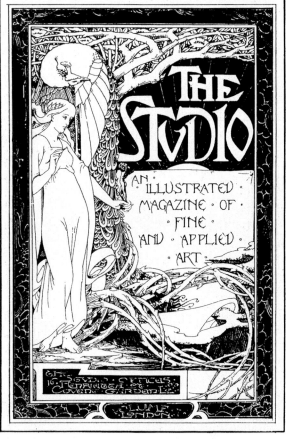

Above. The winner of a competition held by The *Studio* to design a title page. The judges were favourably impressed by the standard of design but deplored "the absence of merit" in the lettering.

Left. The *Studio*, title page, 14 March 1914. The *Studio* was influential in spreading the arts-and-crafts message among the bourgeois.

One of a series of devices produced by Gustav Stickley. The motto *Als ik kan*, first used by Jan van Eyck, is indicative of Stickley's deeply felt attachment to the guild ideals of Morris and the British Arts and Crafts Movement.

Harper's Weekly, Cover, 17 April 1897. Harper's was one of the American general interest magazines to experiment with the new graphic ideas put forward by Stickley and other design reformers.

outlines, flat areas of colour and two-dimensional figures, are clearly evident in the posters of the 1890s. Keyed to the most progressive tastes, they were the ideal advertising medium for magazines. *Harper's*, in 1893, was the first monthly to commission an artist, Edward Penfield, to create a new poster for every issue. Other magazines and the publishers of books, as well, soon adopted this exciting new device. Publishing posters became a major industry on its own; contests were organized to discover new talents, and collectors went poster-mad.

🐦 🐦 🐦

The Commercial Houses

ALTHOUGH THE IMPETUS FOR the revival in the graphic arts came from idealists in the Morris mode, commercial book publishers, too, were instrumental in fostering it. A few of the old established houses had, of course, kept the tradition of fine printing alive, seeking to achieve artistic effects through the use of appropriate types and simplicity and elegance of design.

Now others followed suit. The Bodley Head, a London literary publishing company founded in 1887 by John Lane and Charles Elkin Mathews, embodied the tenets of the revival. They used old-face types, Caslon or Basle, rather than the modern types generally associated with mass-produced books. The page layout followed that advocated by Jacobi, and later by Walker and Morris. Their most distinguishing characteristics, however, were their title-pages and bindings.

Lane, who also published the influential periodical, *The Yellow Book*, commissioned artists as his designers. Some, such as Image, Crane and Horne, were already established; others, including Ricketts, Laurence Housman and Aubrey Beardsley, received their first important assignments from him. They produced some of the most beautiful title-pages of the time, satisfying the dictum of Walter Bigger Blaikie at T & A Constable that the title-page must be "the crowning glory of the book...express[ing] clearly and at first glance the character of the book". Housman's title-page for Francis Thompson's *Poems* masterfully integrates type and stylized decorative design and, with its asymmetric arrangement and ingenious use of off-red colour, provides a striking example of the new style. His design for Katharine Hinkson's *Cuckoo Songs*, with its flowing lines, is pure Art Nouveau, as is the title-page designed by J Illingworth Kay for Norman Gale's *Orchard Songs*. Among Ricketts' masterpieces is his cover for *Silverpoints*, a book of poems by John Gray: airy green leaves superimposed on a geometric pattern of wavy gold lines.

The revival gained a foothold among commercial publishers

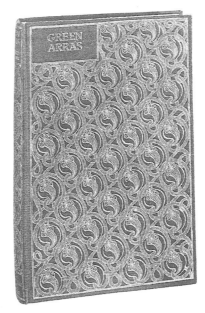

Above. *The Yellow Book*, Poster for Vol 1, April 1894. Aubrey Beardsley was art editor of the magazine until 1895. It was a forum for a broad group of artists and illustrators from the conservative Frederic Leighton to Walter Sickert.

Left. L Housman *The Green Acres*, published by The Bodley Head, 1896.

in the United States, as well. In 1891, Morris's American publishers, the Roberts Brothers in Boston, issued a facsimile of his *The Story of the Glittering Plain*, which proved a revelation to a new generation of publishers and printers who became more receptive to the idea that a book could be intrinsically beautiful. The Boston firm of Houghton Mifflin, according to Fred Holland Day, writing in *The Knight Errant*, did more than any other in America to improve the art of book-printing.

In the early 1890s, they began to publish books directly influenced by Morris and printed at their Riverside Press under the direction of DB Updike. FH Smith's *A Day at Laguerre*, which they brought out in 1892, was the first American book with a title-page in the Morris manner, although it was otherwise in an aesthetic format. Several years later, they produced one of the most Gothic volumes of the period, RB Aldrich's *Friar Jerome's Beautiful Book*, with decorations by WS Hadaway. It was designed and printed under the direction of Bruce Rogers who, like Updike and many others, was originally heavily swayed by Morris and Kelmscott. As he matured, Rogers' style became more Renaissance-orientated, as can be seen in his later Riverside Press limited editions.

The Holy Bible published by Merrymount Press, 1904. This bible, designed and printed by DB Updike for RH Hinkley, shows Updike's evolution towards the classical look with sparing use of decorations and a lighter feel to the page.

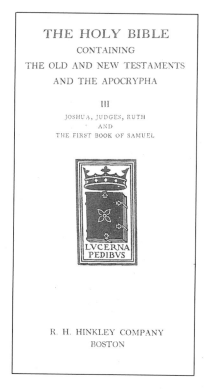

THE HOLY BIBLE

CONTAINING

THE OLD AND NEW TESTAMENTS

AND THE APOCRYPHA

III

JOSHUA, JUDGES, RUTH
AND
THE FIRST BOOK OF SAMUEL

LVCERNA
PEDIBVS

R. H. HINKLEY COMPANY
BOSTON

In 1893, Updike founded the Merrymount Press in Boston, where he produced magnificent books in the arts-and-crafts style. His designs too eventually shed the heavily ornamented influence of Morris to acquire a more restrained and classical look, with sparing use of decoration and a lighter feel to the page. His major work in the Kelmscott mood was the *Altar Book* of 1896, which was bound in blind-stamped pigskin, closed by three metal clasps, and beautifully printed by De Vinne.

The general movement towards more thoughtful design, coupled with the emergence of new technologies, resulted in a surge of stunning multi-coloured bindings and covers. One designer in particular, a New York woman, Margaret N Armstrong, came, more than all the others, to typify this burgeoning development. She designed and decorated trade-bindings for Houghton Mifflin, AC McClure, Bobbs Merrill, Charles Scribner and GD Putnam, among others. Her designs, many reminiscent of stained glass, are strongly geometric and rhythmic, tightly integrated, making effective use of colour in combination with gold, and of stylized floral elements. Her greatest achievements were her designs for the books of Myrtle Reed, published by Putnam, and those of Henry Van Dyke, published by Scribner. The Reed covers, in white, gold and pastels on a light-blue background, are light and airy. The Van Dyke designs are more forceful and dense, with white and gold combining with deep red and greens on dark blue. Armstrong gradually abandoned design and turned to writing, becoming a best-selling author in her later years.

❦ ❦ ❦

Literary Houses

FIN DE SIÈCLE Boston, teeming with intellectual activity, propagated not only arts-and-crafts magazines and commercial publishers, but literary houses, as well, dedicated to producing contemporary works in handsome formats. The most successful was founded in 1893 by two recent Harvard graduates, Herbert Copeland and Fred Holland Day, who published finely made limited editions which maintained the highest standards of craftsmanship and typography. Many, designed chiefly by Bertram G Goodhue, were Kelmscott-inspired, among them a series entitled *English Love Sonnets* and *Sonnets* by Louise Guinney. Others, such as John Bannister Tabb's *Poems* and William Bliss Carman and Richard Hovey's *Songs from Vagabondia*, were in the aesthetic style.

Copeland and Day were the American distributors of *The Hobby Horse* and the publishers of Lane's *Yellow Book* and of

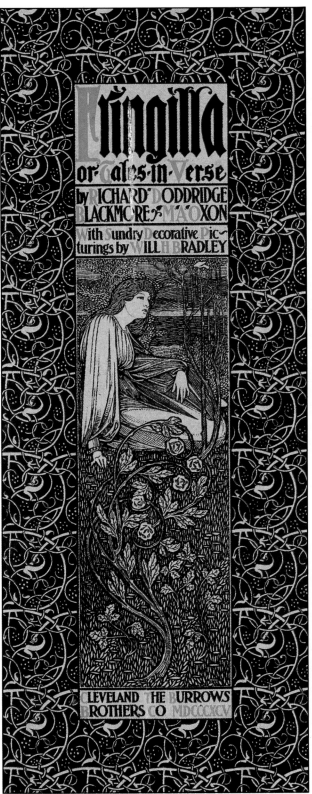

Far left. RD Blackmore, *Fringilla*, published by Burrows Brothers, 1895; one of 600 copies. Will Bradley's illustrations and decorations for this book reflect his masterful assimilation of Morris's and Beardsley's influences in creating a powerfully original work of art.

Left. Alice Brown, *Meadow Grass*, published by Copeland and Day, 1895. This is one of Louis Rhead's most impressive compositions. His use of green and gold alone evoke the title. The cover was issued separately as a poster.

Below left. Lilian Bell, *Little Sister to the Wilderness*, published by Stone and Kimball, 1895. Bruce Roger designed two covers for Stone and Kimball. This one is a clever interpretation of the cover Ricketts created for the Bodley Head's *Silverpoints*.

numerous Bodley Head titles. Following Lane's example, many of their books are characterized by lively title-pages and covers, created mostly by young designers who lived in the Boston area, including Will Bradley, the English-born Louis J Rhead, and Maxfield Parrish.

Chicago, which had also become a major intellectual centre by the last decade of the century, produced not only the influential *Inland Printer*, but was the home for more than fifty commercial printers and for two of the era's most significant literary houses. The first of these had been founded in Boston by Herbert Stuart Stone and Hannibal Ingalls Kimball while they were still Harvard undergraduates and later transplanted to Chicago. Emulating the Bodley Head, some of whose books they also published, Stone and Kimball followed the aesthetic canon with small formats, old-style type, deep tail margins and decorations restricted to title-page and cover. They also produced one of the period's most successful "little" magazines, *The Chap-Book*.

Chicago's second major literary house, Way and Williams, was founded by W Irving Way and Chauncey Williams, the former an ardent bibliophile who wrote perceptive articles for the *Inland Printer*, and the latter, co-founder of still another firm, the Auvergne Press, which published only two books, both designed by Frank Lloyd Wright. During a visit to England, Way had secured from John Lane the American rights to six Bodley Head books and from William Morris the exclusive American rights to a Kelmscott book, Rossetti's *Hand and Soul*. Many of the company's own volumes were clearly influenced by Morris, with designs by Bradley, Hazenplug and Rogers, but others were just as distinctively aesthetic, with covers and title-pages by Maxfield Parrish and by JC Leyendecker.

JJ Bourase *The Miracles of Madame Saint Katherine de Fierbois*, published by Way & Williams, 1897. The book has a splendid woodcut title page and illustrations by Selwyn Image.

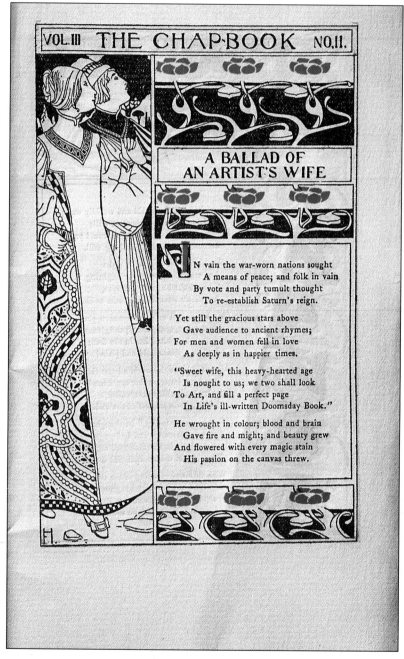

Left. *Lo Inferno di Dante Alighieri fiorentino*, published by Ashendene Press, 1902; one of 135 copies with woodcuts by C Keates and initials in gold and colour. The Subiaco type, the illustrations and the page layout combine harmoniously to provide an elegantly restrained whole.

The Private Presses

MORRIS'S CONCEPT OF THE BOOK as a work of art was expressed perhaps most excitingly through the private-press movement which began in England and spread gradually to the United States. There are many definitions of a private press. Ransom stresses the aspect of individual endeavour: "A private press is the typographical expression of a personal ideal conceived in freedom and maintained in independence." While such freedom sometimes encouraged "vanity" publishers, the majority of private presses were genuinely motivated by Morris's credo that "the activity of making is as important as the thing made". Hand-printed, their editions were of necessity limited. Some produced unabashed and unoriginal Kelmscott imitations, but the best of them – more conspicuously in Britain than in the United States – rarely followed the heavily ornamented Kelmscott lead.

Somewhat outside the Arts and Crafts Movement was the Daniel Press of the Reverend Charles Henry Olive Daniel at Oxford. He had started the press as a childhood hobby, progressed to printing church and community announcements and eventually to producing the works of his literary friends. In the 1870s, he discovered a cache of the magnificent Fell types which had been given to Oxford University Press in the seventeenth century by Bishop Fell, and thereafter he used nothing else for the elegantly crafted volumes that he created in

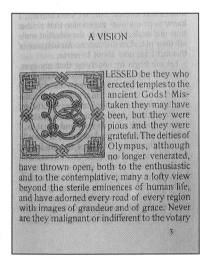

Above. *The Convivio* by Dante Alighieri published by Ashendene Press in 1895. The typeface used here was based on that developed by Sweynheim and Pannartz at Subiaco in 1465.

Far left. WS Landorf, *A Vision*, published by Handcraft Shop, 1901. Will Ransom, the leading chronicler of the private press movement, was inspired by the Roycroft books to start his own press in Snohomish. He printed three wonderful hand-illuminated books before helping Gaudy found his Village Press.

Left. *Lo Inferno di Dante Alighieri fiorentino* published by ashendene Press, 1902; one of 135 copies with woodcuts by C Keates and initials in gold and colour. The Subiaco type, the illustrations and the page layout combine harmoniously to provide an elegantly restrained whole.

collaboration with his wife, Emily. Their most famous was the *Garland of Rachel*, a collection of poems by contemporary literary lions, which they published in 1881 in an edition of 35 to honour their daughter.

The Ashendene Press, founded in 1894 by CH St John Hornby, a director of the booksellers WH Smith and Son, outlived all the other private British presses, continuing to publish until 1935. Hornby, another hobbyist who began to print as a child, was stongly inspired by Daniel, even borrowing the Fell type. He was even more significantly motivated, however, by Morris and Morris's associates, Emery Walker and Sydney Cockerell, who persuaded him to develop his own typeface. He evolved what he called Subiaco, based on a fifteenth-century Italian face. Hornby's style, less massive and exuberant than Morris's, owes more to the Renaissance than to the Gothic. The layout is restrained and the spacing of the lines tight. He used woodcut illustrations sparingly, but these were exquisite, as evidenced by those created by FM Gere and WH Hooper for *Un Mazzetto Scelto dei Fioretti di San Francisco*. He employed little colour, usually only red or blue, which was restricted to initials designed by leading calligraphers such as Graily Hewitt and Eric Gill. The few illuminations were almost always the work of Florence Kingsford.

Charles Ricketts and Charles Shannon moved into book publishing after they sent a copy of their magazine, *The Dial*, to

M Drayton *The Nymphidia and the Muses* published by Vale Press, 1896; one of 210 copies; Vale type. The flowing lines of the decorations and the illustrations, designed by Shannon and Ricketts, and their elegant typeface, combine to provide a vigorous masterpiece of bookmaking.

Oscar Wilde. Impressed, Wilde urged his publishers, first, Osgood McIlvaine and Co, and later, John Lane, to commission Ricketts to design his own books. Ricketts, who shared Morris's conviction that a book must "show design in each portion of it, from type to paper, from build to decorations", soon began to assume control over all the elements, producing books for others besides Wilde. He was responsible for binding, layout and initials for Gray's *Silverpoint*. Together with Shannon, he conceived the title-page, layout, woodcuts and illustrations for the Bodley Head *Hero and Leander* in 1893 and, more importantly, for those of *The Sphinx* in 1894, which was printed by the Ballantyne Press on paper bearing the Vale watermark, named for their London home, the Vale, which had formerly belonged to Whistler.

With *The Sphinx*, they had in effect established their Vale Press, although it was not formally founded until 1896. It existed for less than a decade, but produced 46 outstanding examples of the art of the book, printed by Ballantyne, but creatively theirs, from the delicate layouts to the three Gothic-influenced types designed by Ricketts and to the sinuous line of the decorations which bore a touch of Art Nouveau.

Lucien Pissarro, the son of the painter Camille Pissarro, who became associated with the Vale group, shared their enthusiasm for the woodcut as a medium for illustration and not merely as a means of reproduction. He and his wife Esther, both talented wood-engravers, founded their own house, the Eragny Press, in 1894 with the goal of "printing illustrations with a suitable text rather than books with illustrations". At first they used the Vale types, but Pissarro later designed one of their own called Brook. The Brook face was more legible than the Vale on which it was based and harmonized beautifully with Pissarro's woodcuts.

Their books were in small format and beautifully designed with effective use of colours. In *Songs by Ben Jonson*, the woodcut frontispiece is in four colours and the printing in red and black. Their *Riquet à la Houppe* by Charles Perrault has woodcut initials and illustrations in four colours with the printing in black and red. They also produced five copies in delicate grey and orange.

When the Kelmscott equipment was sold off in 1898, CR Ashbee bought the printing press for his Guild and School of Handicraft, which had its workshops in Essex House, a Georgian mansion in the East End of London. There he established his Essex House Press, and, with the help of the Kelmscott printers and of WH Hooper, who cut the illustrations as he had done for Morris and Hornby, Ashbee produced books

From
The
Forest

 From
The
Forest

✤ XVII. THAT WOMEN ARE BUT MEN'S SHADDOWES.

OLLOW a shaddow, it still flies
you,
Seeme to flye it, it will pursue:
So court a mistris, shee denyes you;
Let her alone, shee will court you.
Say are not women truely, then
Stil'd but shaddowes of us men?

At morne, and even, shades are longest;
At noone, they are or short, or none:
So men at weakest, they are strongest,
But grant us perfect, they're not knowne
Say, are not women truly, then,
Stil'd but shaddowes of us men?

✤ XVIII. TO CELIA.

RINKE to me, onely with thine
eyes,
And I will pledge with mine:
Or leave a kisse but in the cup,
And Ile not looke for wine.
The thirst, that from the soule doth rise,
Doth aske a drinke divine:
But might I of Jove's Nectar sup,
I would not change for thine.
I sent thee, late, a rosie wreath,
Not so much honoring thee,

24

As giving it a hope, that there
It could not withered bee.
But thou thereon did'st only breathe,
And sent'st it backe to mee:
Since when it growes, and smells, I sweare,
Not of itself, but thee.

✤ From
Joseph
Ritson's
Collection
of English
Songs.
18th Cen-
tury air.

25

The Songs of Ben Jonson published by Eragny Press in 1906. The use of the second colour for the capitals at the beginning of each song and the decorative motifs created a medieval feeling.

that were loyal to arts-and-crafts principles. Although his enterprise has been faulted by some for its imperfect presswork and its mannered typefaces (Endeavour and Prayer Book), the books have great vitality. In striving to give each its own character, Ashbee chose artists whose woodcuts would blend with the layouts, among them Reginald Savage, Laurence Housman, Paul Woodroffe, William Strang and Thomas Sturge Moore.

Ashbee himself designed many initials and illustrations, including those for the press's most lavish and ambitious work, *The Prayer Book of King Edward VII*. He used colour extravagantly on the title-page, as well as in the text and running heads, and the initials were gilded and painted by Florence Kingsford. Essex House books were usually printed on Batchelor hand-made paper, with the press's emblem, a flowering pink, as the watermark. Some editions had a separate run on vellum, and a few were printed on vellum only. The bindings were either grey board or vellum, often with a pink embossed on the cover.

The lawyer, Thomas James Cobden-Sanderson, took up bookbinding at the suggestion of Morris's wife Jane, eventually setting up his Doves bindery next door to Kelmscott. Dedicated to "transforming the workshop into a place where the greatest pleasure and the greatest honour in life are to be aimed at", he became one of the leading figures in the revival of the art of bookbinding. His work is characterized by exquisite craftsmanship and innovative design, such as that for the Kelmscott *Chaucer*.

Eventually, wanting to create books in their entirety, Cobden-Sanderson set up the Doves Press, assisted by Emery Walker. They chose a Batchelor handmade paper with a watermark of two doves and both their initials, designed a typeface based on the sixteenth-century Jenson, and hired JH Mason, the former pressman at Ballantyne. Their first book, Tacitus's *Agricola*, was published in 1901. From the beginning, the Doves style appeared fully defined and remained unchanged until 1916,

 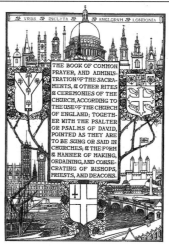

The Prayer Book of King Edward VII published by the Guild of Handicraft in 1903. A medieval depiction of Edward VII surrounded by his predecessors of the same name.

when Cobden-Sanderson closed the press and threw the types into the River Thames, having parted company with Walker seven years earlier. Their books relied on austere layout, superb clarity of type and faultless presswork. The sole concession to ornamentation was the occasional use of a calligraphic initial, dramatically printed in the purest red, as in the opening page of Genesis in their five-volume Bible of 1905.

An inspired teacher, Cobden-Sanderson trained many artists. Chief among them was a Chicago woman, Ellen Gates Starr, who stressed the importance of relating the cover design to the text. She produced superb bindings for the Doves Press, including an outstanding one for *Paradise Lost*.

Among other memorable private presses was the Pear Tree, established by the painter and wood-engraver James Guthrie in Sussex in 1901. Type to him was secondary to the printing of his woodcut blocks. He personally designed, decorated and illustrated all the Pear Tree books, which were printed in black often enlivened by a second colour — green, blue, red or gold. A notable example of this treatment was *Songs and Verses* of 1901. Guthrie also wrote and designed a magazine, *The Elf*, whose coloured covers and decorated endpapers demonstrate his devotion to the woodcut.

More pertinent than the Pear Tree within the context of the Arts and Crafts Movement was the Cuala Press, despite the fact that artistic achievements are uneven. It was created in Dundrum, Ireland, by Elizabeth and Lily Yeats – "Lily" and "Lolly" – the sisters of William Butler Yeats, as part of the Dun Emer Industries, which were established "to find work for Irish women's hands in the making of beautiful things". Originally called the Dun Emer Press, its name was changed when the sisters founded their own Cuala Industries. WB Yeats was their editorial adviser and Emery Walker their adviser on type. Although the books were well designed, with restrained decorations by Elizabeth Yeats, among others, and woodcuts designed by another brother, the painter Jack, they are important primarily for their literary

The Elf, title page, published in 1905 by Pear Tree Press. The beautiful woodcuts by James Guthrie were typical of the work of the press.

value. The Cuala Press still exists today.

An explosion of private presses took place in the United States, as well, over 50 being established between 1895 and 1910. While many produced magnificent books, others were remarkable more for their intentions than for their quality. Most clustered around the major publishing centres, with two important exceptions: Elbert Hubbard's Roycroft Press in East Aurora, New York, and Thomas Bird Mosher's in Portland, Maine. Although the Roycroft Press was part of a successful crafts community with financial gain at its core, and Mosher's books were outside the mainstream of the Arts and Crafts Movement, both contributed substantially to the public's appreciation of well-made, attractively printed books.

Hubbard set up his Roycroft Press after a visit to England which imbued in him the urge to walk in the footsteps of

Print of the Roycroft Shops of Hubbard's crafts community in East Aurora, near Buffalo, New York.

Morris. His early books, such as *The Song of Songs*, are clumsy adaptations of Kelmscott tenets: old-style type closely set on thick paper with ornate borders and clumsily hand-printed initials, usually in red, and bound in grey boards with cloth spines. Hubbard, however, apparently recognized their deficiencies, and began to employ gifted designers, decorators, printers and binders through whose talents Roycroft began to produce outstanding books in a variety of styles, but sharing many characteristics.

The type is antique, heavy and deeply inked; the paper is thick, usually made in Italy, and watermarked with the Roycroft logo; a second colour, usually red, combines with antique ornaments and borders to decorate the pages. Medievalized initials, sometimes hand-coloured, also appear; this was a typically American device which is seen in the work of other private presses. The early bindings soon made way for green, red or brown limp suede for the standard editions. Limited

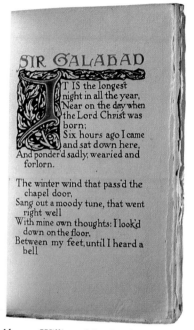

Above. William Morris, *Sir Galahad,* published by Blue Sky Press, 1904; one of 25 copies on Japan vellum (500 on regular paper). The initial represents TW Stevens' homage to Kelmscott.

Left. Elbert Hubbard *A Man of Sorrows,* published by Roycroft, 1904, one of 100 copies on Japan vellum bound in hand-tooled leather. Limited editions were often bound in full levant, or embossed leather, such as this binding, which was probably designed by Harry Avery, one of Louis H Kinder's talented pupils at the Roycroft bindery.

editions, printed on Japan vellum, were elegantly bound in levant, or hand-tooled, leather, in Roycroft's own bindery. They were produced under the supervision of Louis Kinder, one of the foremost practitioners of the art, and the author of *Formula for Bookbinders*, a Roycroft publication.

Among the designers who helped transform the Roycroft books were William W Denslow, who became famous as the illustrator of *The Wizard of Oz* and Samuel Warner. But the artist most responsible of all for placing Roycroft books among the most prestigious of the period was Dard Hunter, who eventually founded his own private press where he published,

entirely by hand, authoritative books on paper-making. During the Roycroft days, he took sabbaticals to study in Vienna and England, and some of his most successful volumes fell under the sway of European Art Nouveau: Washington Irving's *Rip Van Winkle*, *Justinian and Theodora* by Elbert and Alice Hubbard and *White Hyacinths* by Elbert Hubbard.

Mosher, the son of a wealthy sea merchant, had no intention of making a design statement when he set up his press, and cared only to publish good literature in a pleasing format, at an affordable price. He was not above appropriating successful designs from England, and rarely acknowledging them. Nor

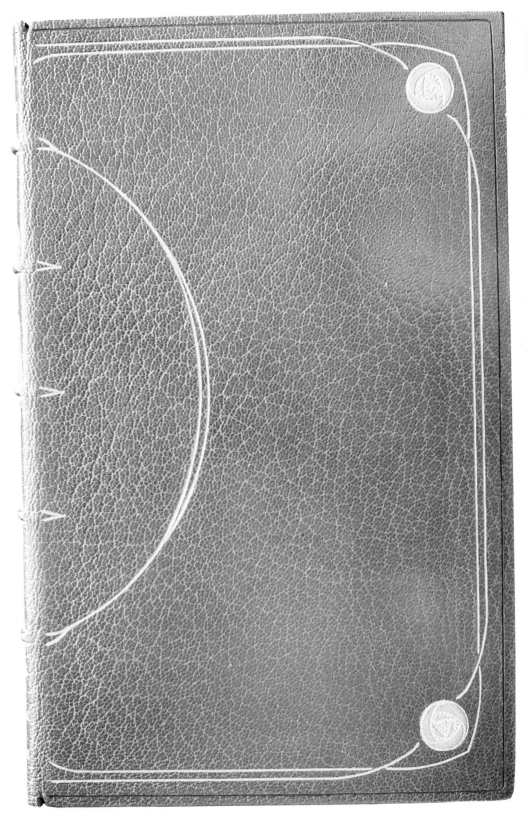

Oliver Goldsmith *The Deserted Village*, published by Roycroft, 1898; one of 470 copies with watercolours by Clara Schlagel. Elbert Hubbard understood the value of "signed" limited editions to collectors and judged, correctly, that hand illuminations would increase the book's appeal. Watercolour paintings on the title page, margins and colophon page were a logical extension of this practice.

Ralph Waldo Emerson. *Nature*, published by Roycroft, 1905. The full levant binding was designed and executed by Louis H Kinder. This elegantly restrained design epitomizes Kinder's mastery of his craft.

was he above reprinting entire books without permission, including a number published by Morris. He produced mostly in the aesthetic style – small volumes, exquisitely printed, the dainty format acknowledging the Aldine books of the fifteenth century, which he much admired. Two, Rossetti's *Hand and Soul* and *Empedocles on Etna* by Matthew Arnold overtly plagiarize the Kelmscott style.

All of his books were issued in limited editions of between 450 and 950 on Van Gelder or Kelmscott handmade paper, with even smaller runs on Japan vellum, and with a few on pure vellum. Decoration and second colours were rare, but his covers were often brilliantly designed by leading artists – Frederic W Goudy, Bruce Rogers, Earl Crawford and Thomas M Cleland, among them.

Mosher's chief contribution to the publishing scene was his dissemination of well-crafted books that were inexpensive enough to reach a relatively wide public.

Among the leading private presses in Chicago was the Blue Sky Press, which was founded in 1899 by Alfred G Langworthy, Thomas W Stevens and Alden Noble, all students at the Armour Institute of Technology. Blue Sky produced a little magazine of the same name, as well as a number of charming books. Although the format was small, designs were Morrisian, as can be seen in Browning's *Balcony*, created by Goudy and William Addison Dwiggins, and in the spirit of Art Nouveau, as evidenced by Edward Moore's *Spoil of the North Wind*, for which Frank B Rae was the designer. Rae, who had briefly worked at Roycroft, eventually moved to New Jersey, where he established the Alwill Press which produced expertly crafted books in a unique combination of arts-and-crafts and Art Nouveau styles. Blue Sky books were printed in limited editions on Ruisdael or Van Gelder paper, with a few titles, such as

Anodos, *Fancy's Following*, published by TB Mosher; one of 50 on Japan vellum (450 on Kelmscott paper). The cover designs for Mosher's books play a strong role in the delight they afford. This cover, along with those for *Primavera* (1900) and *Mimes* (1901), is one of the most successful of the time.

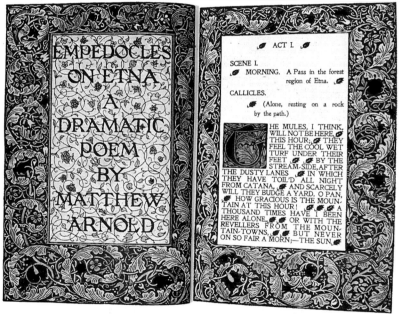

Matthew Arnold, *Empedocles on Etna*, published by TB Mosher, 1900; one of 450 copies. Mosher made spare use of a second colour as a design element: this superb homage to Morris, hand-coloured by Bertha Avery is a very rare example of Mosher's use of full colour. This copy belonged to his secretary Flora Lamb.

Omar Khayyam, *Rubaiyat*, published by TH Mosher, 1897; one of 100 copies on Japan vellum. The cover was designed and executed by Christia Gaskell for the Guild of Women Binders. Bookbinding increasingly became the province of women who formed well-organized groups to promote their crafts.

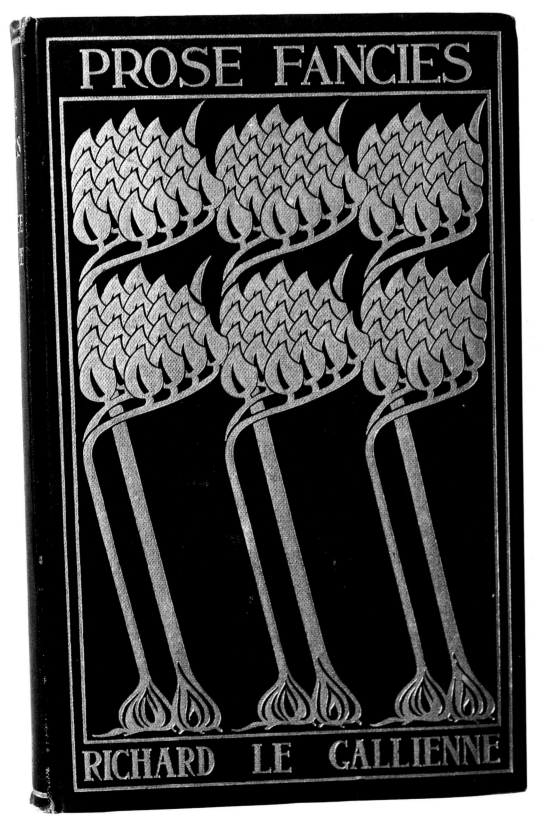

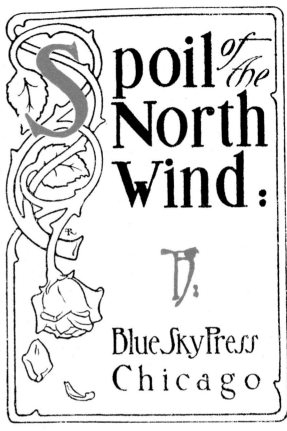

Above. Edward M Moore, *To Omar, Spoils of the North Wind*, published by Blue Sky Press, 1901; one of 500 copies on regular paper. The title page demonstrates awareness of the contemporary European art movements. His design for the cover of the book is one of the outstanding works of that period.

Left. R Le Gallienne *Prose Fancies*, published by The Bodley Head, 1896. The Chicago designer Frank Hazenplug created many books for Stone and Kimball and memorable cover designs, such as this one, for Stone and Kimball.

Morris's *Sir Galahad*, printed in editions of 25 or less on Japan vellum, and hand illuminated. The appealing quality of these books rests to a large extent on the perfect harmony between content and cover.

A lesser Chicago private press, the Alderbrink, came into being simply because its founder, Ralph Fletcher Seymour, wanted to help raise printing standards. His books paid direct homage to Morris, but rarely went beyond exuberant imitation. Seymour designed a type, the Alderbrink, based on Morris's Golden, that substantially contributed to the Kelmscott look of his books.

The most important member of the entire Chicago group was Frederic W Goudy, who was not only to become one of America's leading type designers, but was also a prolific designer of title-pages and covers for a wide range of publishers, including Mosher, Blue Sky, Seymour, and Stone and Kimball. In 1903, he and his wife Bertha established the Village Press, with the chief aim of promoting his own Village typeface. Their books show a distinct Kelmscott influence; their version of Lamb's *Dissertation on a Roast Pig* could indeed have been published by Morris himself. In 1904, the Goudys moved to Hingham, Massachusetts, where they were joined by W A Dwiggins, a former student of Goudy's, who was by then himself a distinguished designer.

Also in Boston was the Craftsman's Guild which was responsible for extraordinary books in the pure arts-and-crafts spirit, which were reminiscent of medieval illuminated manuscripts. Typical is Tabb's *Two Lyrics*, designed by Theodore B Hapgood. The type is Gothic and forceful, and the text, set tightly on the page, is surrounded on three sides by hand-illuminated floral borders. There were 350 copies on paper and 50 on vellum, printed by Carl Heintzemann and bound in gold-stamped vellum with silk ties.

Will Bradley, after his triumphs in Chicago, returned to his native Massachusetts, where he established his Wayside Press in 1895. His style, with its brilliant manipulation of negative space, its flowing lines, medievalized borders and decorations, and its use of old-style type, is a uniquely American combination of Morris and Beardsley. As a freelance, Bradley had designed spectacular posters for the *Inland Printer* and *Chap-Book*, among others, and brilliant covers for many publishers, including the Bodley Head, most notable of which was *The Quest for the Golden Girl* by Richard Le Gallienne, with its swirling background in green on which is superimposed the gold profile of a woman. His masterpieces of book design were CD Blackmore's *Fringilla*, published by Burrows Brothers,

APOLOGY *of* SOCRATES.

MONG all the great characters of antiquity who have come down in history not one is more familiar to us today than the figure of Socrates — he of the fat body, the thick lips, the bulging eyes and upturned nose – Socrates the moralist, educator, philosopher — the man who died for his principles - a martyr who died without heroics, tragic or otherwise, but with serene calm. "We owe a cock to Æsculapius. Do not fail to pay the debt."

Socrates was the son of a sculptor whose profession, and not without success, he is said in the early years of his manhood to have followed. His mother was a midwife whose art he later, humorously, also professed to practice. He did not long however carve marble statues, but following his bent of ethical speculation, he turned himself loose upon his fellow man as a moralist & a teacher. He never after the manner of the professional philosophers of his day established a school nor did he undertake to teach or instruct in any formal or methodical manner — he just met those who sought his wisdom and discussed with them matters of interest. He served as an hoplite in several campaigns. In his dress he was plain to an extreme – one set of clothing answering for summer & winter – and as to foot

13

The Apology of Socrates, published by Alwil Press, 1901; one of 475 copies. Rae's decorations are a charming mixture of arts-and-crafts and Art Nouveau. His use of hand-illuminated initials is typical of the American private press movement.

Top. Charles Lamb, *Dissertation on a Roast Pig,* published by the Village Press, 1904; one of 215 copies. Goudy's early work, while original, shows William Morris's influence. Goudy's wife Bertha was his full partner, helping with typesetting and binding.

Above. John Keats, *The Eve of St Agnes,* published by Alderbrink Press; one of 800 copies designed, illustrated and hand-lettered by RF Seymour, this is but one example of work by Chicago's young publishers, who, inspired by Morris's calligraphy, often produced hand-lettered books.

Left. Maurice Maeterlink *XII Songs,* published by Alderbrink Press, 1902; one of 400 copies. RF Seymour produced this vigorous design for the title page; however, Doudelet's sober illustrations for the text clash with Seymour's exuberance.

which is markedly reminiscent of Kelmscott, and Stephen Crane's *War Is Kind*, published by Frederick A. Stokes, where the stark Art Nouveau line echoes faithfully Crane's grim vision.

At his own Wayside Press, in which advertising work was the mainstay, he also produced the monthly magazine *Bradley, His Book*, as well as superb posters with which to advertise it. Although he published only nine issues, the magazine showed how his style evolved from the Morrisian to something more distinctively American, through the use of Caslon type and heavy woodcuts. He continued to produce in this so-called "colonial" manner at a second press, the Sign of the Vine.

Important, too, however, were the Marion Press of Frank E. Hopkins and the Elston Press of Clarke Conwell. Hopkins shared with Theodore De Vinne, for whom he had worked, a passion for simple design, spare use of ornament, tasteful typography, and impeccable printing on hand-made paper, all of which are exemplified in Huntington's *Sonnets and a Dream* of 1899. Clarke Conwell and his wife, the graphic designer Helen Marguerite O'Kane, also produced remarkable books at their Elston Press in New Rochelle. Although they were not immune to the Morris effects, their books carry a decisive stamp of originality, especially such later volumes as *Samson Agonistes* and *L'Allegro and Il Penseroso*. The designs are simple; the type, Caslon, is light; the second color, red, is frugally used; and the decorations and illustrations are restrained.

The heritage of Morris is still very much with us today. One sees it in the very handsomely produced private press books, such as those of the Allen and Pennyroyal Presses. The very use of wood-engravings is a direct tribute to the Arts and Crafts Movement. But this heritage can even be seen in magazines, such as Andy Warhol's *Interview* or Ricci's *FMR*, whose attention to design and graphics can be traced back to the heightened awareness of design that was the goal of the Arts and Crafts Movement.

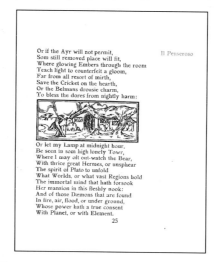

John Milton, *L'Allegro and Il Penseroso* published by Elston Press, 1903; one of 160 copies. Clark Conwell's design is restrained, and he makes sparing use of the red second color. The elegant woodcuts are by H.M.O. Kane.

Chapter Eight

METALWORK

❧ ❧ ❧

IRONWORK ❿ BRASS AND COPPER WORK ❿ THE NOBLE METALS

HE DECORATIVE METALWORK of the mid-nineteenth century was condemned by A.W.N. Pugin with such passion that his beliefs became enshrined in the very dogma of arts and crafts. Honesty, in both work-manship and design, was evoked as a prime article of faith. Things, in other words, should always be what they seemed: there should be no fire grates disguised as medieval castles; no iron painted to look like marble. Decoration should beautify, never conceal, and a metal should never be made to do anything out of character.

The character of most materials, as with wood or pottery, is greatly determined by their limitations. Metals can be made to do almost anything, from shaping a jug to roofing a steeple, and their nature is a matter of interpretation. The craft revival formed its own arbitrary rules and taboos about the metals and the way that they should be handled – rules that they frequently ignored to good effect. Gold, silver, and bronze might be cast, but iron never. Wrought iron should not be bolted or welded. Saw-piercing was *infra dig*, platinum frowned upon;

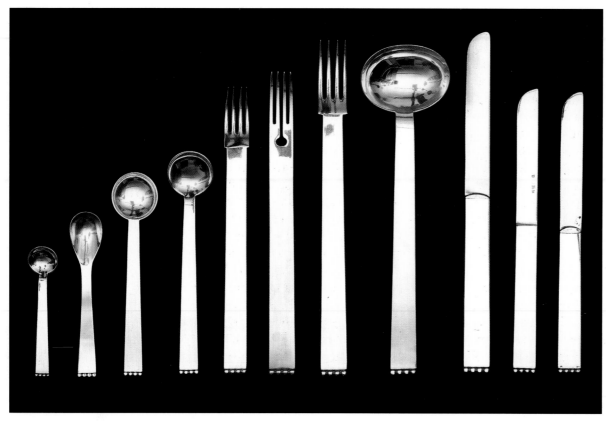

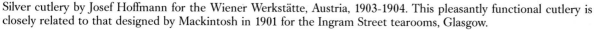

Silver cutlery by Josef Hoffmann for the Wiener Werkstätte, Austria, 1903-1904. This pleasantly functional cutlery is closely related to that designed by Mackintosh in 1901 for the Ingram Street tearooms, Glasgow.

A silver gilt and enamel candlestick by AWN Pugin, England.

gems, companions to the noble metals, should be semiprecious and uncut. No machinery should be used, a prohibition which, in a modern world, it was impossible to observe to the letter. On the other hand, arts and crafts played havoc with orthodox trade practices by mixing base and precious metals, setting domestic silverware with gems and enamels and embellishing furniture with decorative metal plaques and the sort of hinges used on outhouses.

Metal has no visible grain like wood or leather and mechanical methods cannot reveal its hidden nature. In arts and crafts, great store was set by the hammer finish, the skin of calloused metal that grows under the worker's hand in the rough-and-tumble of creation. The artist/craftsman tolerated inequalities of surface or form – even encouraged them; they held the eye in a way that the precision and symmetry of a machined object could never do. In this lay the charm and appeal of arts and crafts and also one of its great weaknesses. Birthmarks and beauty spots were all very well; but if the blemish was a badly soldered joint the job fell apart.

The versatility of the metals suited them to multiple production and in the first half of the nineteenth century mechanical techniques largely took over from handcraft. Wrought iron was almost entirely replaced by cast iron in architecture and the home. Hollow-ware, instead of being hand-beaten into shape over an iron stake was either "spun" – squeezed into shape on a lathe against a suitably formed "chuck" – or stamped out on a press. Jewellery too was punched out wholesale. Competition was savage and production was geared to what the factory owners thought the public wanted – novelty, ostentation and cheapness. The specialization implicit in mass-production meant that the vital connections between designer and workman, and workman and metal were being loosened; it was these bonds that arts and crafts longed to see re-made. Ideally, the designer of an object should also be its maker. Although in arts-and-crafts practice he rarely was, the link between designer and workman was nevertheless extremely precious and sometimes highly intuitive.

Few arts-and-crafts designers had any background in their

chosen skills. Like Pugin, the majority were architects. A purist such as CR Ashbee would have regarded a formal apprenticeship in the trade as the corrupting influence of a withered tradition. His men came from the most diverse backgrounds: Arthur Cameron, the enameller, began as his office boy and he claimed apocryphally to have met William Hardiman, his chief modeller, pushing a cat's-meat barrow in Whitechapel. They learned as they went along, by trial and error, by teaching each other and by studying ancient texts – Ashbee himself translated the workshop notes of Benvenuto Cellini into English. For this reason there is often a marked difference between early and late pieces produced in the same workshop.

The object of this almost mystical approach was a total identification of the craftsman with the medium. "He must get inside it…", said the enamellist Alexander Fisher, "and live at ease there." This attitude to the materials showed in the freshness and charm of a craftsman's early work and, when he or she had acquired the skill, in a "good fit" between design, technique and material, a sense of rightness. Of the many influences which shaped arts and crafts, the strongest and most elusive arose spontaneously from the creative process itself and the interaction between the worker and the metal. Emphasis was on this process as much as on the final product: It was felt that knowledge was less important than the manner in which it was acquired, and that an object should not only gratify its owner but ennoble its creator.

Ironwork

BY THE MIDDLE OF THE nineteenth century the craft of wrought ironwork was fast giving way to cast iron in the decorative arts. As a decorative medium, cast iron had serious limitations. Its intense heat in the molten state often caused it to burn the surface of the sand mould when it was poured, with a consequent loss of depth and precision. Nor was there any chance of chasing in the lost detail with hammer and chisel, cast iron being much too brittle. Pugin detested the medium: "All castings", he maintained "must be deficient of that play of light and shade consequent on bold relief and deep sinkings." The traditional way to create relief in ironwork was by building it up layer by layer in laminations of pierced and fretted metal, or by forging, filing and chiselling it to shape, methods which gave great richness of detail but were quite unsuited to multiple production. The most effective use of cast iron in the decorative arts is in the simple rhythmic patterns seen in railings and balustrades.

A wave of church restoration in the second part of the century encouraged the revival of wrought ironwork. Architects such as Sir George Gilbert Scott replaced the vanished screens of medieval church buildings with versions of their own. The fashion for wrought iron grew as the Arts and Crafts Movement gained momentum, particularly in fire-irons for the fashionable inglenook to which the heat-resistant metal was well suited. A pair of firedogs in London's Victoria and Albert Museum by the Guild and School of Handicrafts is in a scrolled design, topped with the wild rose of the Guild in copper and brass. The furniture maker Ernest Gimson designed fire-irons to be made up in brass and iron by Alfred Bucknell, a son of the village blacksmith of Tunley, Gloucestershire. Bucknell was a man who could breathe life into iron by the simplest possible means, using no more decoration than a few licks with the file or punch. He had an intuitive understanding of the plastic qualities of forged iron and his partnership with Gimson was a close one.

Although iron is liable to corrosion and needs to be painted to protect it from the weather, its great strength makes it suitable for architectural work. Cryptic and elegant, Charles Rennie Mackintosh's ironwork for the Glasgow School of Art has remained the subject of discussion and reinterpretation until our own times. The brackets to the studio win-

Candlestick of forged iron by Ernest Gimson and Alfred Bucknell, England, c1908. A combination of sound engineering and good design utilizes the characteristics of the metal simply and naturally: the polyhedral faceting of knop and stem reflects the candlelight, and the strength of iron allows thin metal to be used in the central lozenge.

One of a pair of wrought iron bronze-headed andirons designed by C.R. Ashbee and made by the Guild of Handicraft, c.1903. The rose design occurs throughout Ashbee's work.

Detail, ironwork from the North Front of the Glasgow School of Art, by Charles Rennie Mackintosh, Scotland, 1897 to 1899. The tall staff rising above the railings is decorated with a pierced disc, believed to have been based upon a Japanese heraldic shield.

dows in the north-west façade combine support and decoration with the prosaic function of holding up the window-cleaner's planks. Their tops end in curious knot motifs which have been compared with the hilt of a Scottish broadsword. The railings below are tipped with the spear-shaped leaves which CFA Voysey introduced to arts and crafts and supported by tall, iron staffs crested by pierced roundels which have been positively identified as *mon*, Japanese heraldic shields.

Inside the building, a balustrade is strengthened by vertical bands of iron punched with oval holes like those in well-worn harness, a complement, perhaps, to the wagon-chamfering that decorates the woodwork. The T girders supporting the roof are split and scrolled into knots, a device in the true arts-and-crafts spirit which emphasizes rather than disguises the nature of the object. The ironwork gives the school an embattled look, as though it were defending the Glasgow arts against all comers. It exists not only as an outgrowth from the building, but in its own matrix of light and weather poised in the thick Clydeside air.

Antonio Gaudi, architect of the fantastic, incomplete cathedral of the Sagrada Familia in Barcelona, well understood how light could be interrupted and transformed by a skeletal membrane of wrought iron. The iron gates which he made for the grotto in the Parc Güell, with their meandering patterns and paired wing forms, were intended to be seen looking out against the harsh Catalan light. Gaudi was the son of a coppersmith of the city of Reus in Tarragona and had grown up with metalwork and metal workers. He knew exactly what to expect, not only of the materials, but of the man in the workshop; often, in his younger days, he had worked side by side with him at the anvil.

This total familiarity allowed him to push the metal to its limits. His iron drifts, twirls, squirms and tangles; it beguiles and repels, soothes and lacerates, but it always behaves like iron. The wings of the Jabberwock-like guardian of his dragon gate were made of iron mesh to give them a vibrant translucency. The gates of the entrance to the Mila house in Barcelona were designed like the veining of a leaf or an insect's wing

Detail, dragon gate, by Antonio Gaudi for the Güell Estate, Barcelona, 1884. The wrought-iron work was carried out in the workshops of a Barcelona locksmith under Gaudi's supervision. It was originally intended that the dragon should raise one claw when the gate was opened.

and glazed – an effective mixture of iron and glass. His finest work is to be seen in Barcelona and it is charged with the raw energy of that anarchist city.

In the United States the best ironwork was made in the competitive hurly-burly of the commercial workshops. There was a keen demand for hand-wrought architectural ironwork in America during the first third of this century and superb work was done then by such craftsmen as Frank Koralewsky in Boston, Cyril Colnik in Milwaukee and Samuel Yellin of Philadelphia. Yellin was born in Poland and emigrated to Philadelphia in 1906, opening his first workshop in the city three years later. A sensitive and cultivated designer, much of his work was based on medieval originals, using the same traditional techniques – the collared joints not only clenching the scrollwork together, but picking out its melodic pattern with a simple counterpoint. Although he did not hesitate to use the latest technology to save time and drudgery, Yellin believed that "there is only one way to make good decorative ironwork and that is with the hammer at the anvil, for in the heat of creation and under the spell of the hammer the whole conception of a composition is often transformed". He was successful commercially as well as artistically, and the studios he had purpose-built in Arch Street in 1915 included showroom, library, museum room and accommodation for more than 60 forges and over 200 workers.

Frank Koralewsky, who worked in Boston, was also an immigrant and had served his apprenticeship in the Pomeranian town of Stralsund. He sailed for Boston in his late teens and took a job with the Krasser iron company. It was Koralewsky's belief that it was possible, in the twentieth century, to match the magnificent metalwork of the late Middle Ages and the Renaissance. To prove his point, he devoted his spare time for some six or seven years to producing the handsome and intricate Sneewittchen lock which retold the fairy tale by the Brothers Grimm of "Snow White and the Seven Dwarfs". Relief panels inlaid with gold, silver and bronze

Detail, Carson Pirie Scott store, Chicago, by Louis Sullivan, 1899-1904. Using plaster models and refined moulding techniques the American ironfounders at the turn of the century achieved the excellence of detail and surface usually associated with cire-perdue bronze casting.

illustrated episodes in the story, and even the hidden parts of the lock were decorated.

Although the use of cast iron ran squarely against the doctrines of arts and crafts, in the hands of the Chicago architect, Louis Sullivan, the medium transcended its own nature. The buildings he designed were often richly and fantastically decorated in a distinctive style which combines Renaissance and Gothic elements with angularities and webbed plane surfaces. The magnificent Carson Pirie Scott department store in Chicago was ornamented in this way. The intention was to set the display windows almost like jewels in frames of delicate cast iron ornament, rather feminine in mood. Apart from being a brilliant success visually, the decoration was a technical *tour de force* which burst through all the constraints hitherto regarded as implicit in cast iron. No more than a shell half an inch (one centimetre) thick, it combined meticulous detail with deep modelling, some of it even free-standing. The models were carved from plaster by Kristian Schneider, working off pencil drawings by George Elmslie, who, at that time, was Sullivan's chief designer.

🖝 🖝 🖝

Brass and copperwork

THE WARM GLOW OF copper, with its suggestion of a rural dairy or a farm kitchen, was a part of the ambience of the arts-and-crafts home. Copper is easy to work and a metal with few vices, appealing strongly to the amateur. Many craftsmen learned its use by the standard arts-and-crafts method of just getting on with it. John Pearson, of the Guild and School of Handicrafts,

was claimed by Ashbee to have been an unemployed potter from the De Morgan factory who taught himself by studying the copperwork in the British Museum. It has also been suggested that Pearson may have had access to one of the metalworking manuals of Charles G Leland, an American who lived in Britain. Designs of Pearson's earlier work have been compared with those published by Leland, but there is more than a passing resemblance to the decoration used on tiles from the De Morgan pottery.

His large copper platters were boldly ornamented with big fishes and birds and familiar motifs of the Guild, such as the ship and the peacock. It seems to have occasioned a little fluttering in the dovecotes of the Guild and School of Handicrafts' Essex House in 1890, when he was expelled for supplying Morris and others with metalwork and employing two outsiders to help him. Although he was reinstated, he finally resigned in 1892 to set up his own shop in the West End of London.

There was nothing the arts-and-crafts coppersmith liked less than the blank "grin" of a smooth and perfect surface. The process of beating out a vessel over a round-headed steel stake inevitably left hammer marks. The smith would either let them remain or work the surface over with a smooth planishing hammer, achieving a pleasing effect like that of evening sunlight on water. Copper was joined either by brazing or riveting. Wherever it was appropriate the arts-and-crafts coppersmith preferred the latter method, allowing the rivet heads to stand proud like visual punctuation marks, so that, in the words of Morris, it is "difficult to tell where the mere utilitarian part of his work ended and the ornamental began". This guideless device was used by many workers in both copper and silver, especially by the Birmingham Guild of Handicrafts.

Birmingham, so-called city of a thousand trades, was a great centre for the mass-production of brass and copper goods, turning out everything from bedsteads to cooking pots. The Birmingham Guild of Handicrafts was founded in 1890 on the principles laid down by Ashbee and Morris. No machinery was used except the lathe, essential for the satisfactory production of domestic lighting fittings in which the Birmingham Guild seems to have specialized. Lugs and handles and other additions fitted to their vessels were often fixed with rivets in this frank and pleasing fashion. Silver boxes made by the Guild were assembled in the same way.

Domestic copperwork was perhaps even more popular in the United States than in Britain, although there were many points of comparison in the work produced on both sides of the

Copper platter, by John Pearson of the Guild of Handicraft, England, c1890. Deer are a recurring motif in arts and crafts. The primitive vigour of the trees and animals is typical of the self-taught craftsman. The somewhat heraldic quality of the central stag recalls the work of the De Morgan pottery with whom Pearson is believed to have been associated.

Copper electric desk lamp by Dirk van Erp, USA, c1901. The stained isinglass panels of the shade transmit a soft natural light. The rivetted handle and dished socket holder suggest a traditional chamber candlestick, the conical shade echoes the wide-eaved roof of a prairie-style house.

A copper repoussé vase, from the workshops of the Keswick School of Industrial Art, England, c1900. The Keswick School was founded in the Cumberland town of Keswick by Canon and Mrs Rawnsley in 1884 as an evening institute and later extended to day classes. The simple repoussé decoration is typical of the work of the school.

Atlantic. The Roycroft Guild's copper workshop employed as many as 35 souls under the leadership of the Viennese Karl Kipp, a former banker, and Dard Hunter, who is probably better known as a bookbinder. The Roycrofters' many links with the British Arts and Crafts Movement are nowhere more apparent than in their robust hammer-finished copperwork with exposed rivet heads; these were sometimes translated into a mere blip on the surface of the metal with no pretence at being anything more than a modest decoration. Kipp eventually left to set up his own enterprise, the Tookay shop, in 1911.

By no means all American coppersmiths were self-taught. Dirk Van Erp learned his trade producing hand-made milk churns and kitchen utensils for the family business in Leeuwaarden, in the Netherlands. At the age of 26 he migrated to California where he worked as a coppersmith in the San Francisco shipyards. He began his career as an art metalworker by hammering brass shell cases into vases. These found a ready market with a firm of San Francisco art dealers and in 1908, at the age of 49, he opened a shop in Oakland. Back in San Francisco two years later he began a short-lived partnership with a Canadian woman, Eleanor D'Arcy Gaw, a designer, weaver and metalworker who had trained with Ashbee, and created a highly successful range of ornamental copperware, including the table lamps with tinted isinglass shades for which Van Erp is best known.

The introduction of electricity to the home, and with it a clean and silent lighting system in which the lamp hung by dainty strands of wire rather than from a gas pipe, offered opportunities and challenges to the designer. As early as 1895 electricity was installed in Ashbee's home, the Magpie and

Copper jardinière, by Gustav Stickley, produced in the Craftsman Workshops, Eastwood, New York, c1905. Stickley began producing metalwork in 1902. This piece shows the exposed rivet heads typical of arts-and-crafts metalwork, although the square form is perhaps indicative of a designer accustomed to working in wood.

Stump, Cheyne Walk, Chelsea. The lamps hung by strands of twisted wires from roses of beaten metal (one of the emblems of the Guild and School of Handicrafts) or were grouped with pendent spheres of glowing translucent enamel. For the Glasgow School of Art, Mackintosh made a fall of 13 copper lamps, each like a tower pierced with a grid of square windows and lined with purple glass. In the lecture theatre, his boat-shaped lampshades of hammered brass exuded just enough light to allow the students to take notes.

Brass is less easily raised into hollow-ware than copper and its traditional use has always been in illumination. Some of Bucknell and Gimson's finest work is to be seen in their brass candle sconces, the flat backplates pierced with simple, vigorous decoration. Robert Riddle Jarvie of Chicago specialized in candlesticks and lanterns. Jarvie, who called himself "The Candlestick Maker", was the archetypal self-made craftsman, employed as a clerk by the City of Chicago and working with metal in his own time. His candlesticks were typically modelled in forms which subtly suggest tall stemmed flowers, cast in brass, copper or bronze and either brush-finished or patinated. The work was so popular that he was emboldened to give up his municipal job and launch the Jarvie Shop, which was immensely successful. He later made silver presentation pieces, some of them after designs by George Elmslie, Sullivan's designer.

True to the arts-and-crafts dictum that the function of an object should be celebrated rather than hidden, a great deal of care was given to hinges and fittings around the home. Pugin had been quite specific about hinges; the only way to make them, he maintained, was so that one leaf could be fitted across the surface of a door and the other along the jamb in a way that

Jewel casket, brass on wood, set with cabochons of opalescent glass and containing a fitted tray, by Charles Rennie Mackintosh, Scotland, c1896. The casket was designed and made by Mackintosh for his fiancée Jessie Kepple, whom he jilted to marry Margaret Macdonald. The repoussé decoration is of peacock eyes.

Brass candlestick, by WAS Benson, England. Trained as an architect, William Benson was encouraged to take up metalwork by William Morris. Although closely identified with arts-and-crafts — he became a director of Morris & Co. when the great man died — he was firmly committed to mechanical production and his London workshops were filled with the latest machinery.

161

would decorate as well as reinforce. The fact that such hinges were most commonly employed in barns and outhouses would in no way have militated against their use in an arts-and-crafts setting. Copper was rather soft for this purpose, but hinges were often made in brass which looked attractive on oak.

The hinges Voysey designed for William Morris's Kelmscott Chaucer Cabinet, with their heart-shaped tips and openwork decoration of birds, are a fine example of his work. He made neat and cunning use of this naïve style of decoration, piercing his hinges with motifs familiar from folk art: people, birds, trees, hearts and flowers. Voysey was a great admirer of Pugin and it seems quite possible that he was influenced by the latter's brass door furniture in the Westminster Houses of Parliament. Although Voysey designed other metalwork, he is probably best known for his hinges.

Mackintosh designed shallow repoussé metal plaques to decorate his furniture and interiors, using the same vocabulary as in his other two-dimensional designs: ellipses, peacock eyes and the familiar girls, either gravely bowing with immense roses or with skirts billowing like aerial balloons. His influence

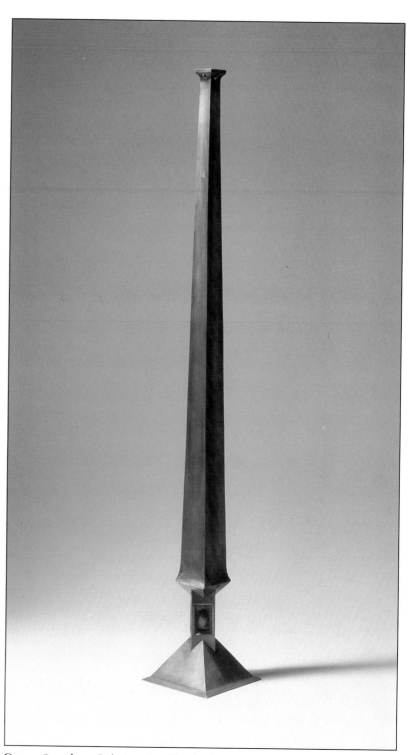

Copper urn, by Frank Lloyd Wright, made by James A Miller, Chicago, c1900. The formal decoration of repoussé panelling was designed as a complement to Wright's geometrical interiors. James Miller began in the roofing trade but later graduated to fine decorative metalwork such as this.

Copper "weed vase", designed by Frank Lloyd Wright, made by James A Miller, Chicago, c1894. Dissatisfied with contemporary decorative objects, Wright set about designing his own. This flower holder was one of his earlier creations.

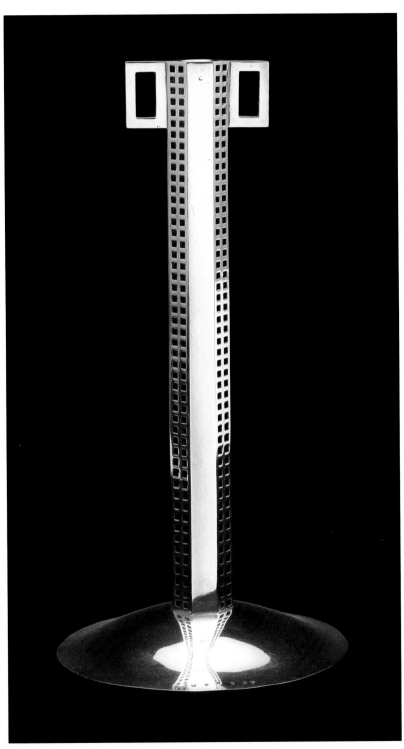

is seen strongly in the early metalwork designed by Josef Hoffman for the Wiener Werkstätte, particularly the window-like piercing, the strong perpendiculars and 90-degree angles. Although Glasgow designs remained significant in the Wiener Werkstätte, after Koloman Moser left in 1906 they gave ground to an agreeably blowsy Viennese style: brass and silver tea-sets, smoking sets and fruit bowls, their tapered and fluted bodies like well-boned corsets, the handles cusped like Cupid's bows.

At the 1878 Paris Exposition, the New York firm of Tiffany & Co showed wares made of base metal alloys laminated with fine gold and/or silver, causing a sensation by breaking a Western convention against marrying the base and noble metals that went back to the Middle Ages and often actually had the force of law.

Eccentric, eclectic and empirical, Tiffany & Co broke rules, invented new ones, built altar candlesticks of thick bronze wire and set them with uncut quartz pebbles, made a Red Indian loving cup of pink metal with handles of rocky mountain sheep horns. Even when Tiffany used a traditional technique, the approach was so fresh as to make it seem as though it had just been discovered. The firm began experimenting with enamel before 1900 as a decoration for the bases of lamps. The enamelled copper vessels they made have the tactile precious quality of the stoneware bowls used by the Japanese in the tea ceremony, the enamel seeming to grow on them like a luminescent skin.

Silver vase, by Josef Hoffmann for the Wiener Werkstätte, Vienna, c1904. The simple geometry and perpendicularity of form, and the pattern of window-like piercing with which it is decorated, illustrate the strong link that existed between Glasgow and Vienna.

Brass teaset, with handles of pale wood, by Josef Hoffmann for the Wiener Werkstätte, Vienna, c1905.

163

The noble metals

BECAUSE OF THE PRECIOUS nature of gold and silver, more time and skill is customarily spent on fashioning them than on the base metals. Arts-and-crafts jewellers and silversmiths at their best were skilled, versatile and sensitive, and they evolved a great variety of individual styles. Nevertheless a family likeness runs through their work, partly because of the international grapevine of arts and crafts along which ideas were transmitted. In even larger measure, it was the outcome of a common code of workshop practice. Arts-and-crafts precious metalworkers lived according to their own beatitudes and commandments. Most of their work was in silver with some jewellery in 18-carat gold. Platinum was hardly ever used although it was freely available at that time. Steel, copper and aluminium also sometimes appear in jewellery.

There was a characteristic aversion to the slick finish. The hammered surface was universal in silver and sometimes, instead of being polished, the metal was lightly rubbed with fine emery. Riveting often replaced soldering. Gems and enamels were set quite promiscuously in both jewellery and silverware, but according to strict conventions. The domed cabochon style of cutting was almost invariably used in simple close settings, giving a natural spontaneous effect as though the stones were budding from the metal. The palette was restricted to the more subdued semiprecious stones, especially opal, moonstone, veined turquoise matrix, cat's eye, garnet, amethyst and the irregularly shaped Mississippi pearl. Star rubies and sapphires were acceptable. The purpose was not simply to lend colour, but a mood of mystery and glamour to the object.

The jewellery and silver trades were mechanized early in the nineteenth century. Although in the best London firms, which catered for the top end of the market, traditions of hand-craftsmanship were maintained, in the factories of Birming-

From left to right. Silver candlestick, probably by Archibald Knox for the Silver Studio, manufactured by WH Haseler of Birmingham for Liberty and Co., London, 1906-1907. Stamped 'Cymric', this pieces evokes a living plant not only in its decoration but in its design and structure.

Silver, enamel and mother-of-pearl biscuit box, probably by Archibald Knox, England. The tightly interlaced and compressed decoration has a Celtic flavour.

Silver and enamel cup and cover set with opals, by Archibald Knox, England, c1900. Here the interlaced motif is given a quite different interpretation, and the sinuous, sharply elbowed scrolls are related to Art Nouveau.

ham and Sheffield designs were all too often pretentious and swamped with over-decoration. Theorists had already diagnosed the problems and prescribed the remedies, but it was left to Christopher Dresser to do something about it. Dresser believed that the machine had come to stay and that it was up to the human race to make the best of it. Despite the fact that his own designs were aimed specifically at factory production, the enthusiasm and common sense of his writings had a considerable influence on the Arts and Crafts Movement.

Dresser was trained as a botanist and in the *Art of Decorative Design* he urged his readers to examine and to meditate upon plants. The study of living plants profoundly affected arts and crafts, not simply in terms of their beauty but because of their structure and engineering. There were examples in the set of a stem and the coil of a tendril which could show the craftsman how to assemble a jewel or bring a spout on to a teapot. Even in designs which were not specifically of botanical inspiration, the base of a pitcher might spread out like the base of a tree-trunk, and the stem of a cup branch out to support its bowl. The elements of jewels sprouted, foliated, grew into and around one another; they were built up piece by piece like stalks and stems and were hardly ever pierced out of sheet metal with a saw.

The naturalistic botanical designs of Arthur and Georgina

Gaskin had many imitators. These unassuming jewels of lush willowy foliage, touched with enamel and inhabited by little birds, emerged from one of the husband-and-wife partnerships notable in British arts-and-crafts jewellery. Although credited to the team, many jewels were made by Georgina alone. Arthur was the principal of the Vittoria Street School of Jewellery and Silversmithing in Birmingham, where plant drawing was a vital part of the curriculum. His former pupil Bernard Cuzner headed the metalwork department of the Birmingham School of Art. Cuzner made a rose bowl for Lord Ilkestone which is encircled by a broad zone of leafy sweet-briar branches in firm repoussé: the floral decorative frieze is repeated in every aspect of arts and crafts from costume to interior design and recurs in slightly different form, supported by an arcade of slender tree trunks, in the tea and coffee set made by Louis Rorimer of Cleveland, Ohio, for the use of his own family. Craft teaching in the Birmingham schools was initiated by the jewellery trade for training its apprentices. Cuzner had a background in the trade as did his equally influential contemporary, WT Blackband, who took over from Gaskin in Vittoria Street. In consequence, Birmingham arts and crafts have a popular, down-to-earth quality which sets them apart from the scholasticism of London and the modernity of Glasgow.

Plant designs were subject to many interpretations. They were in a sense the touchstone to differences, often subtle, that existed between one arts-and-crafts community and another. Beautifully observed and realized, Henry Wilson's stylized roses, figs and pomegranates are not so much caricatures of Nature as tokens of her power. Wilson was a London architect who trained with JD Sedding and took over his practice when

Silver claret jugs, by Christopher Dresser, England. The functional handles are typical, angled for a good grip and easy pouring. Although designed for the machine, this silverware embodies in its simplicity and fitness many of the fundamental aesthetic principles of arts and crafts.

Jewels, by Arthur and Georgina Gaskin, made between 1902 and 1911. The silver, turquoise and chrysoprase necklace is reminiscent of some Italian peasant jewellery and is typical of the Gaskins' early work. The brooches and pendant, with their minute tracery of leaves and blossoms, are more characteristic of their later style. The stones throughout are semi-precious, or even paste, and are painstakingly put together piece by tiny piece without recourse to the piercing saw.

he died. He began metalworking around 1890 and became an inspired creator of jewellery. His work is not only finely conceived but elegantly engineered, so that every part contributes strength to the whole, and even the enamel adds rigidity to the paper-thin gold. The borders of chequered enamel give Wilson's jewels a heraldic feeling, as though they were the badges of some arcane order of chivalry. Wilson is unusual among British arts-and-crafts jewellers for using gem-stones carved to fit his designs. His book, *Silverwork and Jewellery*, remains essential reading for anyone interested in the precious crafts. Besides plants and animals, particularly stags, finely modelled human figures appear in his work. This tendency, together with a literary element, and a leaning towards the classics and to images which are not entirely visual can sometimes be seen in London arts and crafts.

The jewels that Otto Czeschka designed for the Wiener

Pendant and chain in gold, enamel, pearl, opals and emeralds, by Henry Wilson, England, c1910. The enamelled barley-sugar twists which form the necklace often appeared in orthodox Edwardian jewellery, and the symbolic rose makes little concession to naturalism.

Werkstätte are as Viennese as the work of Wilson and the Gaskins is English. Coolly stylized, these pretty and wearable two-dimensional patterns of holly-like leaves and toy birds, set with random groupings of cabochon gems and composed with arrangements of thin chain, have the brittle charm of Christmas decorations.

Wild flowers – dandelion, nightshade, blackberry – were prominent among the art jewellery made by Tiffany & Co before World War I. The collection also included Byzantine and Art Nouveau designs, and the gems with which the pieces were set were often of American origin: Mexican opal, Mississippi pearl, Montana sapphire or turquoise from the south-west.

In its simplicity and nearness to nature, the work of Arthur J Stone, seems to represent everything that Europeans admired about America in Thoreau, Audubon and Walt Whitman. Although Stone served his apprenticeship in Sheffield, his plain, classical silver is obviously in the New England tradition. Some of his work was decorated with finely observed chasings of the plants he gathered on expeditions to the nearby ponds and meadows. The barbed leaves of the arrowhead were a particular favourite. He carried out the chasing himself, occasionally adding touches of gold inlay. Even the hammer finish on his sure, quietly spoken silver was barely perceptible.

Coffee set, in silver and mixed metals, by Tiffany, New York. The firm was the first to introduce Japanese designs and techniques to western metalwork. This work anticipates arts-and-crafts in the hammer-finished silver backgrounds, and Art Nouveau in the treatment of the vine decoration.

Stone was making silver before most of the leading lights of the craft revival were even born, but he ran his workshop in Gardner, Massachusetts, according to the highest principles of the guilds. Every piece carried the mark of the person who had made it beside his own; no worker was ever laid off, and the profits were shared out every six months.

Although wild-flower designs are important in the craft revival, they were by no means its exclusive property. Sprays of diamond hedgerow blooms had been a distinctive feature of conventional jewellery since the middle of the nineteenth

century. Arts-and-crafts designers remained responsive to the same stimuli as the rest of society, however deliberately they tried to insulate themselves from it. Eighteenth-century fashions were popular with most Edwardians and they appear also to have infiltrated the silverware of the craft movement. The most distinctive work by Arthur Dixon, who designed much of the silver at the Birmingham Guild of Handicraft, is in the Queen Anne style – round-bodied vessels, vases, jugs, teapots and coffee-pots with sensible fruitwood knobs and handles, devoid of any decoration other than a hammer finish.

Eighteenth-century American domestic silver appealed to crafts revivalists in the United States because it was both home-grown and handmade. Tiffany & Co launched a fine range of table silver inspired by Queen Anne designs and enlivened by individual touches of arts-and-crafts decoration. The simple panelled and globular domestic silver produced and sold in her Chicago Kalo shops by Clara Barck Welles was probably linked to the same Anglo-American tradition. She was also possibly influenced by Ashbee, who had lectured and exhibited in this city. Welles's earlier pieces were set with cabochon semiprecious stones in the manner of British arts and crafts. Most of her silver was decorated with the elaborate monograms which, together with an exaggerated hammer finish, were characteristic of Chicago work. In Copenhagen, Georg Jensen's rich but unpretentious domestic silver, with its plump hand-hammered surfaces ornamented with succulent clusters of fruits and flowers, evokes the bourgeois comforts of the Age of Reason. Jensen's designs still exert considerable influence, not only in Scandinavia, but throughout Europe and America.

Since the prophets of the craft revival were mainly gentlemen of classical education, the influence of antiquity is inescapable. The bowl that Ashbee designed for jam or butter, with its round, shallow body, double handles and trumpet-shaped foot, has features in common with drinking vessels used by the Greeks. This enchantingly simple but striking design, with its wide-looped handles which part at the top and cling to the body with little suckers like ivy to a wall, is an arts-and-crafts classic. It was successfully imitated by Marcus & Co of New York and it is made in Chipping Campden, home of the Ashbee's guild, to this day. For the most part, it was the nature worship of antiquity that appealed to arts-and-crafts designers, rather than its material culture. Vine, fig and pomegranate often appeared in jewellery, as did the great god Pan himself. The jewels that Edward Spencer had a hand in creating for the London-based Artificers' Guild may have recounted Greek myths such as

Silver casket, by Richard G Hatton and made by the Newcastle Handicrafts Co. for presentation to Queen Alexandra, England, c1906. The enamels represent scenes from Edmund Spenser's *The Faerie Queene* and the base carries an inscription from the same work; inscriptions abound in arts-and-crafts metalwork.

Silver and ebony tea service, by Jensen of Copenhagen, c1915-1920. The lobed forms are inspired by eighteenth-century patterns. The decoration of beading and plump volutes is typical of Scandinavian arts and crafts.

those of Ariadne or the Golden Fleece in images and symbols, but they bore no relationship to Greek personal ornament in either design or technique.

Although "Brummagem Gothic" was a powerful force in nineteenth-century decoration, the medieval element in arts and crafts came in a direct line of descent from Pugin, for whom Italian medieval art was "the beau ideal of Christian purity". Pugin's immediate successor in time if not in spirit was his disciple, William Burges. Addicted to opium and alcohol, and of a grotesque appearance, he was nicknamed "Ugly Burges".

His silver designs were as eccentric as his personality. Brilliantly playful and idiosyncratic, totally unlike Pugin's chaste silver, they teem with living creatures – cats, spiders, mermaids and mice. He often blends a kleptomaniac assemblage of coins, enamels, Chinese hard-stone carvings and Japanese ivories, and contrasts suave engraving with sharp relief, quiet *champ-levé* enamel with showy *émail en ronde bosse*, in a way that makes every element act as the antidote to another. Such a mixing of materials was founded on historical precedent which existed up to the eighteenth century. It can also be seen in the

Dessert service, silver set with enamel and gems, by William Burges for the Marquess of Bute, made by Barkentin and Krall, England, 1880-1881. The style is an architectural Gothic and the bottom of each branch is formed as a tiny otter-like head with a cornelian bead pendant from its jaws.

mazers made by Omar Ramsden and Alwyn Carr in their London workshop. Although this partnership produced a great deal of work in Art Nouveau style, they are perhaps better known for these medieval drinking bowls turned from maple wood and mounted in silver.

Nostalgia for the past lay deep in the psychology of arts and crafts, a yearning for lost innocence, for the intensity and single-mindedness of the Middle Ages, and the simple peasant life. The latter was still very much alive on the European mainland. In the nineteenth century, European folk art was not only still evolving, but experiencing something of an Indian summer before the wintery blight of urbanization. This was

Cope morse in silver and gold set with semi-precious stones and a champlevé enamel, by Alexander Fisher, England, c1902.

Left. Silver salt cellar, by CR Ashbee, made by the Guild of Handicraft, England, 1899-1900. The figure was probably worked by William Hardiman, Ashbee's chief modeller. The roughness of finish may be deliberate, intended to show that the work was hand done, but may also owe something to inexperience.

partly because country people were now relatively well off, and because middle-class town dwellers were becoming aware of their threatened rural heritage. In Sweden particularly, there was a great interest in Slöyd, or traditional handicraft. Folk costume was increasingly worn together with the magnificent jewellery which traditionally accompanied it. Having no indigenous peasant jewellery to speak of, British arts-and-crafts jewellers borrowed snippets from others. In their early days, the Gaskins not only took ideas from rural Italy and Sweden, but made ring brooches which were unmistakably of North African origin. The peacock favoured by the Guild of Handicraft as a decoration was an ancient protection against the evil eye and often appeared in vernacular jewellery. The heart, a religious as well as a sentimental emblem in folk art, which was also borrowed by arts and crafts, had always been popular in jewellery of every kind.

In Japan, the same distinctions made in the West between the fine and the applied arts did not exist. Western designers went to visit, and Japanese craftsmen came to teach enamelling and metalwork, exerting a deep influence on such leading figures as Mackintosh and Dresser. Henry Wilson devoted a section of his definitive book to Japanese metalworking methods. Tiffany & Co began to make silver decorated in the Japanese style, hammer-finished and applied with gold and copper butterflies, bottle gourd vines, wisteria and subaqueous waterscapes full of fishes, frogs and weeds. Never one to shrink from mixing design metaphors, Tiffany used Japanese technology to express the aesthetics of the American south-west. The firm made bowls and vases of Japanese inlaid silver and copper which at the same time reproduced the baskets used by the Hopi, Zuni and Navajo Indians, even giving some of them handles *pavé*-set with native turquoise. Although Japanese techniques did not have the same direct impact in Britain, John Paul Cooper made tentative use of *mokume*, a technique of laminating metal.

Relationships between the "Glasgow Four", Mackintosh, the Macdonald sisters and Herbert MacNair, were so intimate that it would be impossible to conclude where among them any particular jewel originated. All have in common an eerie quality. The plump figures of children are glimpsed through entanglements of briar. Faces peer out of leafy head-dresses like

Gold, enamel and gem-set pendant, "The Love Cup", designed and made by Phoebe Traquair, England, 1907.

opening buds, half-woman, half-plant. Similar creatures, together with little stylized birds, appear on the much analysed poster that Mackintosh designed for the *Scottish Musical Review*. Birds, accompanied by unmistakable Mackintosh roses, also appear on the decoration of a buckle designed for Liberty's by another Glaswegian, the book illustrator Jessie M King. Little Glasgow jewellery has survived, and the city's importance in the precious crafts lies more in its influence abroad than in any tangible legacy. In 1901 Mackintosh designed an unusual set of cutlery for the Ingram Street tea-rooms, which was as functional as surgical instruments with slim tapering handles and pear-shaped spoon bowls. This concept was used and developed by the Wiener Werkstätte and enjoyed a new lease of life when it was rediscovered in the 1960s.

Until well into the second half of the nineteenth century, enamel was used in much the same way as precious stones – simply to bring colour to metalwork. That it had in the past been a two-dimensional art medium in its own right had long been forgotten. Its revival began in France and it was a Frenchman, Dalpeyrat of Sèvres, who introduced enamel to British arts and crafts. In 1886, he was invited to give a series of demonstrations to selected students in London, among whom was Alexander Fisher, who ultimately mastered all the exacting techniques of enamelling on metal: *champlevé*, *cloisonné*, *basse taille* and *plique à jour*. His painted enamels are of extraordinary quality, the colours rich and subtly graduated. He won an international reputation as enameller, metalworker and teacher. The girdle that he made for Lady Horniman – now in London's Victoria and Albert Museum – recounts the legend of Tristan and Isolde, the enamels painted in Pre-Raphaelite style, the steel mounts pierced with Celtic zoomorphic interlacements.

The challenge of enamelling is not simply that presented by a technically demanding medium, but of working on a small and often unconventionally shaped "canvas". In the Tristan and Isolde girdle, Fisher creates the visual sense of peeping through the setting – like Alice peeping into another world in which everything happens just out of sight. In the exquisite Love Cup jewel, by the Irish-born, Edinburgh-based Phoebe

Traquair, the scene is finite and complete, totally contained within the gold border, like the illumination in a medieval manuscript. The flesh tints are made slightly opalescent, the hair brushed with gold, the brilliancies of silk and jewellery evoked by embedding *paillons* of foil in the enamel. Her enamels, bespeaking her Scottish origin, have the shimmering mystery of Celtic legend.

Nelson Dawson learned enamelling from Fisher and taught it to his wife Edith. The couple formed one of those intimate working relationships which emerged so naturally at the time. In the jewels that they made, Edith created the enamel — colourful ideographs of growing plants, poppy, iris, love-in-a-mist, all conveying a deceptive illusion of simplicity. Phoebe and Harold Stabler, another husband-and-wife-team, apparently had the help of a Japanese craftsman named Kato. They worked in the *cloisonné* technique at which the Japanese excelled, producing charming enamels which depicted fairies, piping fawns and naked children mounted on wild beasts.

The impressive amount of jewellery made throughout the craft revival was due to the great number of women working during those years, on both sides of the Atlantic. In Britain, Georgina Gaskin's naturalistic foliage, Madeleine Martineau's minute figures and May Hart's gem-like enamels occupied an important place in the arts-and-crafts scene. In the United States, Madeline Yale Wynne taught herself jewellery and enamelling long before the crafts became fashionable. She learned about metal in the workshops of her father, Linus Yale, the inventor of the Yale lock. The ideas for her jewels grew out of the metal itself, from what happened when she hit a coil of silver with a hammer or drove a blunt punch into sheet copper — a similar approach to that of Alexander Calder half a century later. Her witty and intuitive jewellery was sometimes set with unpolished pebbles. Florence Koehler of Chicago was a natural jeweller who had the happy gift of arranging gems so that they looked as though they had just fallen into place. In her relaxed designs of clusters and foliage, which seem to owe something to the English Renaissance, emeralds, rubies and sapphires appeared far more often than was usual in arts-and-crafts settings, a comment on the wealth of the clients by whom she was commissioned. Her favourite medium was 22-carat gold, which she left unpolished.

No matter how much the pundits of arts and crafts reviled Art Nouveau for its decadence and lack of tradition, it left its mark. It would have been impossible not to have had cross-fertilization between styles so dynamic and so much at one with the spirit of the time. The influence shows in much of Rams-den's and Carr's work, in the sinuous entwinements of Edgar Simpson's pendants, in the metalwork of Alexander Fisher. It permeates Liberty's famous Cymric collection, whose principal designer, Archibald Knox, was dismissed from an art college for teaching Art Nouveau design to his students.

Liberty's store in Regent Street, London, which was closely identified with contemporary taste, launched the Cymric collection in 1899. It was machine-made, but finished by hand to appeal to the increasingly fashionable market in arts-and-crafts jewellery and silver. The title Cymric, with its Celtic overtones, was suggested by the native name for Wales. The enterprise drew in some of the brightest talents of the day in addition to Knox, among them Rex Silver, Oliver Baker, Jessie King, Bernard Cuzner and Arthur Gaskin.

Although Liberty's insisted that the designers must remain anonymous, some of the pieces can be positively attributed. The designs which dominated the collection (and served to justify its title) are Knox's Celtic interlacements. In his hands this basic decoration appears in different variations, tightens in little knots, stretches like muscles or tendons, becomes a whip-scroll or a grave figure of eight. The silver of the Birmingham painter, Oliver Baker, is also distinctive, a flamboyant baroque, punctuated with rivets and tight *cuir roulé* scrolls and with Voysey-esque touches. His waist clasps, with their scrolls, contrastingly fleshy and sinuous, swerving returns and coiling entwinements also carry a suggestion of Art Nouveau.

In the same year that Liberty introduced their Cymric line, the first Martelé silver was put on sale in Chicago by the Gorham Manufacturing Company of Rhode Island. They had imported an English artist, William Christmas Codman, to design a range of jewellery and silver which was to be called Martelé from the French word meaning hammered. A school was set up in the factory to familiarize craftsmen with the traditional techniques to be used in its making. Martelé silver was in the Art Nouveau idiom with swirling liquid scrollwork and flowers, and women with floating hair. Its surfaces were finely textured with the eponymous hammer finish.

After World War I the new wave of craftspeople (and some of the older generation) joined in an accelerating drift towards the cut and dried formalism of Art Deco. Emphasis was now upon design for industry and it was painfully clear that in its primary objective of reforming the world by honest toil the Craft Revival had been a gallant failure. Perhaps history was simply not ready for it, and this is the reason for our awakening interest in arts and crafts as both collectors and creators.

AFTERWORD

N THE HISTORY OF design, the Arts and Crafts Movement is more remarkable for what it inspired than for what it actually accomplished. Few of its supporters were able to produce, in quantity or economically, work that satisfied its own exacting technical and aesthetic standards. But, despite their limited success, they remained convinced of the necessity for design reform, and the strength of their convictions encouraged others to continue their efforts into the twentieth century.

One of the movement's accomplishments was to raise important questions regarding the character of form, ornament and materials; the nature of the design process, and the interrelationship between the fine and the applied arts. Those questions were in part responsible for directing the course of design well into the twentieth century; designers, manufacturers, consumers and critics continued to ponder their

Arthur Heygate Mackmurdo was one of the most enigmatic figures of the design reform movement. His work is dichotomous in character, at times angular and pragmatic, and at other times curvilinear and highly ornamental. Thus, he was equally influential upon practitioners of arts-and-crafts and Art Nouveau styles.

implications into the 1970s.

Their questions particularly affected the work of turn-of-the-century designers throughout Britain, Europe and America. Although they rejected the political aims of the Arts and Crafts Movement, they welcomed the opportunity for stylistic experimentation that it seemed to present. But interpretations were varied and unpredictable, since the campaign raised aesthetic and technical questions without offering specific answers.

During the period between 1890 and 1910, for example, Art Nouveau designers in France viewed the campaign as an opportunity to free their work from the constraints of historicism and revivalism. They developed a new style, featured at Samuel Bing's Paris gallery and retail store, La Maison de l'Art Nouveau, which was based almost entirely on natural

Left. The work of Hector Guimard, a leading Art Nouveau architect and furniture designer, was characterized by sinuous lines, employed both as structure and ornament. His eccentric entrances designed for Paris Metro stations resemble in form the antennae of gigantic insects or the traps of exotic, carnivorous plants. Right. Emile Gallé, a leading Art Nouveau designer, worked in Nancy, France, with Louis Majorelle and others. Gallé was known primarily for blown-glass objects, which were expressionistic in character. His metalwork and furniture were more conservative, recalling in form and ornament the rococo style.

elements. The work of such designers as Georges de Feure, Edward Colouna and Eugene Gaillard was characterized by waxen curvilinear forms, sinuous ornamentation derived from stems, vines, ribbons or human hair, and a daring exploitation of traditional and newly developed materials.

The progressive inclinations of these designers were tempered by an awareness of their artistic heritage. This was especially true in the aftermath of the Paris Universelle Exposition of 1900, at which they made their international début. Bing suggested that contemporary designers must re-examine their approach to form, ornament, structure and materials, encouraging experimentation but, at the same time, advising a degree of conservatism. This may explain why many French Art Nouveau designers tried with varying levels of success to apply their new naturalistic vocabulary to waxen forms that were adapted from Louis XV and XVI models.

American arts-and-crafts designers tended to reject the Art Nouveau style as disjointed, frenetic and lacking in integrity. Although a few flirted with it after viewing French Art Nouveau and German Jugendstil exhibits in St Louis at the Universal Exposition of 1904, the style never gained an extensive following. Americans were too pragmatic to embrace the contorted forms of the "new art", perhaps agreeing with C Howard Walker, a Boston architect and critic for the jury of the Society of Arts and Crafts, that Art Nouveau was "the work of the untrained, underdeveloped, unstocked brain and the faltering hand".

Some British designers seemed to have been able to absorb the nuances of the Art Nouveau style without jeopardizing the lessons learned from the Arts and Crafts Movement. They adjusted their forthright rectilinear forms to appear slightly softened or attenuated. They enlivened surfaces selectively with networks of sinuous interlocking lines or knots of whip-lash curves that appear to be unravelling. They judiciously borrowed motifs from the decorative vocabulary of the Art Nouveau designer to serve as an eccentric counterpoint to their own more conservative systems of ornament. Among these were designers for Liberty & Co, such as Archibald Knox and Rex Silver, and practitioners of the Glasgow Style led by "the Four", Charles Rennie Mackintosh, Margaret MacDonald Mackintosh, Francis MacDonald MacNair and Herbert MacNair.

Designers in Vienna also viewed the campaign for design reform as an opportunity for stylistic experimentation. Feeling restricted by the conservative aesthetic promoted by the Viennese Kunstlerhaus, they broke away from the mainstream in 1898 to form the Vienna Secession, a group which included Josef

In its use of fluid, curvilinear elements and naturalistic motifs, Charles Rennie Mackintosh's work resembles continental Art Nouveau. However, it does betray its arts-and-crafts heritage, stressing the right angle, the straight line and the grid. The unpredictable, "whiplash" curves that threaten to overwhelm Art Nouveau examples are applied by Mackintosh as energized ornament to otherwise forthright forms.

Hoffmann, Joseph Maria Olbrich, Otto Wagner and Koloman Moser, and which was influenced by both the Arts and Crafts Movement and Art Nouveau. It encouraged artistic collaboration among architects, painters, sculptors and applied artists in an effort to unify design from large-scale to small and to integrate art with industry.

As did reformers elsewhere, the members of the Vienna Secession tried to eliminate historicism from their work, cultivating instead simplified forms and ornament suitable for machine production. Initially, they emulated Mackintosh's interpretations of European Art Nouveau which they viewed firsthand at the 1900 Vienna Secession Exhibition and in the pages of *Die Kunst*. Eventually, however, their infatuation with windblown, whiplash curves gave way to a more rational approach: they selected precise geometric forms and ornament, and clothed them in expensive or unusual materials, achieving an effect of understated elegance.

Their efforts led to the formation in 1903 of the Wiener Werkstätte, a co-operative workshop organized by Hoffmann, Moser and their business partner, Fritz Warndorfer. The Werkstätte specialized in hand-made furnishings, metalwork and finishing materials, including textiles and leatherwork.

The design reform movement became most visible in Austria at the turn of the century, when the work of the Vienna Secessionists and the Wiener Werkstätte received acclaim in widely published journals and at international exhibitions. Their activities between 1897 and 1910 often overshadow the fact that the campaign for design reform in Austria had begun relatively early. In 1873, Vienna had hosted an international exhibition which stimulated interest throughout the country in improving standards of mass-produced objects by means of design education. This in turn had led to the founding of museums devoted to industrial art and had also launched an expanded programme of art education in schools.

Germany, during the last quarter of the nineteenth century, instituted similar programmes of art education and established museums of industrial art in cities such as Berlin, Stuttgart, Munich, Weimar and Gotha. Eventually, the German campaign for design reform led to the founding of the Vereinigte Werkstätten für Kunst im Handwerk (United Workshops for Art in Handwork), which spread from Munich to Dresden, Berlin and other cities.

Fearing that it had embraced the reform ideal belatedly, the German government eagerly sought aesthetic input from other countries. In 1899, the Grand Duke Ernst Ludwig von Hesse established an artists' colony at Darmstadt which became a

A professor of the Academy in Vienna, Otto Wagner promoted the philosophy that "Nothing that is not practical can be beautiful". Interacting, as one of the major contributors to the Secession movement, with colleagues such as Olbrich, Hoffmann and Adolf Loos, caused Wagner to abandon his reliance upon historical styles. Instead, he explored a progressive approach based upon simplicity and geometry.

Mecca for progressive designers such as Joseph Maria Olbrich. The architect Hermann Muthesius was seconded to the German Embassy in England from 1896 to 1903, specifically to study the work of arts-and-crafts architects and designers, an assignment that resulted in the publication of his definitive book, *Das englische Haus*. And in 1904, the Weimar Werkstätte appointed the Belgian Art Nouveau architect and designer Henri Van de Velde as a professor.

Olbrich, Muthesius and the Belgian architect and designer Henri Van de Velde were among the founding members in 1907 of the Deutsche Werkbund, an organization devoted to uniting designers, craftsmen, manufacturers and others involved in the production of utilitarian objects. As did design reform organizations elsewhere, the Werkbund sponsored an influential annual exhibition to promote the work of its members and to attract support from the public. But its exhibitions differed notably from those of such groups as England's Arts and Crafts Exhibition Society or the Society of Arts and Crafts in Boston, since they displayed utilitarian appliances and transportation vehicles alongside furniture, metalwork and textiles.

The growth of the Werkbund was remarkable, especially in view of the attrition suffered by most arts-and-crafts organizations during the second decade of the twentieth century. In 1907, the Werkbund had attracted only about 500 members, within six years the number had more than tripled. The strength of the German organization was evident as well from the quality of work displayed at such exhibitions as that held in Cologne in 1914. The Werkbund was one of the forces credited by H Langford Warren, the president of the SACB, with stimulating a "remarkable industrial renaissance" throughout Europe before World War I.

The Arts and Crafts Exhibition Society, which had existed for three decades by 1918, was conscious of the impressive advances made by the Werkbund during its *first* decade. Nervous of the competition posed by the Werkbund, whose "openly avowed objective", according to the British, was "to capture the world market for German art and German wares alone", the Arts and Crafts Exhibition Society organized a large show at Burlington House in London in the autumn of 1917. This featured two galleries of contemporary handicrafts, another devoted to textiles and their methods of production, and a fourth filled with the work of William Morris, Edward Burne-Jones, Walter Crane and other design leaders. Instead of inspiring universal admiration, however, the venture was said by a reporter from Boston, to be permeated with an "air of faded

and useless grandeur".

The newspaperman criticized both the appearance and the cost of most of the objects on display. The work of English design reformers, he implied, could not successfully compete with the Werkbund until a fundamental change in philosophy had taken place. "Here we touch on the fault of our arts and crafts movement", he wrote. "It is too exclusive, too arty: It appeals to the rich, rarely to the needy. The ideal at which we should aim is beautiful things, well designed, well made and inexpensive. More thought must go toward supplying the half-articulate needs of the democracy. The plutocrat can look after himself." The 1917 Burlington House exhibition marked the end of England's supremacy in the campaign for design reform. The leading role for the next two decades was assumed by the relative latecomer, Germany.

Between 1919 and 1933, the chief impetus for design reform in Germany came from the Bauhaus, an educational institution which evolved from the defunct Weimar Werkstätte. Its director was Walter Gropius, an architect renowned for industrial structures such as his prototype factory in Cologne for the 1914 Deutsche Werkbund Exhibition. Gropius, the creative as well as administrative power behind the Bauhaus, not only designed

the classroom, dormitory and administrative buildings when the institution moved to Dessau in 1925, but also developed the curriculum and the philosophy that guided its efforts.

Supporting the notion that "architecture is a collaborative work of art", the Bauhaus trained fine and applied artists to respect each others' fields. All students received essentially the same training at the beginning of their studies, thus establishing comprehensive bases for their speciality areas. At the heart of the curriculum was the concept of "learning by doing": students were encouraged to apply the design theories acquired in lectures to practical studio projects in weaving, ceramics and metalwork. Gropius believed, with Morris, that architects and designers should be thoroughly versed in all the techniques of the crafts and trades with which they would be associated as professionals.

The proponents of the De Stijl Movement, which dated from 1917, advocated an exploration of a pure international style. As a reflection of that approach, Gerrit Rietveld's furniture utilizes flat planks and straight supports, assembled with precise, articulated joinery, and conceived more as sculptural forms in space than as functional supports.

Detroit publisher, George Booth, founded the design school at the Cranbrook Academy along Bauhaus principles. The building is designed around a series of quadrangles, and blends elements of the English Domestic Revival with Finnish vernacular architecture.

As a furniture designer, Alvar Aalto rejected new materials such as metal and plastic. Convinced that the human body should come in contact only with natural materials, he utilized laminated birch plywood, moulded to follow human contours. In 1933, Aalto founded the firm, Artek, to produce inexpensive, well-designed textiles, light fixtures and furnishings.

Consistent with the history of the design reform movement, the Bauhaus was plagued by its share of ironies. Its students were trained to focus on developing prototypes for industrial production, yet Bauhaus studios had few machines for students to use, forcing them to construct their models by hand. Nevertheless, the precise geometric forms devoid of ornamentation which characterized Bauhaus products established an aesthetic of "design by subtraction" that guided twentieth-century designers until the advent of postmodernism in the 1970s.

Although the Bauhaus came to an end in 1933, it continued to influence developments in art, industry and education for the next four decades. It prompted the establishment of educational institutions such as the Cranbrook Academy in Bloomfield Hills, Michigan. It was the driving force behind industrial design and production in Scandinavian countries in the 1940s and 1950s, and inspired such designers as Charles Eames and such American companies as that of Herman Miller to produce furniture that was "adequately and handsomely designed for a typical American middle-income group family". But it was the crafts revival of the 1960s and in the establishment of stores such as Habitat in London in the 1970s that revived the joint spirits of arts and crafts and the Bauhaus. These enterprises were, in their own ways, dedicated to improving the quality of life for a majority of consumers by restoring integrity to the objects common to daily living. Interpretations of integrity varied from decade to decade, but most designers of the proto-modern and modern periods still equated it with the arts-and-crafts ideals of simplicity, beauty, honesty and usefulness.

In the 1970s and 1980s, however, those ideals have been questioned by advocates of post-modernism, whose work is characterized by the addition of ornamentation rather than by the modernist subtracionalist concept. Some of the most radical of contemporary theoreticians are challenging the allegiance of twentieth-century designers to these four basic arts-and-crafts tenets and suggesting that such ideals are outmoded. But, trend forecasters, citing the increasing interest in the works of the Arts and Crafts Movements, suggest that the quest for integrity in design may return in the 1990s, as the home becomes a refuge from the assault of increasingly intrusive technology, and consumers once again seek to follow Morris's advice to surround themselves with the "useful" and the "beautiful".

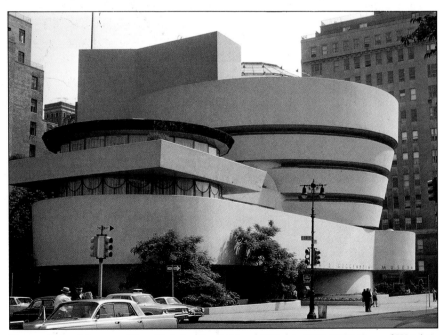

Guggenheim Museum, New York by Frank Lloyd Wright, 1946-1959. One of Wright's most famous buildings. A fascinating development from the arts-and-crafts roots of his earlier work.

BIOGRAPHIES

ASHBEE, Charles Robert
1863-1942
Architect, silversmith, jewellery designer
English architect of some of the finest small houses to break the mould of High Victorian historicism, including his own, the Magpie and Stump in Chelsea, London (1895). In 1888 he founded the influential Guild of Handicraft, which produced leatherwork, woodwork and excellent jewellery and manufactured M.H. Baillie Scott's furniture for the Grand Duke of Hesse's palace at Darmstadt. The Guild moved to Chipping Campden, Gloucestershire, in 1902, and was forced into liquidation in 1907 partly because of competition from machine-made, mass-produced copies of its jewellery. From 1908 Ashbee concentrated on architectural design.

BAILLIE SCOTT, Mackay Hugh
1865-1945
Architect and designer
Eldest of 14 children, he studied at the Royal Agricultural College, Cirencester, England, intending to run his father's Australian sheep farm. From 1886 he trained as an architect instead, and set up a practice on the Isle of Man after marrying in 1889. He is best known for his cottagey houses with flexibly planned interiors and simple furniture with bold, floral motifs. Decorations and furnishings commissioned in 1897 for the Grand Duke of Hesse's palace at Darmstadt won him an international reputation and commissions abroad, including furniture, tapestries and interiors for the Deutsche Werkstätten between 1900 and 1914.

BARNSLEY, Sidney
1865-1926
Architect and furniture designer
Leading cabinetmaker of the English Arts and Crafts movement. He co-founded Kenton & Co in 1890 with Ernest Gimson, WR Lethaby, Reginald Blomfield and Mervyn Macartney. After the firm went bankrupt in 1892, Barnsley moved to Gloucestershire with Gimson and set up a workshop producing the simple, well-crafted furniture for which he and the other Cotswold designers were best known.

BARNSLEY, Ernest
1863-1926
Architect and designer
Articled to the architect JD Sedding, where he met Ernest Gimson. In 1893 he followed Gimson and his brother, Sidney, to Gloucestershire where he designed and furnished houses. From 1902 to 1905, he worked with Gimson at the Daneway workshops, hiring Peter van der Waals, a Dutch cabinetmaker, to execute the furniture designs. The partnership broke up in 1905, after which Barnsley concentrated on architecture, undertaking work for William Morris's Society for the Protection of Ancient Buildings.

BATCHELDER, Ernest A
1875-1957
Ceramist
Born in New Hampshire, USA, he was educated in Boston and later studied at the School of Arts and Crafts in Birmingham, England. A renowned teacher and theorist, he wrote for *The Craftsman* from 1904 to 1909, and taught at the Minneapolis Guild of Handicrafts and Throop Polytechnic Institute. In 1909 he established his own School of Design and Handicraft in Pasadena, California, and is best known for ceramic tiles decorated with Gothic, Art Deco and Native American Revival motifs.

BRADLEY, Will
1868-1962
Graphic artist
Began his career as a wood engraver in 1879 in Chicago, USA, and by the 1890s had gained an international reputation for his bold typography, poster design, magazine covers and book illustrations. In 1901-1902 he published influential designs for furniture and interiors in the *Ladies' Home Journal* in a style much influenced by the work of CFA Voysey and MH Baillie Scott. He subsequently built three homes for his family in Massachusetts and New Jersey. From 1915 he was Art Director of the Hearst publishing and film empire.

BURNE-JONES, Sir Edward Coley
1833-1898
Painter and designer
Met William Morris at Oxford University, England, in 1853. From 1857 he designed stained glass and painted furniture for Morris and Philip Webb. In 1861 he helped found Morris, Marshall, Faulkner & Co and designed stained glass, tiles, embroideries and all the figurative tapestries produced by the firm from 1881 to 1894, including the "Holy Grail" (1894). In 1895 he designed 87 striking illustrations for the renowned Kelmscott Chaucer, and in 1897 produced his expressive stained glass designs for Birmingham Cathedral. He is best known as the leading Pre-Raphaelite painter

BRANGWYN, Sir Frank
1867-1956
Painter and interior designer
Born in Bruges, Belgium, moved to London in 1875 and worked for Morris & Co from 1882 to 1884. From 1885 he regularly exhibited paintings at the Royal Academy. Both Samuel Bing and LC Tiffany commissioned stained glass from him, and in 1905 and 1907 he furnished the British pavilions at the Venice Biennale. Later work included a major decorative scheme for Rockefeller Center, New York.

COOPER, J. Paul
1869-1933
Metalworker and jewellery designer
Trained as an architect in JD Sedding's London office, but subsequently devoted his life to craftwork. Cooper produced a monumental oeuvre of nearly 1400 items of gesso-work,

metalwork and jewellery between 1892 and 1933. He acquired his metalworking skills in Henry Wilson's workshop and their jewels, incorporating Byzantine architectural and floral motifs, are some of the most original arts-and-crafts designs, distinguished by exceptionally fine workmanship on the reverse.

CRANE, Walter
1845-1915
Painter, designer, book illustrator
Achieved fame in Britain in the 1870s as a nursery book illustrator. He went on to design ceramic vases, plates and tiles for Wedgwood, Minton, Maw and Co, and Pilkington's Tile and Pottery Co, tapestries for Morris & Co, and over 50 wallpapers as well as plasterwork, mosaics and stained glass. He was a founder member and Master of the Art Workers' Guild, and President of the Arts and Crafts Exhibition Society from 1888 to 1893 and 1896 to 1912.

DE MORGAN, William Frend
1839-1917
Potter and novelist
Trained at the Royal Academy Schools in London and worked for Morris & Co in the 1860s designing stained glass and tiles. He re-discovered the secret of lustre glazes, setting fire to his studio in the course of the experiments. In 1872 he established a new showroom, workshop and studio in Cheyne Row, London, transferring the business to Merton Abbey in 1881 to be near Morris's workshops. He returned to London in 1888 and went into partnership with Halsey Ricardo. Towards the end of his life he turned to writing fiction and won acclaim as a novelist.

DRESSER, Christopher
1834-1904
Designer
Botanist and academic, who became one of the leading commercial designers of the 1860s and 1870s, creating stark and functional metalwork, pottery and furniture for mechanized industrial production. He was a prolific writer and constant campaigner for industrial design reforms. *Japan, its Architecture, Art and Art Manufactures*, his magnum opus, was published in 1882, and his own designs owe much to the geometry and ornamental restraint of Japanese art.

During the 1890s he ran a studio in Barnes, a suburb of London, designing glass for James Couper & Sons of Glasgow.

ELMSLIE, George Grant
1871-1952
Architect and interior designer
Born in Aberdeenshire, Scotland, emigrated to the USA in 1884, and joined JS Silsbee's practice in Chicago where he met Frank Lloyd Wright. From 1889 to 1909 he worked for Adler & Sullivan, executing most of Louis Sullivan's ornamental designs, notably on the Carson Pirie Scott building in Chicago. In 1909 he set up his own practice, designing Prairie-style houses. For the most important commissions, including the Charles A Purcell house, Illinois (1909), he also designed leaded glass, terracotta ornaments and furniture.

FISHER, Alexander
1864-1936
Silversmith and enamellist
Leading enamellist of the British Arts and Crafts Movement, best known for his "Wagnerian" girdle of wrought steel links and plaques enamelled with scenes from Wagner's operas. He wrote extensively for *The Studio*, taught at the Central School of Arts and Crafts, London, from 1896 to 1899, and in 1904 established his own school of enamelling, influencing a generation of designers including Arthur and Georgina Gaskin, Edith Dawson, Phoebe Traquair and Florence D Koehler.

GIMSON, Ernest
1864-1919
Architect and designer
Entered JD Sedding's office in 1886 on Morris's advice, where he met Ernest Barnsley. In 1890, with Barnsley, Lethaby, Reginald Blomfield and Mervyn Macartney he founded Kenton & Co. He designed furniture for the company, but his chief interest was decorative plasterwork, which he executed for Lethaby's house, Avon Tyrell in Hampshire. In 1892, he moved to Gloucestershire with the Barnsleys and in 1902 set up the successful Daneway House workshops which produced his designs for chamfered and inlaid furniture, firedogs, iron sconces and hinges, often in a cottagey seventeenth-century style.

GREENE, Charles Sumner
1868-1957
Architect and designer
and
GREENE, Henry Mather
1870-1954
Architect and designer
Brothers and leading exponents of the American West Coast arts-and-crafts ideal, both studied architecture at the Massachusetts Institute of Technology in Cambridge, Massachusetts, and set up their practice, Greene & Greene, in Pasadena, California in 1892. The arts-and-crafts philosophy is reflected in their designs for contextual Prairie-style houses with finely crafted wooden interiors, and in the exquisite dowelling and pegging of Greene & Greene furniture. Between 1907 and 1909 they designed their best-known houses, for Robert R Blacker and David B Gamble in Pasadena, and Charles M Pratt in Ojai, and their work was regularly featured in *The Craftsman*.

GRUEBY, William H
1867-1925
Potter
Leading American art potter, who revived and popularized matt glazes. He trained at the J & JG Low Art Tiles Works in Chelsea, Massachusetts, and founded the Grueby Faience Company in 1894. After seeing French pottery at the Chicago World Fair in 1893 he began to experiment with matt glazes, and around 1900 perfected his characteristic style of heavy vase decorated with leaves in low relief and a "watermelon" green glaze. The company also produced architectural faience, making tiles for houses, churches, stations and even zoos.

HOFFMANN, Josef
1870-1956
Architect and designer
Born in Moravia, studied architecture in Munich and Vienna. In 1897 he joined the Vienna Secession, but around 1900 moved away from Art Nouveau towards a more rectilinear style, influenced by CR Mackintosh. After a visit to England in 1903 he founded the Wiener Werkstätte with Koloman Moser, based on CR Ashbee's Guild of Handicraft, and he designed for the workshops until 1931. He produced jewellery, furniture,

metalwork, textiles and glass in addition to many exhibition pavilions and major architectural commissions, including Palais Stoclet, Brussels (1905-11).

HUBBARD, Elbert
1856-1915
Publisher and founder of craft community
Born in Illinois, spent 20 years as a soap salesman then settled in East Aurora, near Buffalo, New York, founding the Roycrofters in 1893. The phenomenal success of Roycroft's Mission furniture, leather and metalwork gifts and chamois-bound books established him as the arts-and-crafts cultural messiah in America. After visiting William Morris and seeing the Kelmscott Press in 1894 he bought his own press and published *The Philistine* magazine, *The Song of Songs* and *Little Journeys*, a series of interviews with famous people. His commune attracted important designers such as Dard Hunter and Karl Kipp. He drowned on the *Lusitania* in 1915, but the Roycroft Shops survived until 1938.

HUNTER, Dard
1883-1966
Furniture designer, metalworker, papermaker
Studied at Ohio State University, joined the Roycrofters in East Aurora, New York, in 1903, and set up a studio there designing some of the most sophisticated Roycroft furniture, metalwork, leaded glass and books. He travelled to Vienna in 1908 and 1910, after which he set up an independent school of handicraft. He became a leading authority on papermaking, and from 1928 to 1931 revived the hand-made paper craft at Lime Rock in Connecticut.

JARVIE, Robert Riddle
1865-1941
Metalworker
Born in New York, moved to Chicago and made his name designing copper, brass and patinated bronze candlesticks. In 1904 he opened the Jarvie Shop and by 1906 had outlets for his sleek, organic candlesticks in more than ten states. With George Grant Elmslie, he became a founding member of the Cliff Dwellers Club in 1909 and under Elmslie's influence developed a more

architectonic style, using Celtic motifs reminiscent of the Glasgow School. From 1912 he concentrated on commissions for presentation silver trophies, many of them given to cattle raisers at the Chicago fairs.

KNOX, Archibald
1865-1941
Metalworker
Born on the Isle of Man, in the Irish Sea, studied from 1878 to 1884 at the Douglas School of Art and probably in BaillieScott's Isle of Man office. In 1897 he moved to London and worked for Liberty designing its popular "Cymric" silverware and "Tudric" pewter range in 1899 and 1900. His designs influenced the widespread Celtic Revival. From 1904 to 1912, he designed carpets, textiles, jewellery and metalwork for Liberty, as well as Arthur Lasenby Liberty's tomb in 1917.

LA FARGE, John
1835-1910
Painter and stained glass designer
Seminal figure in the development of American arts-and-crafts glass. In 1872 he travelled to France and studied medieval stained glass windows, then to England in 1873 where he met William Morris and Edward Burne-Jones. From 1875 he experimented with a novel technique of fusing different coloured layers of glass, anticipating LC Tiffany's opalescent glass. He collaborated with architect Henry Hobson Richardson, designing windows for Trinity Church, Boston, the Crane Library in Quincy, Massachusetts, and the William Watts Sherman House, Newport, Rhode Island.

LETHABY, William
1857-1931
Architect and designer
Worked for architect R Norman Shaw from 1879 to 1889, when he left to set up his own firm. He designed furniture, interiors and wrought iron and his small architectural output included Avon Tyrell, Hampshire (1889-91), and Melsetter House, Orkney (1898). His major role was as an influential teacher and propagandist, helping to found the Art Workers' Guild in 1884, the Arts and Crafts Exhibition Society in 1887, Kenton & Co in 1890 and the Design and Industries Association in 1915. *Architecture, Mysticism*

and Myth (1892), his major published work, was widely read and influenced CR Mackintosh.

MACKINTOSH, Charles Rennie
1868-1928
Architect and designer
Trained as an architect in Glasgow, Scotland, working for Honeyman and Keppie from 1889 to 1913, where he met Herbert MacNair. They joined forces with Margaret and Frances Macdonald (the "Glasgow Four"), designing posters, metalwork and furniture in a mannered Art Nouveau style which attracted criticism in England, especially at the 1896 Arts and Crafts Exhibition, but was enormously influential in Vienna. In 1897 Mackintosh won the competition for the new Glasgow School of Art, built between 1897 and 1909, and from 1897 to 1916 he also decorated Miss Cranston's Ingram Street and Willow Street tea rooms and designed his best private houses, drawing on the vernacular traditions of Scottish castle architecture: Windyhill at Kilmacolm (1900) and Hill House, Helensburgh (1902).

MACLAUGHLIN, Mary Louise
1847-1937
Ceramist
An influential amateur art potter, renowned for reviving the "Limoges" technique of underglaze decoration. She studied at the Cincinnati University School of Design, Ohio, from 1873 to 1877. In 1876 she saw the French ceramics at the Philadelphia Centennial Exhibition, and subsequently began experimenting with coloured slips applied to unfired earthenware. She first exhibited her faience in 1878, in New York, Cincinnati and Paris, and in 1879 organized the Women's Pottery Club, using Rookwood's facilities until 1882. Her technique was adopted at Rookwood, and imitated at many other American art potteries.

MACKMURDO, Arthur Heygate
1851-1942
Architect and designer
Studied architecture, and in 1874 travelled to Italy with Ruskin. In 1875 he set up a practice which lasted until 1906, undertaking a commission for the Savoy Hotel, London (1889), and building his own house, Great Ruffins

(1904). In 1882 he established the Century Guild, and designed much of the furniture, metalwork and interiors made by the Guild until 1888. Century's Music Room and Stand for Cope's tobacco company, shown at the Liverpool Exhibition in 1886, had a lasting impact on interior design and many of Mackmurdo's designs were plagiarized. The stylized title page of his book *Wren's City Churches* (1883) is recognized as one of the first Art Nouveau documents.

MACNAIR, Herbert
1868-1955
Architect and designer

Worked for Honeyman and Keppie in Glasgow, Scotland, where he met CR Mackintosh in 1889 and became one of the "Glasgow Four". In 1895 he established himself as an independent designer, concentrating on furniture, book plates and posters. In 1898 he was appointed Instructor in Design at the Liverpool University School of Architecture and Applied Art. He lived in Liverpool with his wife, Frances Macdonald, until about 1908, but continued the association with Mackintosh, collaborating on interior designs for the Vienna Secession Exhibition in 1900 and the Turin Exhibition in 1902. After his wife's death in 1921, he abandoned his career and sank into obscurity.

MAHER, George Washington
1864-1926
Architect and designer

Worked in the offices of Sullivan and Adler, and JL Silsbee, assimilating the Prairie School style. In 1888, he set up on his own and designed houses according to his "motif rhythm theory", using a repeated decorative motif to unify exteriors, interiors and furnishings. The lion and the thistle were used as linking motifs at the John Farson House, Oak Park, Illinois (1897). From 1905 to 1915 he moved away from figural motifs and heavy carving, and designed less monumental houses, including Rockledge (1912), which reflected the influence of CFA Voysey.

MORRIS, William
1834-1896
Wallpaper, textile and interior designer, printer and novelist

A lifelong admirer of John Ruskin and the creative impetus behind the whole Arts and Crafts Movement. In 1856 he entered GE Street's office in Oxford, England, to train as an architect and met Philip Webb, who built and furnished Red House for him in 1859-60. In 1861 he founded Morris, Marshall, Faulkner & Co and designed furniture, stained glass, wallpapers, chintzes, hand-tufted and woven carpets, fabrics and tapestries for his firm. From 1870 to 1876 he illuminated manuscripts and in 1889 to 1891 set up the influential Kelmscott Press to print "beautiful" books, notably the Kelmscott *Chaucer* (1896) with illustrations by Edward Burne-Jones. Morris's designs were widely plagiarized, but he had an even greater influence as a teacher and propagandist of international stature. He was also a novelist and poet.

MOSER, Koloman
1868-1918
Graphic artist and designer

Born in Vienna, began his career as an illustrator and in 1897 was a founder member of the Vienna Secession. He designed stained glass windows for Josef Maria Olbrich's celebrated Secession Building (1898) and organized the Secession's contribution to the Paris 1900 Exhibition. In 1903 he founded the Wiener Werkstätte with Hoffman, and designed furniture, metalwork, jewellery, toys and bookbindings. He left the workshops in 1907.

MUTHESIUS, Hermann
1861-1927
Architect and writer

Studied architecture in Berlin and practised from 1887 to 1891 in Tokyo. In 1896 he was appointed to the German Embassy in London and began to research and disseminate information on contemporary English architecture and design. The vernacular traditions influenced his own designs for houses. Articles published in *Dekorative Künst* and his widely read book *Das Englische Haus* (1904-5) spread the ideals of leading arts-and-crafts designers. He was the impetus behind the formation of the Deutsche Werkbund in 1907, and tirelessly campaigned for design reforms in Germany.

NICHOLS (STORER), Maria Longworth
1849-1932
Ceramist

American, the contemporary and rival of Marie Louise McLaughlin. She established the highly successful Rookwood Pottery, Cincinnati, in 1880, and after 1882 Rookwood had a virtual monopoly on the underglazing technique developed by McLaughlin. Her own "Nancy" ware was partly inspired by the shapes and motifs of Oriental pottery. Rookwood trained a group of renowned ceramists including Laura Fry, Artus Van Briggle, William P MacDonald and Matthew A Daly. In 1889, Rookwood pottery took the Gold Medal at the Paris Worlds Fair.

OLBRICH, Joseph Maria
1867-1908
Architect and interior designer

Studied architecture in Vienna, and joined Otto Wagner, Josef Hoffmann and Koloman Moser as a Secessionist. In 1898 he designed the remarkable Secession Building in Vienna, and wallpapers and a poster for their second exhibition. The following year he left for Darmstadt and became the prime creative force of the artists' colony established by the Grand Duke of Hesse. He produced numerous designs for houses and interiors, furniture, light fittings, metalwork, embroidery and cutlery in a refined, geometric style, shedding the extravagance of his early Secession work.

RICHARDSON, Henry Hobson
1838-1886
Architect and interior designer

One of the most influential and widely imitated American arts-and-crafts architects. Raised in New Orleans, studied at the Ecole des Beaux Arts in Paris and set up an architectural practice in New York in 1865. In 1874 he moved to Massachusetts to supervise the building of his Trinity Church, Boston (1872-77), one of the best examples of "Richardson Romanesque". In 1881 to 1882 he designed ornamental Romanesque furniture for the New York State Capitol, and his later work reflected the growing interest in the American Colonial era. From the 1870s he also designed and furnished houses, including residences for William Watts Sherman in Newport, Rhode Island, and the Glessners in Chicago.

RICKETTS, Charles de Sousy
1866-1931
Book designer
Born in Geneva, studied wood engraving at the City and Guilds Technical Art School, London, where he met Charles Hazlewood Shannon. Together they published an occasional magazine the *Dial* (1889-1897). Ricketts designed innovative book bindings, frontispieces and illustrations, including those for John Gray's *Silverpoints* (1893) and Oscar Wilde's *The Sphinx* (1894). In 1896 he founded the Vale Press, which published over 40 books largely influenced by the style and superb woodcuts of the *Hypnerotomachia Polifili*, a fifteenthcentury architectural treatise.

ROHLFS, Charles
1853-1936
Furniture designer
Born in New York, began his career as a designer of cast-iron stoves, and subsequently became a well-known Shakespearian actor. In 1884 he married the novelist Anna Katherine Green who insisted that he give up acting, so he turned to woodworking. He opened a small workshop in Buffalo, New York, where he made simple oak furniture, close in style to Mission furniture but incorporating pierced Gothic and Art Nouveau motifs. He exhibited work at the Buffalo Exposition in 1901, Turin, in 1902 and St Louis in 1904.

RUSKIN, John
1819-1900
Critic and writer
Champion of the Gothic style and medieval craft values, he was the most influential critic of his era. His idealistic views on handcraftsmanship, creativity and their importance for the worker were taken up by William Morris and became the foundation of the whole Arts and Crafts Movement. In 1871, he established the short-lived Guild of St George, a pioneering model for subsequent guilds. Among his most influential books were *The Seven Lamps of Architecture* (1849) and *The Stones of Venice* (1851 and 1853), which included his seminal essay "On the Nature of Gothic".

SEDDING, John Dando
1838-1891
Architect and designer
Articled to GE Street in 1858, where he acquired a deep knowledge of Gothic architecture and ornament, handed on to his own pupils. In 1874 he established a practice in London and employed many of the leading arts-and-crafts designers, including Ernest Barnsley, J Paul Cooper, Ernest Gimson and Henry Wilson. In 1887-9 he built Holy Trinity Church, Sloane Street, London, an influential monument for ecclesiastical arts-and-crafts design. It was flamboyantly furnished and decorated, after he retired, by Henry Wilson, Morris, Burne-Jones and sculptor Alfred Gilbert among others.

SHAW, Richard Norman
1831-1912
Architect and designer
The most inventive architectural exponent of the English Domestic Revival movement. In 1859 he became GE Street's chief assistant and produced designs for furniture in the Reformed Gothic style. From 1862 he had his own practice and evolved the characteristic Old English style of his country houses, as evident in Leys Wood, Sussex (1869) and Grims Dyke, near London (1872). His emphasis on vernacular English styles, on contextuality and on the use of regional building materials was very influential. During the 1870s, he revived the "Queen Anne" style for city offices and town houses.

STICKLEY, Gustav
1857-1946
Furniture designer
From 1875 trained in his uncle's chair factory and opened a furniture store in New York in 1883. After visiting Europe in 1898, he designed plain oak furniture, adopting the Shaker ideal of rustic simplicity. His "Craftsman" furniture was highly successful, and frequently publicized in *The Craftsman* magazine which he published from 1901 to 16. The magazine became the best-known American forum for arts-and-crafts philosophy. By 1913, he had franchises from Boston to Los Angeles, and purchased a 12-storey skyscraper in New York as the flagship of the Craftsman empire, but he overestimated the market and by 1915 he was bankrupt.

SULLIVAN, Louis Henry
1856-1924
Architect and designer
Trained at Massachusetts Institute of Technology, in Cambridge, Massachusetts, the Ecole des Beaux Arts in Paris, and settled in Chicago in 1875. He formed a partnership with Dankmar Adler in 1881, and executed numerous public buildings and offices, stamping Chicago with his influential palazzo skyscrapers and vigorous organic ornament and dominating the Chicago School. Prestigious commissions included the Stock Exchange and Auditorium Building in Chicago, the Getty Tomb, and the Guaranty Building in Buffalo, New York. His best known works — the Carson Pirie Scott department store and the Gage Building in Chicago — are notable for their horizontal lines and fluidity.

TIFFANY, Louis Comfort
1848-1933
Glass and interior designer
Son of Charles Tiffany, the founder of Tiffany & Co, jewellers. He trained as a painter but in the late 1870s became interested in the decorative arts and in 1879 founded Louis C Tiffany & Associated Artists with Candace Wheeler. It became one of the most popular decorating firms in New York, specializing in stained glass and mosaics, and won a commission to decorate rooms at the White House in Washington (1882-83). In 1885 he founded the Tiffany Glass Company and developed the iridescent "favrile" glass that won international acclaim.

UPDIKE, Daniel Berkeley
1860-1941
Book designer
Influential leader in American arts-andcrafts book making. He worked for Houghton Mifflin's Riverside Press, Cambridge, Massachusetts, before setting up his own office in 1893. *A Day at Laguerre's* (Riverside Press, 1892) was probably the first American book to reflect the designs of Morris's Kelmscott Press publications. In 1896, he designed the monumental arts-and-crafts book, *The Altar Book* (Merrymount Press), with Merrymount type designed by architect Bertrand Grosvenor Goodhue. It was hailed as "the perfect book" by the *New York Tribune*.

VAN BRIGGLE, Artus
1869-1904
Ceramist
Born in Ohio, studied painting at the Cincinnati Academy of Art and painted vases at the Avon Pottery for a living. In 1887 he joined Rookwood, but left for Paris in 1893 to study sculpture and painting at the Académie Julian. He returned to Rookwood briefly, and set up his own studio in Colorado in 1901. His sensuous sculptural vases, which achieved commercial and critical success, reflect the European Art Nouveau idiom which he absorbed in Paris.

VAN ERP, Dick
1860-1933
Metalworker
Born in Holland, emigrated to the USA in 1886 and worked as a coppersmith in San Francisco's shipyards. His hobby — making vases out of copper shell casings — was put to commercial use in 1908 when he opened The Copper Shop in Oakland, California. He moved the shop back to San Francisco in 1910 where it flourished. His products, especially the characteristic riveted and hand-beaten copper lamps with mica shades, were widely bought to complement the oak interiors of American arts-and-crafts bungalows.

VAN DE VELDE, Henri
1863-1957
Architect and designer
Belgian. Abandoned his early career as a painter under the influence of Ruskin and Morris in 1892. He designed furniture and interiors, silver, cutlery, books, jewellery, textiles and porcelain. Interior decorations at the Folkwang Museum in Hagen, Germany (1900-1912), were the culmination of his early curvilinear Art Nouveau style. From 1901 to 1914 he worked at The Weimar Werkstätte and in 1908 became director of the school of arts and crafts which later developed into the Bauhaus. In 1920, he went to Holland and designed the Kröller-Müller Museum (1937-54). Prolific writings on design and ornament made him an influential propagandist for the decorative arts.

VOYSEY, Charles Francis Annesley
1857-1941
Architect and designer
Worked in architect JP Seddon's London office from 1874 to 1880 and set up his own practice in 1882. His talent for flat pattern design produced many wallpapers, printed fabrics and carpets which were commercially successful. In 1888 he designed his first house, and in 1900 completed The Orchard at Chorley Wood, Hertfordshire, his own home, for which he also designed furniture and fittings. Articles in *The Studio* and *Dekorative Künst* publicized his "enchanted cottage" style abroad, and it was widely imitated. He also designed hinges and door furniture, cutlery, tableware and light fittings.

WEBB, Philip
1831-1915
Architect and designer
Entered architect GE Street's office in 1854 and in 1856 met William Morris, for whom he designed and furnished Red House (1858), the seminal arts-and-crafts monument. In 1861 he joined Morris's company and was responsible for much of its stained glass. He also designed the birds and animals in Morris's wallpapers, and furniture in a massive Gothic style. Important country house commissions included Clouds in Wiltshire, decorated by Morris & Co (188186), and Standon near East Grinstead (1891). Like CFA Voysey, his inventive interpretation of vernacular traditions was influential in America and Europe.

WELLES, Clara Barck
1868-1965
Silversmith
Studied design at the Art Institute of Chicago and in 1900 founded the Kalo Shop, which flourished as Chicago's leading outlet for fine handcrafted silver. With husband George S Welles she established the Kalo Art-Craft Community at Park Ridge, producing metalwork and jewellery that was sold in the Chicago shop. The sophisticated, hammertextured silverware, ornamented with cabochon stones and elegant monograms, provoked the renaissance of silversmithing in Chicago.

WHEELER, Candace
1829-1923
Graphic artist
A pioneering spirit in the women's arts-and-crafts movement in America. She founded the Society of Decorative Art in 1877, which provided a model for 30 sister societies. In 1879 she helped establish Louis C Tiffany & Associated Artists, running Associated Artists as a separate business from 1883 to 1907. She designed textiles, embroideries and wallpapers, stamped with a Japanese influence. In 1893 she was appointed Director of the Women's Building at the Chicago World Columbian Exposition.

WILSON, Henry
1864-1934
Jeweller and metalworker
Chief assistant to architect JD Sedding, and took over his practice in 1891. From 1890, however, his interest in metalwork dominated his career. He taught metalworking at the Central School of Arts and Crafts, London, from 1896 and at the Royal College of Art from 1901. *Silverwork and Jewellery*, which he published in 1903, was acclaimed as the finest practical handbook for craftsmen. His

WRIGHT, Frank Lloyd
1867-1956
Architect and designer
Foremost exponent of Prairie School architecture, and a major influence on American arts-and-crafts architecture. From 1887 to 1893 he worked in Louis Sullivan's office in Chicago and took over the residential commissions. The Prairie style houses which followed, such as those for Ward W Willits (1902-3) and Susan Lawrence Dana (1903), reflected the open flat geography of Illinois with their strong horizontals and low overhanging roofs. He also designed dark oak furniture, popularizing tall spindle-back chairs and built-in cupboards in his functional, open-plan interiors. In 1897 he was a founding member of the Chicago Arts and Crafts Society, and by 1900 he had designed more than 50 houses. He went on to become a leading Modernist, and the contrast between the arts-and-crafts buildings and later work such as his fine Guggenheim Museum (1956-59) well illustrates his diversity and range.

INDEX

Page numbers in *italic* refer to the illustrations and captions

ACKNOWLEDGEMENTS
❧ ❧ ❧

Quarto would like to thank the following for their help with this publication and for permission to reproduce copyright material. Abbreviations used: a = above, b = below, c = centre, l = left, r = right, t = top, f = far; Bridgeman = Bridgeman Art Library; Christie's = Christie's Colour Library, England; H. & W. = Haslam and Whiteaway, England; R. C. H. M. = Royal Commission for Historical Monuments, England; S. P. N. E. A. = Society for the Preservation of New England Antiquities, Boston; V. & A. = Victoria and Albert Museum, London. Jean-François Vilain would like to thank Roger S. Wieck for his help and support.

p. 2, Angelo Hornak **p. 8**, t E. T. Archive b V. & A. **p. 10**, E. T. Archive **p. 11**, l National Portrait Gallery, London r Aldus Archive **p. 12**, t William Morris Gallery, London b V. & A. **p. 14**, A. F. Kersting **p. 15**, b Clive Hicks t Alastair Duncan/Volpe **p. 16**, V. & A. **p. 17**, l E. T. Archive r V. & A. **p. 18**, Design Council **p. 20**, l A. F. Kersting r R. C. H. M. **p. 22**, R. C. H. M. **p. 23**, A. F. Kersting b A. F. Kersting **p. 24**, R. C. H. M. **p. 25**, l R. C. H. M. r S. P. N. E. A. **p. 26**, V. & A. **p. 27**, tl Clive Hicks a and b Emett Bright **p. 29**, V. & A. **p. 32-3**, A. F. Kersting **p. 34**, Architectural Association, London **p. 35**, t Architectural Association, London b Christie's **p. 36**, a A. F. Kersting b Royal Institute of British Architects, London **p. 37**, Architectural Association, London **p. 38**, Ed Teitelman **p. 39**, a A. F. Kersting b Museum of Finnish Architecture, Helsinki **p. 40**, a S. P. N. E. A. **p. 41**, A. F. Kersting **p. 42**, A. F. Kersting **p. 43**, l Architectural Association, London r V. & A. **p. 44**, l Architectural Association, London r A. F. Kersting **p. 45-7**, Ed Teitelman **p. 48**, S. P. N. E. A. **p. 49**, Ed Teitelman **p. 50**, S. P. N. E. A. **p. 52**, l Angelo Hornak r Bridgeman **p. 53**, Angelo Hornak **p. 54**, a Paul Reeves, London b Bridgeman **p. 55**, l Christie's r H. & W. **p. 56**, Angelo Hornak **p. 57**, a H. & W. b Simon Tracy, London **p. 58**, E. T. Archive **p. 59**, Museum of Applied Arts, Helsinki **p. 60**, Museum of Applied Arts, Helsinki **p. 61**, l Paul Reeves, London r H. & W. **p. 62**, Christie's **p. 63**, a V. & A. b Christie's **p. 64**, American Museum in Britain, Bath **p. 65**, a High Museum, Atlanta b Alastair Duncan/Volpe **p. 66-7**, Alastair Duncan/Volpe **p. 68**, l Alastair Duncan l Virginia Museum/Lewis coll **p. 69**, Christie's **p. 72**, l Design Council b H. & W. **p. 73**, Design Council, London **p. 74**, l Sandersons **p. 75**, l H. & W. r Aldus Archive **p. 76**, l H. & W. r E. T. Archive **p. 77**, a Design Council, London b H. & W. **p. 78**, E. T. Archive **p. 79**, E. T. Archive r H. & W. **p. 80**, H. & W. **p. 81**, V. & A. **p. 82**, H. & W. **p. 83**, l Paul Reeves, London r Hunterian Art Gallery, Glasgow **p. 84**, Aldus Archive **p. 86**, r Alastair Duncan **p. 87**, Paul Reeves, London **p. 88**, V. & A. **p. 90**, l Angelo Hornak r Bridgeman **p. 92**, Painton Cowen **p. 93**, Angelo Hornak **p. 94**, l Painton Cowen r Christie's **p. 95**, Painton Cowen **p. 96**, r Christie's **p. 97**, Angelo Hornak **p. 98**, Bridgeman **p. 99**, Angelo Hornak **p. 100**, Angelo Hornak **p. 102**, Corning Museum of Glass, New York **p. 103**, a Aldus Archive b Corning Museum of Glass, New York **p. 104**, Corning Museum of Glass, New York **p. 107**, Sothebys **p. 108**, a Bridgeman b Angelo Hornak **p. 109**, l Pilkingtons r Angelo Hornak **p. 110**, Richard Dennis, London **p. 111**, Christie's **p. 112-3**, Angelo Hornak **p. 114**, l Angelo Hornak r Bridgeman **p. 115**, Richard Dennis, London **p. 119**, Alastair Duncan **p. 120**, Gem Antiques, New York **p. 121**, High Museum, Atlanta **p. 122**, l Alastair Duncan r Christie's **p. 123**, Gem Antiques, New York **p. 124**, Virginia Museum **p. 126**, Gem Antiques, New York **p. 127**, Gem Antiques, New York **p. 130**, V. & A. **p. 131**, V. & A. **p. 133-4**, V. & A. **p. 136**, l V. & A. **p. 137**, a V. & A. **p. 139**, l and r V. & A. b Jean-François Vilain **p. 140**, Jean-François Vilain **p. 141**, a and l V. & A. fl Jean-François Vilain **p. 142-3**, V. & A. **p. 144**, V. & A. **p. 146-152**, Jean-François Vilain **p. 154**, l Sothebys r H. & W. **p. 155**, V. & A. **p. 156**, V. & A. **p. 157**, Architectural Association, London **p. 159**, l Simon Tracy, London r Paul Reeves, London b Angelo Hornak **p. 160**, Alastair Duncan/Volpe **p. 161**, r Paul Reeves, London **p. 162**, l Alastair Duncan r Christie's **p. 163**, Sothebys **p. 164**, V. & A. **p. 165**, l Design Council, London r Bridgeman **p. 166**, Bridgeman **p. 168**, a Bridgeman **p. 169**, Bridgeman **p. 169**, V. & A. **p. 170**, l Bridgeman r V. & A. **p. 171**, V. & A. **p. 174**, c Architectural Association, London **p. 175**, Sothebys **p. 176**, Angelo Hornak **p. 177**, Bauhaus Archiv **p. 178**, a Cranbrook Academy of Art, Cranbrook l Christie's br H. & W.